348

THE EDUCATION
THAT
EDUCATES

THE EDUCATION THAT EDUCATES

Evaluation of Hebrew Education as Compared with Ancient and Modern Systems and an Application of its Principles and Methods to Present Day Educational Problems

By
MARION E. CADY, M.A.
Author of "Bible Nature Series," "Education in the Bible," etc.

"Wisdom is justified of her children"—Jesus

NEW YORK
Fleming H. Revell Company
LONDON   AND   EDINBURGH

370
C11
2

Printed in the United States of America.

New York: 158 Fifth Avenue
London: 21 Paternoster Square

To

Parents, teachers, and educators, everywhere, who recognize that character development is the supreme aim of education, and who are endeavoring to make it vital in the experiences of children and youth, this volume is dedicated.

May it aid in giving clearer vision to those who watch for souls as those who must give account; and may its reading constrain others to unite with those who are engaged in this nicest work ever committed to mortals.

PREFACE

THE supreme desire of every true parent, teacher and educator is that those under their care shall be given an education that really and truly educates. They will be satisfied with nothing less than the "genuine article." They want their children and youth to have a real education, instead of a reel-education, devoid of spontaneity, vitality, and interest.

The daily program of study, recitation, and recreation too often is formal and lifeless and the learning process regarded as a dreaded drudgery instead of a living, joyous enterprise. If each opportunity for learning is not eagerly anticipated then education fails to really and truly educate. Parents and teachers wish their children and youth to secure such an education.

This is the kind of an education the author presents in this volume entitled: *The Education that Educates*. This is not an original invention or discovery of the author. More than a half century ago, it was written and talked about. A number of educators and educational historians have had part in its discovery, but only a few have had the courage to make it known. Hebrew education has not been appreciated, but belittled and criticized, and its devotees have been unpopular for it is out of harmony with the educational program of the day.

This rather recently discovered educational system was carried out by the Ancient Hebrews nearly 3,000 years ago. During the reigns of David and Solomon, it was one of the main causes of national prosperity. The Queen of Sheba, and all the kings of the earth, sought the presence of Solomon to hear his wisdom: "And there came of all people to hear the wisdom of Solomon, from all kings of the earth, which had heard of his wisdom" (I Kings 4: 34). The Queen of Sheba said unto Solomon: "It was a true report that I heard in mine own land of thy acts and thy wisdom. Howbeit I believed not the words, until I came, and mine eyes had seen it; and behold, the half was not told me; thy wisdom and prosperity exceed the fame which I heard" (I Kings 10: 6, 7).

This education that interested the kings and queens of earth in the day of Israel's prosperity as a nation, and which called forth expressions of surprise and admiration, it is the purpose of this volume to consider.

In Part I, a brief survey is made of ancient and modern systems of education to enable the reader to compare the Hebrew system with them as he proceeds in its study. The world situation in education, and its unsolved problems are also briefly considered, so that the reader may have opportunity to note how these or similar problems and situations were met and solved by Hebrew educators. In order that a true and unbiased consideration might be given as to the defects and weaknesses of various systems of education, the educators of the time bear their own testimony as to the working of the system of which they were an integral part. As regards the educational situation in America, the testimony of clergy and statesmen supplements that borne by teachers and educators. The principles and practice of Hebrew education are given full and careful consideration in Parts II and III.

The Bible is the oldest source of information obtainable for the study of Hebrew education. We shall feel free to quote from both the Old and the New Testament Scriptures, as we shall include in our study both Hebrew and Jewish education as revealed in the Bible. In addition, reference will be made to the Talmud, considered by the Jews to be the greatest source of Hebrew educational principles and practice. Other Jewish writings have been consulted, including some of the present day. The writings of educational historians and of educators along various lines have been considered in preparing this volume.

An endeavor has been made to clarify the Hebrew educational program by considering quite fully the various subjects taught both as to content and method of instruction. The following subjects are considered in the order given:

1. The Study of the Holy Scriptures.
2. The Study of Science.
3. Physical Education.
4. Industrial Education.
5. History and Prophecy.
6. The Study of Literature.
7. The Study of Music.
8. Art and Architecture.
9. The Study of Philosophy.

In Part IV we consider the product of Hebrew education and some of its contributions to modern civilization. An important chapter of this section deals with the following trends of present-day education, viewed in the light of Hebrew educational principles and practice:

1. Creative Education.
2. Educational Determinism.
3. Methods of Instruction.

Some educators believe that the principles and practice of Hebrew education, intelligently injected into present-day systems of education with such modification as changed world conditions consistently require, would prove a cure of our educational ills, and that civilization would soon rise to a higher level.

The author believes that wherever Hebrew educational principles and practice are given full and free opportunity of expression, the same fruitage will appear as was borne in their native land. The children and youth were taught to be clean and strong in body, clean and keen in mind, clean and pure in heart. For such an education no price is too high to pay; no sacrifice too great to make.

M. E. C.

Takoma Park, Washington, D. C.

CONTENTS

PART ONE

Educational Evaluation and Justification

PART TWO

Theory of Hebrew Education

9

Part Four

Influence of Hebrew Education

EDUCATIONAL EVALUATION AND JUSTIFICATION

I

HAS EDUCATION FAILED TO EDUCATE?

A Vital Question

IN all civilized nations down through the centuries, the well-being and prosperity of the children have been first and foremost in the minds and hearts of parents. The combined efforts to bring about these desirable results have usually been included in the term " education." The people of each country have felt more or less free to justify or condemn the educational program carried on in behalf of their children. They are satisfied with nothing short of an education that really and truly educates, even though they are usually ignorant of the processes involved. Their justification or condemnation of a system of education is largely based on the kind of fruit borne by the educated trees. Parents have planted the trees (brought their children into the world); and they expect teachers and educators to so develop and cultivate them that they shall bear good fruit.

Parents and teachers have not always agreed as to the processes that should be employed in developing the educational saplings; and, what is still more unfortunate, educators have often been critical and intolerant of each other's views as to how the child should be educated. The educational house is divided against itself and cannot stand. This confusion and chaos result in a disappointing product coming from the schools. The stability and efficiency of educational systems have always been matters of public discussion. Never before was American education more seriously on trial before the bar of public opinion.

In this chapter we are considering the vital question, " Has Education Failed to Educate? " In other words, has education failed to " make good " ? Has it justified itself in accordance with the standard given by the " Prince of Educators," who said, " Wisdom (education) is justified of her children."

We here give opportunity for those most vitally concerned to express their opinions. We first give opportunity to educators whose hands have operated the levers of their educational machinery, to pass judgment on their own work. This is to be a world forum, the testimony not being limited to any particular system of education of any country at any period of its history. Here ancient and modern systems of education will weigh themselves in their own balances to see if they are found wanting. They will answer to the world the question: "Has Education Failed to Educate?"

Greek Education

The first opportunity to bear testimony will be given to Aristotle, recognized as the prince of Greek educators. Concerning the educational situation in his day he wrote:

" What education is and how the young should be educated, are questions that require discussion. At present there is difference of opinion as to the subjects that should be taught; for men are by no means in accord as to what the young should learn, whether they aim at virtue or at getting the best out of life. Neither is it clear whether education is more concerned with intellect or with character. And the question is brought no nearer solution by reference to actual practice of contemporary education; no one knows whether the young should exercise themselves in those studies which are useful in life, or in those which tend toward virtue, or in those of essentially theoretical interest. All these opinions have found supporters. Furthermore, there is no agreement as to the means of cultivating virtue; for different people, starting from different conceptions of virtue which all respect, naturally differ as to how the practice of it should be cultivated." [1]

Aristotle's diagnosis of the educational situation in Greece indicates uncertainty, disagreement, ignorance, and inability to carry out the educational program as the following expressions clearly show:

1—" Education requires discussion "
2—" Difference of opinion "
3—" By no means in accord "
4—" Neither is it clear "
5—" No nearer solution "
6—" No one knows "
7—" There is no agreement "
8—" Different people . . . naturally differ "

The Greek educational system, as viewed by its greatest scholar, has been weighed in the balance and found wanting.

Education in England

Doctor J. Welton, a modern educator, of Leeds University, England, in his book *What Do We Mean by Education*, opens the first chapter with the above quotation from Aristotle. Commenting on this indictment of Greek education, Doctor Welton says:

" So wrote Aristotle more than two thousand years ago, and in our own day his remarks are as truly descriptive of current opinions as they were in his own. Now as then, there is no general agreement as to what is meant by education, for there is no agreement as to its aim. Learning for its own sake, acquisition of knowledge and skill likely to be useful in life, training in morality, development of individuality,—each has its own advocates.

[1] Aristotle, *Politics*, v (VIII) 2.

Nor are those advocates tolerant of each other's views. A liberal education is often opposed to a utilitarian training, a primary reference to the
needs of adult life is contrasted with the immediate requirements of child
nature, and though the upholders of each may grant the importance of
moral goodness, none of them seems to be prepared to make this the
determining factor in the educative process.'' [2]

The Doctor in the preface of his book gives a graphic word picture of the serious conditions prevailing under England's system of
education:

'' We live in an age of great educational unrest. For many years en-
thusiasts have preached ' education ' as a cure for all social ills, and vast
sums of money have been expended on schools. Yet the result is general
dissatisfaction, and the voice of the doubter becomes more insistent as the
demands on his purse increase. Parents are often apathetic, sometimes
hostile. Employers of all grades complain that young people come to them
from the schools badly trained, wanting in initiative and adaptability, and
in power of serious concentration. Social reformers confess that there is
little sign of a general elevation of the national character, even when they
do not lament its decadence. Everywhere it is frankly questioned whether
the country is getting an adequate return for the money it expends on the
schools. Yet never have teachers, as a body, been more intelligent, more
enthusiastic, more devoted.''

Let us briefly summarize the appraisal of the educational situation in
England as given by Dr. Welton in 1916:
1. No general agreement as to what is meant by education.
2. No general agreement as to its aims.
3. Educators intolerant of each other's views.
4. Result is very general dissatisfaction.
5. Moral goodness granted, but not made a determining factor in the
   educative process.
6. An age of great educational unrest.
7. Vast sums of money expended on the schools.
8. Yet the result is general dissatisfaction.
9. Parents often apathetic—sometimes hostile.
10. Employers of all grades complain of the product of the school.
11. Wanting in initiative, adaptability, and power of serious concen-
    tration.
12. Little sign of general elevation of national character, and some
    lament its decadence.
13. Everywhere, returns for money expended are frankly questioned.
14. Teachers as a body have never been more intelligent, more en-
    thusiastic, more devoted.

According to this diagnosis the educational situation in England in
1916 was more serious and disquieting than in Greece. Surely the verdict must be " weighed in the balances and found wanting."

The appraisal of England's education was made after the World War

[2] J. Welton, *What Do We Mean by Education?* pp. 1, 2 (Macmillan).

had been waging for two years. Mother England began to sense the weakness and impotency of her educational system in meeting the world crisis. How about her daughter America? Was she at that time able to give a better accounting of her educational system?

American Education

Doctor Holliday of the Montana University, an American educator, gives expression to his views of the workings of the American system of education in the educational journal, *School and Society*, June 30, 1917. This article, entitled "A Return to God in Education," was written about the time that the United States joined other nations in the world conflict, and the writer lays the blame and responsibility of the World War at the door of education, as it was carried on during the preceding century. A quotation from this serious educational indictment follows:

" It would seem that one of the principal lessons of the world conflict is that the efforts of the self-appointed ' classes ' to uplift the ' masses ' as an entirety and at one heave, have met with feeble response. We are discovering today that in spite of the universal intellectual training in Germany, in spite of the universal promulgation of the artistic spirit in France, in spite of the labors of a multitude of societies for this or that form of advancement for the masses in England, the same old primitive savagery, the same wild lust for destruction, the same fiendish hatred as were known in the days of the Babylonians and Carthaginians, have burst forth. The same rapine, the same ruthless and utterly unnecessary destruction of property, the same starvation of children and deportation of defenseless citizens, now occur as in the days when the Ancients left desolation in their wake or carried off whole nations into slavery."

Doctor Holliday then speaks of the esthetic environment provided by the nations, the millions spent annually in " erecting noble buildings, buying statuary, filling art galleries, maintaining beautiful parks, and founding institutions for training the masses to distinguish a pretty thing from an ugly thing," and then sums up the results of this esthetic training and culture in severe and serious terms:

" It is indeed becoming a serious question whether in reality we have advanced greatly over our distant ancestors in the essentials of civilization. We have indeed put a cultural veneer upon ourselves; . . . we may have discovered how to arouse this or that esthetic thrill over the merits of a musical composition or a bit of painted canvas. But in the hour of stress, in the moment of temptation the veneer cracks, or even peels off in large sections, and, behold, there underneath is the raw savage. Something has gone amiss in European education, and in its imitation in America. For nearly ten decades the new education has toiled with unsparing pains, and with colossal confidence, and has produced—*a cultured pagan!* Is that not the festering sore in the educational system of today? "

The article closes with the following strong indictment against the present educational theory:

" As matters now stand, the development of mere intellect has failed. Our educational theory has developed a fatal weakness; in the moment of our greatest confidence in it, it has broken down, and the primitive instincts and practices of savagery have gained the supremacy. No nation in history has been able to survive without a God; it is not probable that America is an exception." [3]

Since the World War, England, Germany, France, and America, have made radical changes in their educational systems. Physical education, especially, has received a new impetus, and strong health courses of instruction are given in all classes of school from the elementary up to and including the university. The World War showed up a generation of youth physically unfit for the hardships of warfare. Educators and responsible men of the nation have strongly urged various lines of educational reforms, and expressed great dissatisfaction with the education of the past. Some idea of the revolt against education can be gathered from the following titles of books and articles that have been published during the recent past, most of which have been written by educators:

" About Face in Education," " New Ideals in Education," " The Old School and the New," " What's the Matter with Education," " Education After the War," " Refashioning of English Education," " Challenge to American Education," " Education the Surpassing Farce," " Plea for Educational Reconstruction," " Topsy-Turvy in Education," " Revolt Against Education," " Educational Revolution in England," " America's Need for Education," " New Dawn in Education," " Chaos or Cosmos in American Education," " Present Educational Discontent," " Educators All at Sea," " Education at the Cross-Roads," " American Education Faces the Storm," " Crisis in Education," " Way Out of Confusion in Education," " This New Education," " Salvaging the Civilization," " Faith in American Education," " Education for Peace," " Great Rift in Education," " Education or Revolution," " New Day Demands New Education," " Deepening Crisis in Our Schools," " Pedagogical Racketeering," " European Criticism of American Education," " Blundering Toward Civilization," " Educational Decline," " Crucifying Christ in Our Colleges," " Current Crime in Education," " Education and the New Deal," " Character Emphasis in Education," " Christ in American Education."

If the above titles of articles and books indicate the contents of these publications, surely the educational situation in America is not reassuring.

Educators Criticize Education

In addition to the above criticisms made against our educational theory and practice some specific criticisms have been made by educators against the results of our educational practice. Doctor Henry Holmes of Harvard University in an article entitled " Chaos or Cosmos in American Education," appearing in the *Atlantic Monthly*, October, 1927, offers the following criticism:

[3] *School and Society,* June 30, 1917.

" Education suffers in America from confusion of purposes. Justified a hundredfold in our faith in schooling as an instrument of democracy, we have cared more for the spread of education, than for its fitness for specific ends. We have been interested in quantity rather than quality. . . . In liberal education we are so far from clarity and agreement as to the ends to be served and the means to be used, that the situation, in spite of certain fixity, is little better than chaotic.

" Our schools form a maze, a labyrinth with any number of entry points and exits. Our procedure lacks not only simplicity, but integrity. It is a sprawling, spineless profusion of educational opportunity. . . .

" What our students learn in school they do not learn well, and they are very far indeed from the point at which learning is transmitted to understanding. They acquire no mastery of subjects as means for interpreting life. Their history does not enable them to view the present broadly in the light of the past, nor does their science enable them to see facts as the outward expression of laws. They develop no general criteria of taste or principles of criticism, no standards of judgment, no grasp of methods. They come to college ' prepared ' but with hardly the beginnings of an education. . . . So far as we aim at thoroughness at all, it is the superficial thoroughness of circumnavigation. Even our college graduates too often secure only a series of passing views of the islands of knowledge, including a view from the air. . . . Our colleges, and indeed our graduate schools, suffer from the disease that keeps our secondary schools permanently enfeebled—' credititis,' the itch for credits, points, units, and semester hours.

" We are in the midst of a generation of students and teachers obsessed with the notion that organization counts more than the educational outcome of the educative process in the intellectual and spiritual condition of the pupil. Educationally we are a nation of credit hunters, and degree worshipers. Even our graduate students preparing to teach, talk of how many semester hours they have taken of Dr. X or Dr. Y. To have had work with Dr. So and So, to say, ' I had his work last semester ' is offered as a substitute for knowledge on the subject and independent views of its issues. Everywhere the emphasis is on machinery, and bookkeeping. Standardization has laid its deadening hand upon us. There is much attention to processes and little assessment of results."

Doctor Holmes realizes that his pen picture of the situation in American education is rather discouraging, and may seem one-sided and unfair, but he believes that an unprejudiced consideration of the facts will indicate that the picture is not overdrawn. He says:

" This picture of American education is undoubtedly discouraging, and may seem one-sided and unfair, but when one stops to examine our educational procedures from the standpoint of its consistent bearings on clearly defined and widely accepted aims, it is difficult to find much that will support a more optimistic view." [4]

Doctor Pritchett, in the " Twenty-eighth Report of the Carnegie Foundation for the Advancement of Teaching," makes the following criticism of the American system of education:

" The defects of the present system are obvious. The school becomes a cramming place, rather than an agency for training boys and girls to

[4] *The Atlantic Monthly*, October, 1927.

use their minds. The most deadening result is the intellectual insincerity of the process. In spite of fine buildings, of an extensive and an ever growing list of studies and the mounting cost, the typical child reads and speaks his native tongue badly. The handwriting is slipshod and formless. His command of elementary mathematical reasoning is weak. He has not learned to read books '' (p. 27).

The criticisms of Doctor Pritchett are very concrete and frankly expressed, and appearing in the report of an organization whose avowed purpose is to discover the strong and weak points of the American system of education, they should have weight with those especially who are responsible for the educational methods and procedures in the schools. Parents will strongly protest against such returns for the means invested in the education of their children.

We conclude the testimonies of American educators by quoting from an address delivered by President Wm. Mather Lewis at a meeting of the North Central Association held in Chicago in April, 1933. Regarding the challenge to education he says:

" Isn't the challenge in America today for a new standard, and a better standard of values than we have had in these days of false prosperity? Isn't it true that perhaps in times of false prosperity the college itself and the school itself drifted away from the real things? I think none of us has fully realized the challenge which now has come to set up new values about what life actually is.'' [5]

This certainly is a clear, clarion call from a veteran educator for a new brand of education, with new and better standards and values about what life really is. This is probably what President Nicholas Murray Butler had in mind when he said: " Education will be entirely revolutionized by the war." Let us summarize the criticisms offered by American educators against our national system of education:

1. Education is held responsible for the World War.

2. The product of education is cultured pagans.

3. The development of mere intellect has failed.

4. England, Germany, France, and America have made large investment in intellectual development but have failed to give proper emphasis to moral and spiritual education.

5. Education has been revolutionized by the World War.

6. Educators are not agreed on the reforms necessary to insure peace, so, confusion and chaos pervade the educational world.

7. There is more interest in the spread of education, than its fitness for certain specific ends.

8. Greater interest in educational quantity than in its quality.

9. In liberal education, educators are far from clarity and agreement as to the ends to be served and the means to be used in directing the activities of the growing child.

10. Educational procedure lacks not only simplicity but integrity, and becomes a sprawling spineless profusion of educational opportunity.

[5] *North Central Association Quarterly*, Vol. VIII, No. 2, pp. 230–1.

11. Student learning is so superficial that it cannot be transmitted to understanding. It is the superficial thoroughness of circumnavigation, consisting of passing views of the islands of knowledge, including a view from the air.

12. Students acquire no mastery of subjects as a means for interpreting life.

13. The study of history does not enable the student to view the present broadly in the light of the past.

14. The study of science does not enable the student to see facts as the expression of law.

15. Students develop no criteria of taste or principles of criticism; no standards of judgment, no grasp of methods.

16. Colleges and universities are suffering from the disease—" credititis "—the itch for credits, points, units, and semester hours.

17. Educationally America is a nation of credit hunters and degree worshipers.

18. Everywhere the emphasis is on educational machinery, and educational standards; much attention given to processes and little assessment of results.

19. The schools have become cramming places instead of agencies for training students to use their minds.

20. The most deadening result of the educational program is the intellectual insincerity of the process.

21. The three R's are poorly taught, and the typical child reads and speaks his native tongue badly; his handwriting is slipshod and formless; and his command of elementary mathematical reasoning is weak.

22. American educators are challenged today to develop new and better standards of values than those set up during the days of false prosperity.

23. The challenge to educators is to set up new standards of value as to what life actually is.

Educational Verdict

What shall the answer be to the question, " Has American Education failed to educate? " The answer must be in the affirmative. The defects of American education apparently are greater in number than those of the systems of other countries. But this is due only to the closer range of study, and the easier accessibility to material for study and observation.

In all English and European countries there is a great longing for an education that will insure peace, and abolish war. The League of Nations was established to aid nations to settle their problems by arbitration, but its efforts have been largely ineffective and the present situation threatens to involve European nations in what might be another world conflict.

Many are seriously asking why the tree of knowledge is bearing such undesirable fruit? In other words, Why has Education Failed to Educate? This question will be answered in the next chapter.

II

WHY EDUCATION FAILS TO EDUCATE

Lack of Educational Unity

IN the previous chapter, Aristotle of Greece, Doctor Welton of England, and Doctor Holmes of America testified to three prevailing weaknesses in education in these three great nations of earth:

1. Educators disagree as to the supreme aim of education.
2. Educators disagree as to the subjects to be taught.
3. Educators disagree as to the best methods of teaching.

In division there is weakness, but in union there is strength. An army with its officers disagreeing as to the purpose of the campaign, the military equipment needed, and the methods of masterful handling, are defeated before they begin the march, for they will fall fighting among themselves. This is true in the erection of a great building. The master mechanics and the workmen must be in agreement; or their efforts will result in an unfinished tower of Babel.

The three weaknesses in the educational building program become pillars of strength in the educational temple:

1. *When* character building is the supreme aim in all the educational effort.
2. *When* the only subjects taught are those that permanently develop and strengthen the whole man physically, mentally and spiritually.
3. *When* the only methods of teaching employed are those which provide for a symmetrical development of the child's threefold powers, giving them opportunity for natural expression in real life in its growth to manhood and womanhood.

Intellect First Place

Note again the indictment made by Doctor Holliday against the education that many are holding responsible for the World War catastrophe: " As matters now stand the development of mere intellect has failed."

The mind had received much attention, the body some, but the heart little or none—so little that there was heart-failure. The spiritual powers were so neglected that both mind and body got out of control. The educational veneer cracked or even peeled off in large sections and, behold underneath the raw savage.

After calling the product of our educational system a " cultured pagan," Doctor Holliday adds: " A cultured pagan may not be a bad sort of creature when he is not tempted. Under favorable conditions he may not be a *bad* husband, a *bad* father, a *bad* voter, a *bad* citizen; but when the hour of temptation comes will he have the moral stamina to stand firmly for the right? "

After concluding his characterization of the cultured pagan, a possible remedy for the appalling situation is suggested: " After all, perhaps our Puritan ancestors were right when they insisted upon instilling into their children ' the fear of God.' "

Doctor Holliday does not attempt, in his article, to give any program or method for developing the moral and spiritual powers of the child, but maintains that if " true civilization is to come, we must breathe into our education the spirit of a joyous, living religion, a confident belief in a benevolent Higher power, who desires justice, decency, honesty, mercy and love to reign on the earth."

Moral Education Neglected

Many educators, clergymen, and men of affairs in the state and nation have regretted the failure in education to develop the moral and spiritual powers of the present generation of children and youth. They are not calamity-howlers and pessimists, but are responsible men and women who while decrying the present serious situation in the educational world because of neglect in character training, are foremost in suggesting plans and methods to remedy the deplorable situation. We here give opportunity to a few of many who because of careful, thoughtful study and long experience are entitled to speak to our minds and hearts.

At Washington, the capital of the nation, in the year 1926, the Department of Superintendence of the National Educational Association held its annual meeting, at which about 12,000 educators throughout the nation were in attendance. The following were a few of the prominent men who addressed the convention:

Calvin Coolidge, President of the United States; Herbert Hoover, U. S. Secretary of Commerce; John C. Tigert, U. S. Commissioner of Education; Bishop Freeman, Episcopal Church, Washington, D. C. We quote the following from the official report:

As a representative of moral and religious education, Bishop Freeman said:

" I venture to tell you that all your mechanisms and all your modern improvements in education so infinitely in advance of anything we knew in our boyhood or girlhood, will ultimately fail of their purpose, unless they are shot through and through with that which alone comes through personalities that are conscious of their high authority.

" I believe profoundly that in answer to the query: ' Who art thou? ' ' What sayest thou of thyself? ', you have to answer more than in terms of education. You have to say that you have something plus knowledge. You have to say that you have something other than scientific skill. You have to say that you have something besides your modern inventions and mechanisms for training the minds and bodies of youth. You have to say that you have so much of moral character, sustained by a profound religious conviction, that your great conception of duty leads you to believe that the primary and not the secondary business of life is the molding, and the shaping, not only of minds, not only of bodies, but of souls; and unless you can see the emergence of the souls of the youth committed to your care, I care not what your genius as educators may be, you are playing false in the most critical time in human history; and if you are unresponding to your high and solemn obligations, you may wreck the civilization that lies ahead '' (pp. 6–8).

Bishop Freeman certainly made a clear and frank statement as to the primary responsibility resting upon the teachers of the children and youth of this nation—to live and help live on a high moral plane—as the only guarantee of the continuance of the temporal blessing of civilized life.

Commissioner of Education, John C. Tigert, representing the educational interest of the nation, said:

" The fact that so many people prefer ' jazz ' to music; the books of the hour, with their sordid appeal to sex and vulgarity, to literature; the trashy and salacious shows to drama, and similar predilections, indicate that we need a real invasion of culture. Illiteracy is such a serious tragedy that one hesitates to suggest that it could have any possible virtue, but a sampling of the popular literary pabulum that is now being swallowed by the American people would lead one to surmise that the illiteracy may have some compensation, and at least serve as a literary vaccination which renders one immune to mental pollution.

" Sharp instruments are needed for surgical operations, but it is far more important that the instruments should be sterilized. Dull instruments that are foul are less dangerous than sharp ones. Modern Society needs enlightenment, but it needs virtue also. An educated criminal is more dangerous than an ignorant one. Progress depends both on knowledge and character '' (pp. 15, 18).

Commissioner Tigert by forcible illustrations made it plain that the springs of knowledge must be pure and clean if the stream of life is to be unsullied and fruitful along its course.

Secretary of Commerce, Herbert Hoover, representing the commercial interests of our country, insisted that morality is basic to success in the business world. He said in part:

" Nor is it enough to have trained minds, or even to have implanted national ideals. Education must stimulate ambition, and must train character. There have been educational systems which trained the intellect while they neglected the character. There have been systems which trained the mind and debauched the character. And there have been educational systems which trained the body and mind and character to effectuate routine jobs, while they failed to give either hope, inspiration or ambition.

" And I am less interested, as you are, really, in what you put into young folks' heads than what you put into their spirits. The best teaching is not done out of a book, but out of a life.

" I would be one of the last people in the world to belittle the importance of the exact knowledge that teachers impart to their pupils (as an engineer I set a high value upon precise information); but knowledge, however exact, is secondary to a trained mind, and serves no useful purpose unless it is the servant of an ambitious mind, a sound character, and an idealistic spirit. Social values outrank economic values. Economic gains, even scientific gains, are worse than useless if they accrue to a people unfitted by trained character to use and not abuse them '' (pp. 64–66).

Danger Signals Raised

Now we listen to the words of one upon whose shoulders at the time rested the chief responsibilities of a great nation. We quote from his book published in 1925, entitled *America's Great Need for Education:*

" It was not education that founded religion, but it was religion that founded education. It was beside the place of worship that there grew up the school.

" This important fact cannot be ignored in our development of education. Without its spirit either civilization will fall of its own weight, and that deep, abiding wisdom which supports society will cease to exist, or we shall have a type of mind keen in intelligence, but greedy and cruel, which armed with the power of modern science in seeking to destroy, will in the end accomplish its own destruction. Without the presence of a great directing moral force, intelligence either will not be developed, or if it be developed, will prove self-destructive. Education which is not based on religion and character is not education.

" In education the whole being must be taken into consideration. It is not enough to train the hand, the eye, to quicken the perception of the senses, develop the quickness of the intellect, and leave out of consideration the building of character, the aspiration of the soul.'' [1]

" We do not need more material development, we need more spiritual development. We do not need more intellectual power, we need more moral power. We do not need more knowledge, we need more character. We do not need more government, we need more culture. We do not need more law, we need more religion. We do not need more of the things that are seen, we need more of things that are unseen. It is on that side of life that it is desirable to put the emphasis at the present time. If that side be strengthened, the other side will take care of itself. It is that side which is the foundation of all else. If the foundation be firm the superstructure will stand. The success or failure of liberal education, the justification of its protection and encouragement by government, and of its support by society, will be measured by its ability to minister to this great cause, to perform the necessary services, to make the required redeeming sacrifice.'' [2]

With more than usual keenness of perception and clearness of vision the then President of the United States charts the true course of the ship of education, pointing out the dangerous rocks and reefs along the way. The supreme end and aim of education is declared to be the development of the whole man, with the moral and spiritual elements ever in the ascendancy and exercising a controlling power over his physical and mental activities in their proper relation to his fellow beings.

[1] Calvin Coolidge, *America's Great Need for Education.* From address on '' The Needs of Education,'' pp. 30, 36 (Houghton, Mifflin).
[2] *Ibid.* From address on '' The Things that are Unseen,'' pp. 74, 75.

Educators Recognize the Problem

It is indeed significant that so much emphasis was placed on moral and spiritual education by leading men of the nation and urgently pressed home to the heart of those most responsible for the training of children and youth. It must have been regarded as a most opportune moment to remind teachers of their most solemn obligation, one which there was great danger of neglecting to the peril of the nation.

Nearly a decade has passed since the adjournment of that memorable convention, and what is the moral and spiritual pulse of the education of today? At the annual meeting of the Department of Superintendence recently held at Atlantic City, N. J., Mary E. Woolley, President of Mount Holyoke College, spoke on " The Child in Its Relation to the Twentieth Century." After stressing the need of cultivating in the child the ability to use its mind, and to control its emotion, she continued:

" There is a third need of the day in which we live, a supreme need, namely, higher moral standards. That is a realization no longer confined to preachers and religious teachers. Men and women of all creeds, of all nationalities and races, who really care for the future of humanity are one on this question. We must build character on the enduring foundations of the moral and spiritual, and the laying of the foundation must begin with the child, that goes without saying. Home and Church are not exempt from responsibility, but, alas, in this modern day, in the lives of thousands of children, neither the home nor church plays its part. Upon the school rests the responsibility." [3]

The moral and spiritual education of the children and youth of the nation is still the greatest unsolved problem in American education. President Henry Lester Smith in his address to educators assembled at the National Educational Association Convention held in Denver, Colorado, July 1, 1935, brings this educational problem to the forefront. After speaking of the necessity of finding employment for the graduate product of schools, he said:

" The second problem with which education is faced *calls for immediate attention.* We have gradually passed over to the schools more and more responsibility for the moral welfare of school children. However there has not been delegated the authority to set up proper procedure. We have had little control over the environment of the child, except for the few hours when the child is in school. And, furthermore, the schools, because of certain restraints placed upon them by society, have not taken seriously enough their delegated responsibility.

" There exists in our society, outside of the control of the schools, a number of agencies which exert a powerful influence on the child for good or for bad. The movies, the radio, the press, the church, adult school organization, the liquor establishments, the advertising agencies, various organizations for youth, such as Boy Scouts,—all of these agencies have little direct connection with the constituted educational authorities of a city or state. Some are contributing creditably to the education of the youth;

[3] Department of Superintendence, *Official Report,* 1935, p. 143.

some are tearing down whatever is beneficial in the interests of commercialism, greed and political favor.

" Certainly there is need for a revising of our social order so that the agencies, which influence the lives of our children, may co-operate to control those factors in any agency which are of known detriment to youth." [4]

Agencies of Moral Education

While religious training is pre-eminently important in the work of education, yet we believe that our nation has acted wisely in leaving this phase of training to the home and the church, not forcing religious instruction upon those who are opposed or indifferent to religious matters. Those opposed to religious instruction in the home and in the church are prohibited from taking steps to intimidate or interfere. Maintenance of private or parochial schools, where religious instruction may be given along with secular studies, was recently upheld by the United States Supreme Court, when the state of Oregon passed legislation prohibiting such schools.

So the doors are wide open for religious instruction in the home, in the church, and in schools conducted by religious organizations provided that these schools meet the standard required by the state in secular instruction. Of course, the vast majority of children and youth living in Christian homes are continually surrounded by the religious atmosphere that pervades both the home and the church. Few of these children and youth will have the opportunity of religious education in any school. This makes it doubly necessary that the home and church shall be very earnest and diligent, watching and praying for souls as they that must give an account for their divine stewardship.

Even though the atmosphere of the home and church is pure and invigorating and the instruction given therein is wholesome and uplifting, yet our children are continually moving and living in the atmosphere of the school and community. They cannot escape the influences that surround them on every side. The influences of the community are not under control and fluctuate from good to better, and from bad to worse. Sad to say,—but the influence of the school is not always what it should be, and often tends to neutralize the efforts of the home and the church. The school should supplement the influence of the home and church and thus aid in lifting the community to a higher spiritual level.

It is true that the teachers in the public schools are not permitted to teach the Bible to the children and youth, but they are unrestricted in the higher and more fruitful privilege and opportunity of living the Bible before them. If all the teachers of the state-supported schools were to live the Bible principles and truths in their daily contacts with their students and the community, as well as in their relations with others of their profession, what a mighty change for the better would take place in a very short time. The character of the parents determines the home; the character of the preachers determines the church;

[4] Journal of the National Education Association, September, 1935.

and to a large degree the character of the teacher determines the school, which in a large degree determines the character of the nation.

In order that we may more clearly understand the question before us in this chapter, let us briefly summarize the reasons offered above:

1. Education has been largely confined to the development of the intellect.

2. The whole being—physically, mentally and spiritually—has not been symmetrically developed.

3. The moral and spiritual education of the child has been almost wholly neglected.

4. The study of music, literature, and dramatics develops in the student a decided taste for jazz, a love for books with a sordid appeal to sex and vulgarity, and a fascination for trashy and salacious shows.

5. Knowledge and skill have been stressed to the neglect of instruction as to their proper and legitimate use.

6. Morals and religion have not been recognized as the foundation of true education.

7. Without this foundation for education, civilization will fall by its own weight, and that deep abiding wisdom which supports society will cease to exist.

8. Without this foundation a keen type of mind will be developed, but greedy and cruel, which armed with the power of modern science, in seeking to destroy, will in the end destroy itself.

9. Material realities have been emphasized to the neglect of spiritual realities.

10. Success or failure of liberal education will depend on its ability to elevate human society, performing the necessary services, and making the required redeeming sacrifice.

Present Educational Confusion

Many heroic and sacrificial attempts are being made to bring order and stability out of the present state of educational uncertainty and confusion. Doctor John Dewey, generally recognized as one of the greatest educational philosophers of our day, recognizes the unsettled and confused state of American education and recently has written a book entitled, *The Way Out of Confusion in Education.* Concerning this state of confusion and uncertainty he says:

" It is unnecessary to say that we are in the midst of great educational uncertainty, one probably unparalleled at any past time. There is nothing accepted as axiomatic, nothing beyond the possibility of questioning, and few things that are not actually attacked. . . . It is not merely this or that method for securing educational results that is attacked, but ideals and aims are under fire. . . . I propose, then, to consider some of the main conflicts in present educational tendencies, hoping that that course may at least clarify vision, although I recognize that I may only add to the confusion." [5]

[5] John Dewey, *The Way Out of Confusion in Education,* pp. 1, 3 (Harvard University Press).

Doctor Dewey endeavors to show that the present unrest and confusion arise from a disagreement as to what should be included in the traditional subjects of study, the methods to be employed in teaching these subjects, which unduly increases the students' work and tends to confusion of mind and lack of efficiency in results. There is no doubt but what this disagreement regarding the organization of subject matter, methods of instruction, and increased number of subjects are serious handicaps resulting in much confusion. But are they primary or secondary causes for failure in our educational programs?

The two most recent expressions regarding educational uncertainty and confusion are the following:

'' How can we hope to improve the state of the nation? Only through education. A strange circularity thus afflicts us. The state of the nation depends on the state of education; but the state of education depends upon the state of the nation. How can we break this vicious circle and make at last the contribution to the national life that since the earliest times has been expected of us?

'' We can do so only if some institutions can be strong enough and clear enough to stand firm, and show our people what higher learning is. As education it is the single-minded pursuit of the intellectual virtues. As scholarship it is the single-minded devotion to the advancement of knowledge. Only if the colleges and the universities can devote themselves to these objects can we look hopefully to the future of higher learning in America.'' [6]

'' The American spirit is opposed to the kind of domination of people's thinking now being attempted by the Old World dictators. While we can and should rejoice in the absence in this country of hampering edicts issued by those who are bent on using the schools for purposes of social and political control, we ought to be aware of the dangers which beset freedom. We ought to face frankly the fact that we have been so occupied with the development of our material resources that uncertainties with regard to what education should be and do have been allowed to accumulate until now there is imminent possibility that these uncertainties will lead to social disintegration. . . .

'' It is my firm belief that confusion in the world of mind is the real cause of the present chaos in the world of concrete happenings. Life has grown so complex and its instruments have become so abstract that human capacities are overtaxed. The result is bewilderment and a type of uneffective action not unlike that which appears when men are lost in the forest and circle round and round looking vainly for the way out.'' [7]

Another modern educational writer gives the following as the main cause of uncertainty and confusion that now exist in the educational world:

'' It is because Christ's words are disregarded, because the Word of God

[6] Robert Maynard Hutchins, President of Chicago University, *Higher Learning in America* (Yale University Press).

[7] Charles H. Judd, Dept. of Education, Chicago University, *School and Society*, Sept. 19, 1936.

is given second place in education, that infidelity is riot and iniquity is rife. Things of minor consequence occupy the minds of many of the teachers of today. A man of tradition containing a mere semblance of truth is brought into the courses of study given in the schools of the world. The force of much human teaching is found in assertion, not in truth. The teachers of the present day can use only the ability of previous teachers; and yet with all the weighty importance that may be attached to the words of the greatest human authors, there is a conscious inability to trace back to the first great principle, the Source of unerring wisdom. There is a painful uncertainty, a constant searching, a reaching for assurance that can be found only in God. The trumpet of human greatness may be sounded, but it is with an uncertain sound. . . . In acquiring earthly knowledge, men have thought to gain a treasure; and they have laid the Bible aside, ignorant that it contains a treasure worth everything else. A failure to study and obey God's Word has brought confusion into the world."[8]

Here the writer plainly points out the great cause of present educational uncertainty and confusion: "The Word of God is given a second place in education," "a failure to study and obey the Word of God has brought confusion into the world," and for these reasons "infidelity is riot and iniquity is rife."

Greatest Educational Guide Book

The above writer goes on to speak of the Bible as an educational book:

"The Word of God should stand as the highest educating book in our world. . . . It should be placed in the hands of the children and youth as the great lesson book." . . . "The education gained from the study of God's Word will enlarge the narrow confines of human scholarship, and present before the mind a far deeper knowledge to be obtained through a connection with God."[9]

It is interesting to note that some of the greatest men of our nation have appreciated the educational value of the Bible. The testimonies of a few of them are here given:

"The studious perusal of the Sacred Volume will make better citizens. So great is my veneration for the Bible, that the earlier my children begin to read it, the more confident will be my hopes that they will prove useful citizens of their country, and respectable members of society."
—JOHN QUINCY ADAMS.

"There is no solid basis for civilization but in the Word of God."
—DANIEL WEBSTER.

"In regard to the Great Book, I have only to say that it is the best gift which God has given to man." —ABRAHAM LINCOLN.

"Hold fast to the Bible, it is the sheet-anchor of your liberties. Write its precepts on your hearts, and practice them in your lives. To the in-

[8] Ellen G. White, *Counsels to Teachers*, pp. 439, 440 (Pacific Press Pub. Assn.).

[9] *Ibid.*, pp. 427, 13.

fluence of this book, we are indebted for the progress made in civilization,
and to this we must look as our guide in the future.''

—ULYSSES S. GRANT.

'' The more profoundly we study this wonderful Book, and the more
closely we observe its divine precepts, the better citizens we will become,
and the higher will be our destiny as a nation.''   —WILLIAM McKINLEY.

'' If a man is not familiar with the Bible, he has suffered a great loss
which he had better make all possible haste to correct.''

—THEODORE ROOSEVELT.

'' I expect to find solution of problems before me as President, in the
proportion that I am faithful in the study of the Word of God.''

—WOODROW WILSON.

'' Science, however important, does not provide a civilization that can
stand without classical ideals. The classic of all classics is the Bible.''

—CALVIN COOLIDGE.

The Greatest Teacher of Morals

Educators are preparing books on character education, and using
material from the Bible for this purpose. The lack of character education in higher institutions of learning, and negative efforts put forth on
the part of some college and university teachers, are given consideration
in a recent publication entitled, *Christ Crucified in Our Colleges* by Dan
Gilbert.

Christ in American Education, by Dr. Gerrit Verkuyl, indicates that
an effort is being made to accentuate the principles and methods of the
" Master Teacher " in American education. Among the practical books
written are the following by Dr. H. H. Horne, holding the chair of
Philosophy of Education, in New York City University: *Jesus the
Master Teacher; Christ in Man Making; The Essentials of Leadership;
Idealism in Education; Jesus our Standard; Modern Problems as Jesus
Saw Them.*

According to the testimonies given by educators, clergy, and statesmen, the prime reason for education failing to educate is the failure to
train and develop the moral and spiritual powers of the children and
youth of the nation. This is true of all nations according to the history
of education impartially and truly written.

Has any nation existed which in its educational system has provided
for the moral and spiritual development of its posterity? If so, are the
principles, methods, and results of that system available for study and
investigation?

Hebrew Moral Education

William T. Harris, U. S. Commissioner of Education, in his report for
1895–6, includes a translation of a Jewish primer written by Rabbi
Akibah, who was living A. D. 70 when the Jerusalem Temple was
destroyed. Concerning the educational value of this Jewish primer,
Commissioner Harris says:

" This article (Jewish primer) is interesting and valuable in the history of education as showing the pains taken in Hebrew education to find a spiritual sense to all natural and artificial objects. Europeans and Americans are content to require their children to study the alphabet and master it as a mechanical affair. The Hebrew is of all people the one chosen by Divine Providence to ponder most carefully the spiritual sense of nature and human life. It would be expected, therefore, that an account of Hebrew education would show some of the devices by which the directive power of that wonderful people should manifest in its sleepless care of the culture of the spiritual sense. . . .

" The student of the philosophy of history and the philosophy of education will read with interest this excerpt from the history of Jewish education, as showing the neglect of what is mechanical and prosaic; what in other words is the letter for the spirit of it,—the spiritual sense which the Hebrew mind finds underlying all in time and space." [10]

Doctor Naphtali Herz-Imber, the translator of the Jewish primer, speaks thus concerning its educational value:

" We can now understand the psychological problem, how the Hebrews, whose religion was void of the idealistic charm which characterized the religion of the Pagans, yet proved to be better devotees to their faith, in spite of the dryness and lack of inspiring motives. The answer to that problem is the Jewish primer, and the idealistic spiritual education which was implanted in the heart of the child by it, and has inspired the grown Hebrew to endure temptations, as well as persecutions. From a historical and educational point of view the Jewish primer is of great value bearing testimony to the great power of education." [11]

We close this chapter by giving the hopeful outlook for American education, as expressed by Dr. William J. Bogan, Superintendent of Schools, Chicago, in his address on " The Schools and America's Future " at the Department of Superintendence Convention held at Atlantic City, N. J., February 23–28, 1935. He said in part:

" Why did the Hebrews abandon their great weapon, the war club? They had made a reputation for military power that extended far over Egypt's dark sea and beyond the borders of Scythia, Assyria, Babylonia, and Arabia. The answer lies in their recognition of the possibilities of a new weapon, a better weapon than the club. Education is the protection of all mankind. It is one blessing which even the severest blows of fate cannot take away from man. Through education the lowest one in the world may mount from the depths to the heights. He may bring with him rich and poor, weak and strong, the lame, the halt, the blind, and people from all kinds of environment. From that little patch in the barren land called Palestine, religious and profane (secular) systems of education, nurturing the highest ideals, have spread throughout the world and influenced the thoughts and actions of all peoples." [12]

---

[10] U. S. Commissioner of Education, *Report*, 1895–6. Vol. I, p. 701.
[11] *Ibid.*, p. 702.
[12] Department of Superintendence, *Official Report*, 1935, pp. 293, 294.

THE EDUCATION THAT DID NOT FAIL TO EDUCATE

The Ancient Hebrew System

ONE of the Oriental systems of education—the Ancient Hebrew—has been very carefully studied in recent years by eminent scholars, and given unqualified endorsement by some of them; and others have deemed it worthy of study because of certain elements in it that might with profit be grafted into present-day educational systems.

For some reason writers of history of education have given very little space in their works to Hebrew or Jewish education. Most of the educational historians have devoted but a few paragraphs or pages to it and have justified this meager mention by saying that the Hebrews made the greatest of all contributions to the field of religion; but very little if anything to education. Now it is being fearlessly asserted that as in religion, so in education, the Hebrews have made the greatest contribution of any nation, ancient, medieval, or modern. A little over a half century ago, when the battle of anti-Semitism in Germany and Austria had reached its culminating point, Doctor M. I. Schleiden, a Christian professor of science, felt moved to write an essay entitled: *The Importance of the Jews for the Preservation and Revival of Learning During the Middle Ages.* The movement he tried to stem, the English translator of his essay says, "had assumed threatening proportions, not stopping short of disfiguring historical truth, trying to rob Judaism of its reputation in the world of letters and learning, which it had well earned by generations of gifted scholars, whose work had left its mark upon the development of almost every field of human research and knowledge."

This essay, written originally in the German, went through several editions and has been translated into French, Italian and English. The author, in the preface of one of the later editions, states his reason for writing the essay, and his appreciation of its kind reception:

" It has given me great satisfaction that this essay . . . has been noticed in a manner which I could hardly venture to expect. This is perhaps partly due to the recognition of the feeling which caused me to pen these chapters, a wish at least to make a commencement to set right a part of the unspeakable wrong which has been done the Jews by the Christians."

Conservators and Contributors of Knowledge

In his essay Doctor Schleiden gives a historical survey of the work done by Jewish scholars among the various nations, from the beginning of the exilic period down to the Renaissance, and then concludes with the following general statement:

" I have shown how during the whole of the Middle Ages, while all European nations stood still or retrograded, or, like the Germanic people, had scarcely advanced at all, the Jews stepped forward energetically on the path of mental progress, and developed every side of scientific life, and how much of their acquisitions had been transferred to the various nations who were commencing a new intellectual life by the end of the Middle Ages."

Speaking of the intellectual contributions made by the Jews to Western nations he continues:

" But the Jews have an additional great merit. At the time when the Western nations began to look longingly toward the valuable results of the old intellectual culture, the Jews had to step forward and act as interpreters, as the ignorant Christians of the period did not understand the languages in which the spirit of the Old World had communicated its gifts.

" Had the Jews not done good work as translators, the darkness of the medieval life would not have been lifted from us for a long time. The first people who developed a fresh intellectual life after the night of the migrations of the nations, and the wild orgies following their wake, were the Moorish Arabs, and they were solely indebted to the Jews who interpreted Greek literature to them. A Jew—Aristobulus—was primarily instrumental in bringing about the translation of the Old Testament into the Greek, the so-called Septuagint, and his grandson, bearing the same name, translated the book of Jesus Sirach (Book of Wisdom) into the same language."

After this general statement regarding the preservation and propagation of learning, Doctor Schleiden enumerates the various branches of knowledge pursued by the Jews:

" We find that during the intellectually dark and slothful Middle Ages, the Jews were the preservers of agriculture, of all large industries, the cultivation of silk, dyeing and weaving works. It was they who carried on an international trade which was and ever will be necessary to the well-being of all nations. We have seen that the Jews left no branch of science or learning untouched, ever searching and developing, and at the end of the Middle Ages handing over the results of their long and arduous labors to the nations who were only commencing to wake up. They are the founders of systematic philology, they . . . are the only people who possessed a penetrating and fruitful knowledge of Holy Writ, as they stood alone for many centuries in their knowledge of the languages of the Orient (partly even of Greek) and the tongues of the West; they were furthermore the only people who freely developed the study of philosophy, and more especially that part of philosophy relating to religious problems; while they cultivated with greater thoroughness than any other nation the field of ethics and practical morality.

" We find, again, that it was a special object of research with the Jews to elaborate a methodical and scientific study of medicine, they participated actively in the progress of Astronomy, they founded the great medical faculties of Salerno and Montpelier, and contributed materially to the flourishing condition of the University of Padua. A few years after the invention of the art of printing, the Jews established printing works in many towns.''

Doctor Schleiden verifies his contention as to the Jews being the conservators of knowledge by the following quotation from what he deemed a worthy source:

'' We are indebted to the Jews for our first knowledge of philosophy, botany, medicine, astronomy, cosmography, no less than for the elements of grammar, the sacred languages and almost all branches of Biblical study.''[1]

Modern Debt to Hebrew Education

Many bear witness to the historical truth that the Jews have occupied vantage ground mid the mountain peaks of learning since they lost their national identity as well as before. To the ancient Hebrews were committed the true principles not only of morals and religion, but also of education. Scholars generally, although somewhat reluctantly, are conceding to this view, for the indisputable evidence brought forward makes any other attitude disquieting and unsatisfactory.

Doctor E. C. Baldwin, while holding the chair of English Literature in the Illinois University, states clearly and briefly the attitude of unprejudiced scholars regarding our educational obligations to the Hebrew peoples, in his book entitled, *Our Modern Debt to Ancient Israel*. He says in part:

'' Undoubtedly the most important result of the new interest in Hebrew literature has been the awakening of the world to a keener realization of the incalculable debt that it owes to Israel and to Israelitish thought. We have at last come to understand that modern culture, both artistic and ethical, goes back to Athens and to Jerusalem, but that English culture owes far more to the Hebrew than to the Greek. By clearly revealing the contributions made to our intellectual and moral life by the leaders of Israelitish thought, modern scholars have shown that we are what we are not only morally but intellectually as a result of the influence of Moses, David, Solomon, Isaiah, of Paul and of Jesus, rather than as a result of the influence of Homer, Hesiod, Sophocles, Aristophanes, Plato and Aristotle.''[2]

Chancellor Matthews of New York City University, in his work, *The Bible and Men of Learning*, expressed the same thought in the following pregnant sentence: "The Hebrews drank of the fountain, the Greeks from the stream, and the Romans from the pool."[3]

Doctor Fletcher Harper Swift of the California University in his book, *The Education of Ancient Israel to A. D. 70*, speaks of the education of the Jews in its relation to Greece and Rome:

'' Despite the fact that the great cultural heritage of Greece and Hellenized Rome was at their very doors, the faithful Jews not only remained

[1] M. I. Schleiden, *The Importance of the Jews for the Preservation and Revival of Learning during the Middle Ages*, pp. 55–57.

[2] E. C. Baldwin, *Our Modern Debt to Ancient Israel*, pp. 6, 7. (Sherman and French.)

[3] Matthews, *The Bible and Men of Learning*, p. 224.

indifferent to the physical, esthetic, and intellectual interest of their pagan conquerors, but studiously excluded them from their schools and from their ambitions. Narrow as this may seem, it is doubtful whether any other course would have saved the Jews from paganism, amalgamation and oblivion.'' [4]

This statement of Doctor Swift indicates the unswerving fidelity and loyalty of the faithful Jews throughout the centuries, not only in the matters of religion, but also to the principles of education given to them by Moses after their exodus from Egypt as Hebrew slaves, long before they were recognized as a people with national standing.

Educational Systems Compared

Louise Emery Tucker, A. M., for many years occupying the chair of education at the College of New Rochelle, writes in the preface of her book, *Visualized History of Education:*

'' In the light of experience, gained through contact with students during my eight years' occupancy of the chair of education at the College of New Rochelle, and through many years of supervisory and lecture work with teachers, I have compressed the leading facts of educational history into outline form in this book. It is an attempt to marshal in orderly form and in small compass the progressive story of the changing educational ideal, and its attempted realization of itself through curriculum and method.''

In this excellent work the author attempts to evaluate the various educational systems of the ancient, medieval and modern periods. This is done by giving the '' strong points '' and '' weak points '' of each system, by the naming of great educational leaders, and by pointing out the contributions to modern educational theory and practice.

Inasmuch as Doctor Baldwin, already quoted, has indicated the superiority of Hebrew education over that of Greek, it will be of interest to note the evaluation by Louise Emory Tucker of the education of this ancient nation. It is as follows:

Greek Education

'' 1. Strong points:
- (1) They exalted the home and magnified the rights of parents over their children.
- (2) They gave the individual an opportunity of free development.
- (3) They had a harmonious education subject to state inspection.
- (4) They produced great men, such as Socrates, Plato, and Aristotle.
- (5) They foreshadowed the kindergarten by recognizing the educational value of play.
- (6) They realized the state ideal through the development of the individual.
- (7) A few were ideally educated.

'' 2. Weak points:
- (1) They tended toward an extreme development of selfish individualism.

[4] F. H. Swift, *The Education of Ancient Israel to A. D. 70,* pp. 78–79 (Open Court Pub. Co.).

(2) Women, slaves, and vast masses of the population were excluded from educational benefits.''

Hebrew Education

'' 1. Strong points:
(1) They exalted the woman and made the home the vital factor
of national life.
(2) They formed a progressive race, lovers and seekers after
knowledge.
(3) They fostered patriotism and obedience to law.
(4) They produced many great leaders such as Moses, Solomon,
Elijah, and Isaiah.
(5) Racial characteristics were conserved and perpetuated through
a troublous history. They furnish an example unparalleled in
history of educational devotion.
(6) The elevation of the teacher to a high social and national
position.
'' 2. Weak points:
(1) Much of the instruction was formal training, rather than
thought training.
(2) Psychologically, they had a mistaken notion of corporal
punishment.'' [5]

Hebrew Education Superior to Greek

In the above evaluation of Greek and Hebrew education the latter
appears to have occupied higher vantage ground. This is positively
asserted by Dr. John A. Maynard, associate professor of Semitic
languages, and the history of religion in Bryn Mawr College. In his
book entitled, A Survey of Hebrew Education, he writes:

'' The Spartans and the old Athenians wanted to be brave men, the old
Romans knew how to obey, but the old Greek education was unable to maintain its hold upon men when Hellas became more civilized and the old
Roman education gave way also before the less virile ways of the new
Hellas. Hebrew education trained servants of God who knew how to be
brave and obedient; except among a minority of wealthy Sadducees,
their educational ideals remained untarnished by Hellenism. This is why
mankind is their debtor. The health of the world came indeed from the
Jews. No decadence affected their educational ideals. . . . The Greek with
his art and his philosophy, the Roman with his law and statesmanship,
the Neo-Greek of the renascence with his erudition and his classicism are
of less real value today than the old Hebrew. They did not understand
as well as he that the most important element of education is moral discipline, that the home is a place of happiness and duty, that true greatness
is in the righteousness which can be found only by faith in God.'' [6]

Doctor Maynard indicates that modern education greatly needs to
learn the valuable lessons taught by Hebrew methods and ideals:

[5] L. E. Tucker, Visualised History of Education, pp. 33, 26 (Hinds, Hayden and Eldridge, Inc.).

[6] J. A. Maynard, A Survey of Hebrew Education, p. 56 ff. (Morehouse
Pub. Co.).

" As for us, we can learn from Hebrew methods at times, from Hebrew ideals very often. In these days of machinery and complexity of crowded tenements, highly strained modes of living, noisy standardized pleasures, we need an education that will provide a way of escape for the heart and mind. The Hebrews knew when to find it, even by the waters of Babylon. Perchance if we are inspired by him we shall know how to deal more effectively with the problems of education in theory and practice. From the point of view of history of education *per se*, we may learn from our study to be less dogmatic, to have little or no faith in labels given to people or great men. . . . We should not say with Davidson that the Hebrews before the exile must be classed as barbarians along with the Phœnicians. Such classifications are meaningless. These barbarians are our masters and our teachers; we use their alphabet; we read their literature; we try to follow their social ethics. If the history of education paid more attention, as it should, to a careful study of racial intelligence it would rate Hebrew education high.'' [7]

Jesus Educated on the Hebrew Plan

Teachers and educators in the elementary schools, in spite of the chaos and confusion that exist as to the best methods of child education, are encouraged and heartened as they study the unfolding and expanding life of the " child " who " grew, and waxed strong in spirit, filled with wisdom, and the grace of God was upon him. . . . And Jesus increased in wisdom and stature, and in favor with God and man."

A very illuminating article on child education, by Lucia Barton Morse entitled: " The Child Grew " appeared in *Progressive Education*. It deals with the Hebrew methods of child training and suggests that their application in modern education will help to solve some of our confusing and perplexing problems:

" Out of the chaos of opinion as to what constitutes the whole child, what may be the real meaning of intelligence, or how opportunity should be provided to develop creative expression, may we not look over the ages to that one Child whose influence has been indelibly stamped upon our time, because in some way He increased toward perfection in mind and body, and in His spiritual and social relationship?

" It is this contact with the spiritual which in the modern world of materialism we fail to make vital. Busying ourselves with providing the means for measuring a child's intelligence, we lose our vision of wisdom. Setting up an environment which invites self-expression, we limit our sense of the real self, ' in favor with God,' to the mere human impulses acting without basic principle. Establishing a school community which may best present social experiences, we try to guide and nurture the relations involved, without the one element which can give them universal value and effectiveness, a knowledge of love as God, as a force apart from human selfish will, and animating every situation. . . . To grow in favor with God is to have the forces within one's self controlled by a higher law. . . .

" Our children of today are free and fine and beautiful, but they lack that poise that comes with the deliberate choice of principle to direct their lives. They think and act independently and creatively, but too often they

[7] *Ibid.*, p. 59 f.

are afforded no background for judgments or for action beyond that intelligence that can be measured. . . .

"It may be a solution to our problem if among other educational activities we faithfully water and nourish this seed which is in the soul of every child, that he may naturally grow and wax strong in spirit. For whatever form the idea of God may take in our diversified minds, we can but know that there are no figures which may determine how much of the kingdom of heaven a child may manifest."[8]

In the above quotation the Hebrew plan and method of educating the child is strongly recommended, and special attention is called to the training and developing of the spiritual powers, which are so sadly neglected in modern education.

Let us now briefly review the evaluation of Hebrew and Jewish education as given by educators in this chapter:

1. The Jews were the conservators, interpreters and propagators of knowledge during the darkness of medieval life.

2. During the intellectually dark and slothful Middle Ages the Jews were the preservers of agriculture, dyeing and weaving works, all large industries, and carried on international trade so necessary to the well-being of all nations.

3. The Jews were diligent students of science and philosophy, and were the founders of a systematic philology.

4. The Jews made a methodical and scientific study of medicine, contributing many valuable books on materia medica; and established medical schools of Salerno and Montpelier.

5. The Jews contributed materially to the flourishing condition of the University of Padua.

6. A few years after the invention of the printing art, the Jews established printing works in many towns.

7. We are indebted to the Jews for first knowledge of philosophy, botany, medicine, astronomy, the elements of grammar, the sacred languages, and almost all branches of Biblical study.

8. Modern culture, both artistic and ethical, goes back to Athens and Jerusalem; but English culture both morally and intellectually owes far more to the Hebrews than the Greeks.

9. The faithful Jews excluded from their schools the esthetic and intellectual culture of their pagan conquerors, thus saving their nation from paganism, amalgamation, and oblivion.

10. In the evaluation of various systems of education (ancient, medieval and modern) by the educational historian, Hebrew education ranks high.

11. Some modern educators give Hebrew education the highest place, not excepting the Greek system of education, which generally has been accorded that honor.

12. The chief element giving superiority to Hebrew education over all other systems is the moral and spiritual training of the child, bear-

[8] *Progressive Education*, Vol. 3, No. 1, 1926.

ing fruitage in the lives of such characters as Joseph, Moses, Solomon, Isaiah, Daniel and Esther, but reaching its fullest and sublimest expression through the parental training of the child Jesus.

It seems very evident that there is a growing interest in Hebrew education on the part of many teachers and educators, and hope is entertained that an application of its principles and methods will prove a panacea to present educational ills. The remaining portion of this book will be devoted to a study of the principles, methods, product, and contributions of Hebrew education, and to an application of the principles and methods to the present modern problems of education.

The author confidently believes that the readers who are engaged in religious education will be most benefited by this study. He also believes that those teachers and educators in secular schools who have faith in the Bible as the inspired Word of God will be greatly benefited by this study of Hebrew education. And more than this, he even believes that those who doubt the inspiration of the Bible, and may go so far as to classify themselves as agnostics, skeptics or infidels will profit by this study. He is so sure that they will not be harmed by this study, that a hearty invitation is given and urgent request made that this group of teachers and educators continue their reading with open minds and hearts until the end of the book is reached. With this invitation gladly and freely extended we now launch into the study of the next chapter on " Foundation Principles " of Hebrew education.

PART TWO

THEORY OF HEBREW EDUCATION

IV

FOUNDATION PRINCIPLES

Educational Systems

IN the previous chapters we have quoted the testimonies of eminent educators and of men carrying responsibilities in church and national affairs, all showing that we live in a period of "great educational unrest," and that in spite of the large educational program being carried out by the leading nations of our day, the results are far from satisfactory.

Educational theorists and historians have in the past given diligent consideration to the Greek and Roman systems of education, as well as to the systems of Oriental nations; but in none of them has been found that wisdom which "is a tree of life to them that lay hold upon her; and happy is every one that retaineth her" (Prov. 3: 18).

One Oriental nation, however, has been given very meager consideration, it seemingly being taken for granted that no good thing in educational theory and practice can come out of Judæa. Many scholars have boldly asserted that Israel made but one lone contribution of value to the world; that was her system of morals and religion. But may it not be that a nation which has bequeathed this best of all gifts holds in her lap other gifts of rare and priceless value?

One reason given for not considering the educational system of the ancient Hebrews is the meager literature we possess describing that system, the Old Testament being the only history preserved contemporary with their national development. Since the Old Testament Bible is a history of the religious life and experience of the Hebrews, it is not regarded as authority concerning their principles and practice in education. But may it not be that this attitude toward the Bible is due to a narrow, restricted, or even erroneous view of what is to be included in education, and that a careful study of the Bible would give a clearer and more comprehensive outlook on this all-important question?

Relation of the Bible to Education

The Bible does not give in detail correct business forms, it does not delineate arithmetical processes or illustrate rapid methods of calculation, for God has given to men the powers of origination, comparison, and judgment for the development of these essentials. But the Bible does give that which is of far greater importance than methods and processes, namely, guiding principles of honesty, fidelity, and thrift illustrated in human experience, without which, however thoroughly other essentials are mastered, no man can pursue a truly successful business career.

The Bible does not give to the linguist rules of syntax and literary criticism, but the chief requisites of language—simplicity, purity, veracity, without which no man can become a master of letters—it repeatedly emphasizes. Even from a purely literary standpoint the Bible generally is regarded as the greatest of all classics.

The Bible does not organize and systematize the observed facts of creation, and from these formulate and state the laws of nature; for man is endowed with powers of observation, reflection, and organization which enable him to classify and systematize into the various sciences the knowledge gained. But it does lift the curtain which divides the seen from the unseen, and the student becomes acquainted with his Maker, the Creator of all things. In all the operations of nature he beholds a revelation of the power, wisdom, and love of God. By beholding the divine character he becomes changed into the same likeness. Godliness—God-like-ness—becomes the one great longing of the soul, until, like David, he speaks to God: "I meditate on all thy works; I muse on the works of thy hands. I stretch forth my hands unto thee, my soul thirsteth after thee as a thirsty land" (Ps. 143: 5).

The Bible does not give a great array of facts, and descriptions of customs and habits of peoples such as are contained in descriptive geographies and secular histories, but it far outreaches them by telling when, how, and why the earth was brought into existence. The Bible, only, tells when and where human history began and how it will end. It traces the hand of God in human history and emphasizes the great truth that "the Most High ruleth in the kingdom of men, and giveth it to whomsoever he will." The Bible is God's history of the world— past, present and future; so that the student who has mastered Bible history is able to view all history from God's standpoint; to study all history at its base, and therefore to become a wiser historian than by the study of secular history alone.

Educational Principles in the Bible

The following are the main educational principles found in the Bible, either directly stated or implied from its teaching:

1. God is to be recognized as the Creator of all things. "Remember now thy Creator in the days of thy youth" (Eccl. 12: 1). "In six days the Lord made heaven and earth, the sea and all that in them is, and rested the seventh day" (Ex. 20: 11).

2. The works of creation are to be studied by man.

(1) *Plant Life.* "Consider the lilies of the field how they grow" (Matt. 6: 28). The method of study is suggested. Study the lilies in

the field where they grow, and learn how they grow. Physiological rather than systematic botany is given the main emphasis.

(2) *Animal Life.*

   a. *The Birds:* "Consider the ravens" (Luke 12: 24). "Behold the fowls of the air" (Matt. 6: 26). The word "behold" suggests field study.

   b. *The Insects:* "Go to the ant, thou sluggard; consider her ways and be wise" (Prov. 6: 6). The method of study is suggested: "Go to the ant." Go where the ants live and observe them. Learn "her ways" (habits) for that is more important than to learn of their structure.

   c. *The Beasts:* "They shall teach thee."

   d. *The Fowls:* "They shall tell thee."

   e. *The Fishes:* "They shall declare unto thee." Study in their natural surroundings these creatures that God has made and hear their message: "that the hand of the Lord hath wrought this, in whose hand is the soul of every living thing, and the breath of all mankind" (Job 12: 7-10).

   f. *Inanimate Nature:* "Speak to the earth and it shall teach thee" (Verse 8).

   g. *The Starry Heavens:* "Lift up your eyes on high and behold who hath created these things, that bringeth out their hosts by number; he calleth them all by their names, by the greatness of his might, for that he is strong in power; not one faileth" (Isa. 40: 26). See more than the stars, "Behold (Him) who hath created these things."

If the above suggestions as to methods were carried out in the study of nature and science, there would be more study in the great out-of-door laboratory which God has provided, and He would be more in the student's thoughts.

3. The works of creation are to be regarded as an exhibition of the love, wisdom, and power of God. "The Lord by wisdom hath founded the earth; by understanding hath he established the heavens. By his knowledge the depths are broken up, and the clouds drop down the dew" (Prov. 3: 19, 20).

4. The operations of nature are direct manifestation of the wisdom, power, and love of God.

"He giveth snow like wool; he scattereth the hoar frost like ashes" (Ps. 147: 16). "He sendeth rain on the just and on the unjust" (Matt. 5: 45). "He giveth to the beast his food, and to the young ravens which cry" (Ps. 147: 9). "He causeth the grass to grow for the cattle, and herb for the service of man . . . and wine that maketh glad the heart of man, and oil to make his face to shine, and bread which strengtheneth man's heart" (Ps. 104: 14, 15).

5. Man's unaided wisdom is not able to comprehend the works of God. "Canst thou by searching find out God? Canst thou find out

the Almighty to perfection? It is as high as heaven; what canst thou do? deeper than hell; what canst thou know?" (Job 11: 7, 8).

6. Wisdom is a gift from God in answer to faith: "If any of you lack wisdom, let him ask of God . . . and it shall be given him. But let him ask in faith, nothing wavering" (Jas. 1: 5, 6).

Examples:

Solomon. "God gave Solomon wisdom and understanding exceeding much" (I Kings 4: 29).

Daniel and His Companions. "As for these four children, God gave them knowledge and skill in all learning and wisdom" (Dan. 1: 17).

Bezaleel and Aholiab. "Them hath he filled with wisdom of heart, to work all manner of work, of the engraver and of the cunning workman" (Ex. 35: 35).

7. Wisdom is primary in importance; knowledge is secondary: "Wisdom is the principal thing; therefore get wisdom, and with all thy getting get understanding" (knowledge) (Prov. 4: 7).

8. Wisdom is given to those who seek for knowledge that they may glorify God. "Give therefore thy servant an understanding heart to judge thy people, that I may discern between good and bad; for who is able to judge this thy so great a people? And the speech (request) pleased the Lord, that Solomon had asked this thing" (I Kings 3: 9, 10).

9. The Holy Spirit is man's teacher and guide in the search for truth. "Howbeit when he, the Spirit of truth, is come, he will guide you into *all* truth" (John 16: 13).

10. The attitude and spirit of the true seeker after knowledge:

    (1) Receptive: "Receive my words."

    (2) Retentive: "Hide my commandments with thee."

    (3) Attentive: "Incline thine ear."

    (4) Applicative: "Apply thine heart."

    (5) Supplicative: "Cryest after knowledge and liftest up thy voice for understanding."

    (6) Active: "Seekest her as silver, and searchest for her as for hid treasures."

    (7) Results: "Then shalt thou understand the fear of the Lord and *find the knowledge of God*" (Prov. 2: 1–5).

11. God is recognized as the source of all true wisdom and knowledge: "The Lord giveth wisdom; out of his mouth cometh knowledge and understanding" (Prov. 2: 6). "In whom (Christ) are hid all the treasures of wisdom and knowledge." "And ye are complete in him" (Col. 2: 3, 10).

12. The book of Proverbs is recognized as the greatest educational book in the Bible, emphasizing the threefold development of man's powers—the physical, the mental, and the spiritual; and the proper social relations of man with man, individually and collectively.

13. The education of the child Jesus is a perfect example of the outworking of the threefold plan of development of the Hebrew system of education. "The child grew (physically), and waxed strong in spirit

(spiritually), filled with wisdom (intellectually); increased . . . in favor with God and man (socially) and the grace of God was upon him" (Luke 2: 40, 52).

14. The pre-eminence of the spiritual development: "Seek ye first the kingdom of God and his righteousness, and all these (temporal) things shall be added unto you" (Matt. 6: 33).

15. Character, the great end in all education: "Bodily exercise profiteth little (somewhat); but godliness is profitable unto all things, having promise of the life that now is and of that which is to come" (I Tim. 4: 8).

16. Give diligent heed to scriptural warnings against false education. "Beware lest any man spoil you through philosophy and vain deceit; after the tradition of men, after the rudiments of the world, and not after Christ" (Col. 2: 8).

17. Discern the workings of false education. "The world by wisdom knew not God."

"For the wisdom of this world is foolishness with God" (I Cor. 1: 21; 3: 19). "When they knew God, they glorified him not as God . . . but became vain in their imaginations (reasonings), and their foolish heart was darkened. Professing themselves to be wise they became fools. . . . Who changed the truth of God into a lie, and worshipped and served the creature rather than the Creator. . . . And even as they did not like to retain God in their knowledge, God gave them over to a mind void of judgment" (Rom. 1: 21–28. Margin).

18. Parental responsibility in the education of the child. "Teach us what we shall do unto the child that shall be born." "How shall we order (train) the child, and what shall be his work?" (Judges 13: 8, 12. Margin). "These words which I command this day shall be in thine heart, and thou shalt teach them diligently unto thy children, and shalt talk of them when thou sittest in thy house, and when thou walkest by the way, and when thou liest down, and when thou risest up . . . and thou shalt write them upon the post of thy house and on thy gates" (Deut. 6: 6–9).

19. The sure reward of faithful training. "Train up a child in *the way* he should go; and when he is old, he will not depart from it" (Prov. 22: 6).

20. Thorough education and training insures opportunity for service. "Neglect not the gift that is in thee" (I Tim. 4: 14). "Stir up the gift of God which is in thee" (II Tim. 1: 6). "A man's gift maketh room for him, and bringeth him before great men" (Prov. 18: 16). "A man's wisdom maketh his face to shine, and the boldness of his face shall be changed" (Eccl. 8: 1).

The foundation principles of Hebrew education enumerated above are generally accepted by all those who regard the Bible as the inspired word of God. That these principles may be better understood and intelligently incorporated into present-day educational theory and practice, the next chapter is devoted to an analysis of Hebrew education.

V

HEBREW EDUCATION ANALYZED

Origin of Hebrew Education

BEFORE making an analysis of Hebrew education, let us first consider its origin. Did it originate with the Hebrews or was it borrowed or copied from Egypt or Babylon, or some other nation with whom they came in contact? We find the question regarding the origin of Hebrew education not only asked, but also answered in the Bible.

The question was asked and answered by Job living sometime between the days of Abraham and Moses, the latter undoubtedly writing the book bearing his name. Job is spoken of in the Scriptures as a man that "was perfect and upright, and one that feared God, and eschewed evil" (Job 1: 1). He had much wealth and "a very great household; so that this man was the greatest of all the men of the East" (Verse 3). It would seem from the Scripture record that he was a king, for he says: "When I went out to the gate through the city, when I prepared my seat in the street, the young men saw me and hid themselves, and the aged arose and stood up. The princes refrained from talking and laid their hand on their mouth. The nobles held their peace and their tongue cleaved to the roof of their mouth. When the ear heard me then it blessed me; and when the eye saw me, it gave witness unto me; because I delivered the poor that cried, and the fatherless and him that had none to help him" (Job 29: 7–12). He was not only a just and compassionate ruler, but he was a wise teacher and educator. Eliphaz, one of his three leading councilors, speaking of him as a teacher said: "Behold, thou hast instructed many, and thou hast strengthened the weak hands. Thy words have upholden him that was falling, and thou hast strengthened the feeble knees" (Job 4: 3, 4). Knowing that Job was both a wise ruler and an inspiring teacher of his people, we shall certainly be inclined to listen with respect and confidence to his answer as to the origin and character of Hebrew education.

First Question: "Where shall wisdom be found? and where is the place of understanding?"

First Answer: "Man knoweth not the price (value) thereof: neither is it found in the land of the living" (Job 28: 12, 13).

He declared man's ignorance regarding the source of education (wisdom and understanding) and also its value. He again repeats his question as to the origin of education, declaring man's utter ignorance of it, and then proceeds to tell of its source and character.

Second Question: " Whence then cometh wisdom, and where is the place of understanding seeing it is hid from the eyes of all living? "

Second Answer: " God understandeth the way thereof, and knoweth the place thereof. . . . And unto man he said, Behold, the fear of the Lord, that is wisdom, and to depart from evil is understanding " (Job 28: 20, 21, 23, 28).

The question and answer are repeated and amplified for the sake of impressing man that true education does not, cannot originate with man, any more than can true religion. It is equally a matter of divine revelation. It is of supreme importance that educators shall recognize that God is the source of true education as well as true religion. True religion is revealed in the Bible; and so is true education. The Bible is authority in religion, and it is equally so in education. In these days of educational confusion and uncertainty there is need of a voice of truth and authority that will bring unity and stability into the educational program.

Education Analyzed

Job declared that wisdom and understanding (knowledge) come only from God, and then he tells of their influence in the life of the possessor:

1. *He fears God.* " The fear of the Lord, that is wisdom."

2. *He departs from evil.* " To depart from evil is understanding " (Job 28: 28).

The very first results in the outworking of the educational process are the instilling of the fear of God in the human soul, and the departing from evil in the human conduct. Reverence and humility are cultivated; and a love of righteousness and hatred of iniquity is developed.

Solomon, the wisest and best educated of all men, agrees with Job as to the true source of education:

" The Lord giveth wisdom and out of his mouth cometh knowledge and understanding " (Prov. 2: 6).

According to Job and Solomon, education is composed of two elements—wisdom and knowledge. Speaking in the terms of chemistry, the educational compound is composed of two elements. Water is a chemical composed of the two elements, oxygen and hydrogen, the first being present in a larger proportion, as represented by the chemical symbol H_2O. Representing the educational compound in the same way we have the symbol WK. Which of these elements is present in the larger proportion, or the more important, or are they of equal importance? We are not left in uncertainty. Solomon gives the true analysis of education and indicates which is the principal element: " Wisdom is the *principal* thing; therefore get wisdom; and with all thy getting get understanding " (knowledge).

According to this analysis, wisdom is the principal element in education and cannot be expressed by less than W_2K. It may be of much greater importance; for wisdom is very highly exalted by the wise man:

" Happy is the man that findeth wisdom, and the man that getteth understanding: for the merchandise of it is better than the merchandise of silver,
and the gain thereof than fine gold. She is more precious than rubies: and
all the things thou canst desire are not to be compared unto her. Length
of days is in her right hand; and in her left hand riches and honor. Her
ways are ways of pleasantness, and all her paths are peace. She is a tree
of life to them that lay hold upon her; and happy is every one that
retaineth her '' (Prov. 3: 13–18).

" Get wisdom, get understanding: forget it not; neither decline from the
words of my mouth. Forsake her not, and she shall preserve thee: love her
and she shall keep thee. Wisdom is the principal thing; therefore get wisdom: and with all thy getting get understanding. Exalt her, and she shall
promote thee: she shall bring thee to honor, when thou dost embrace her.
She shall give to thy head an ornament of grace: a crown of glory shall she
deliver to thee '' (Prov. 4: 5–9).

Wisdom is the Principal Thing

According to the Bible, then, wisdom is the *primary* element in education, and knowledge is *secondary*. Its value is beyond all expression
and comparison. Yet how contrary is this view to that of modern
educators. Knowledge is extolled, and highly exalted; but very little,
if anything, is said as to the value of wisdom. Educational literature
from the many institutions of learning is sent to the youth urging them
to enter their doors to secure knowledge; but little is said about the
importance of securing wisdom. The abundant provision made by
these institutions for imparting knowledge, by means of libraries and
laboratories and other facilities, is graphically represented by pictorial
illustrations in college and university catalogues, calendars, and bul-
letins; but scarcely any representation is made of provisions for
imparting the " principal thing " in education.

Relation of Wisdom to Knowledge

As already noted from the Scriptures, " The fear of the Lord, that is
wisdom." Again the Word of God declares, " The fear of the Lord is
the beginning of wisdom; " that is to say one must *first* reverence and
respect God if he would have wisdom. Unless this attitude of mind
and heart is maintained toward the Creator, there is no basis of co-
operation and communion with the Master Teacher.

A very common and good definition of wisdom is the following:
" Wisdom is the ability to use knowledge aright." But it is more than
to use knowledge aright. Wisdom, when it functions fully, aids in
gathering knowledge aright, and of the right kind. The gathering of
knowledge precedes the using of it. This order of sequence is suggested by Solomon: " I gave my heart to *seek and search out by
wisdom* concerning all things that are under heaven " (Eccl. 1: 13).
Wisdom aided the youthful king in seeking and searching for knowledge, so that he was able to gather only that which was good and
useful, and not to waste his time and energy on that which was false
or of little value in the administration of the affairs of his kingdom.

What an indispensable aid to the student and teacher in the right *gathering* and *using* of knowledge is this wisdom so highly and urgently recommended by Job, Solomon, and other Bible writers.

The author offers the following as his own definition of wisdom, believing that it may help to indicate the utility and value of this primary element in education, as it functions in human life and conduct:

Wisdom is the ability which God gives to man to enable him to do the right thing, at the right time, in the right place, in the right way.

Four unalterable conditions will invariably be met when wisdom functions fully. They are:

1. The right thing.
2. The right time.
3. The right place.
4. The right way.

The conduct guided and controlled by wisdom results, then,

1. In the right thing being done.
2. In its being done at the right time.
3. In its being done in the right place.
4. In its being done in the right way.

A lack of wisdom is manifest:

1. When the right thing is done at the right time, in the right place, in the *wrong* way.
2. When the right thing is done at the right time in the *wrong* place in the right way.
3. When the right thing is done at the *wrong* time, in the right place, in the right way.
4. When the *wrong* thing is done at the right time, in the right place, in the right way.

The full and complete working of wisdom is manifest only when the right thing is done at the right time in the right place in the right way. Four rights, not one, nor two, nor even three. There must be four rights to constitute that righteousness which lifts and elevates. This is what Solomon had in mind when he said: " Righteousness exalteth a nation; but sin (unrighteousness) is a reproach to any people " (Prov. 14: 34).

Without wisdom knowledge will destroy; for, as previously quoted from Ex-President Coolidge:

" It is not only what men know, but what they are disposed to do with that which they know, that will determine the rise and fall of civilization," and " It was not education that founded religion, but it was religion that founded education. . . . This important fact cannot be ignored in our development of education. Without its spirit either civilization will fall of its own weight, and that *deep abiding* wisdom which supports society will cease to exist, or we shall have a type of mind keen in intelligence, but greedy and cruel, which, armed with the power of modern science in seeking to destroy, will accomplish its own destruction." (See p. 24.)

How Wisdom and Knowledge Are Secured

We know that we must seek and search for knowledge. There must be earnest, diligent effort in study and observation if knowledge is to be gained. But how is wisdom, this saving, preserving, uplifting element in education, to be secured? The Apostle James, the philosopher of the New Testament, gives the answer: " If any of you lack wisdom, let him ask of God, that giveth to all men liberally, and upbraideth not and it shall be given him. But let him ask *in faith* nothing wavering " (Jas. 1: 5, 6).

Wisdom, then, is a *free gift* which comes from God in answer to the prayer of *faith*. It is not secured by our study and effort, or learning through experience, but only in response to unwavering faith. There is a wisdom which comes through experience, and there is a wisdom which comes through faith. This wisdom by faith, which is the principal thing in education, is referred to by the Apostle Paul: " We speak not in the words which man's wisdom teacheth, but which the Holy Ghost teacheth " (I Cor. 2: 13).

Hebrew education included more than human teachers. It recognized the teaching and ministry of angels and of the Holy Spirit. This accords with the words of the Master Teacher before He took final leave of His earthly school of twelve: " When he, the Spirit of truth, is come, he will guide you into all truth " (John 16: 13). The angel said unto Daniel: " I will show thee that which is noted in the scripture of truth " (Dan. 10: 21).

The Apostle Paul heads the list of free gifts that come through faith in Christ with wisdom: "Of him are ye in Christ Jesus, who of God is made unto us wisdom, and righteousness, and sanctification, and redemption " (I Cor. 1: 30). When Christ by faith is made unto us wisdom, then we like Him in our conduct will do the right thing, at the right time, in the right place, in the right way. A clean, pure, moral influence will pervade both the home and the school, when parents and teachers regard wisdom instead of knowledge as the principal factor in all educational endeavor.

Educational Theory Applied

In this analysis of Hebrew education, we have thus far considered it only in theory. Now we shall proceed with the application of its principles as recorded in the Scriptures.

In the early years of Solomon we have a good example of the application of the principles of Hebrew education in human life and conduct, and the results in personal achievement. While in his teens (still " young and tender ") (I Chron. 29: 1), Solomon was anointed king over Israel. He was undoubtedly very desirous of ruling his kingdom with wisdom and discretion; for the Lord appeared to him in a dream and gave him opportunity to express the supreme desire of his heart. The following is the narrative somewhat abbreviated:

" In Gibeon the Lord appeared to Solomon in a dream by night: and God said, Ask what I shall give thee. And Solomon said, Thou hast showed unto thy servant David my father great mercy . . . and thou hast kept for him this great kindness, that thou hast given him a son to sit on his throne, as it is this day. And now, O Lord my God, thou hast made thy servant king instead of David my father: and I am but a little child. I know now how to go out or come in. . . . Give therefore thy servant an understanding heart to judge thy people, that I may discern between good and bad: for who is able to judge this thy so great a people?

" And the speech (request) pleased the Lord, that Solomon had asked this thing. And God said unto him, Because thou hast asked this thing and hast not asked for thyself long life; . . . but hast asked for thyself understanding to discern judgment; behold, I have done (not will do) according to thy words: lo, I have given (not will give) thee a wise and an understanding heart; so that there was none like thee before thee, neither after thee shall any arise like unto thee. . . . And Solomon awoke; and, behold, it was a dream " (I Kings 3: 5–15).

This request of the young ruler of Israel was highly approved and immediately answered. No lapse of years, occupied in study and research, was required to fit Solomon to administer wisely the affairs of the kingdom.

After Solomon awakened from his sleep and dream, he at once went to Jerusalem to worship God, who had promised him wisdom to judge the people. " He came to Jerusalem and stood before the ark of the covenant of the Lord, and offered up burnt offerings, and offered peace offerings, and made a feast to all his servants " (Verse 15).

As soon as he took his seat on the throne, he was confronted with a very serious and difficult problem—the maternity of a child: " Then came there two women . . . unto the king, and stood before him " (Verse 16).

As the record indicates, these two women claimed the same child. As they stood quarreling with each other before him, Solomon interrupted them by calling for a sword:

" They brought a sword before the king. And the king said, Divide the living child in two, and give half to the one, and half to the other. Then spake the woman whose the living child was unto the king . . . and she said, O my Lord, give her the living child, and in no wise slay it. But the other said, Let it be neither mine nor thine, but divide it. Then the king answered and said, Give her the living child, and in no wise slay it: she is the mother thereof " (I Kings 3: 24–27).

King Solomon decided the question at once, without taking time to gather evidence; and the wisdom and influence of that decision is recorded as follows: " All Israel heard of the judgment which the king had judged; and they feared the king: for they saw that the wisdom of God was in him, to do judgment " (Verse 28).

As already expressed, the endowment of wisdom which came to Solomon in response to his faith did not inhibit in him the desire and determination to seek for knowledge. On the contrary, he was greatly stimulated to engage in earnest study and research. " I gave my heart to seek and search out by wisdom concerning all things that are done under heaven " (Eccl. 1: 13).

Some idea of the knowledge accumulated by Solomon can be gained by the following:

1. Solomon was a great musician:

" I gat me men singers and women singers, and the delights of the sons of men, as musical instruments, and that of all sorts " (Eccl. 2: 8). " His songs were a thousand and five " (I Kings 4: 32).

2. Solomon was a great literary master:

" He spake three thousand proverbs " (I Kings 4: 32). " He gave good heed, and sought out, and set in order many proverbs. The preacher sought to find out acceptable words: and that which was written was up-right, even words of truth " (Eccl. 12: 9, 10). " Have not I written to thee excellent things in counsels and knowledge, that I might make thee know the certainty of the words of truth; that thou mightest answer the words of truth to them that send unto thee " (Prov. 22: 20, 21).

3. Solomon was a great scientist:

" He spake of (lectured on) trees (botany), from the cedar tree that is in Lebanon even unto the hyssop that springeth out of the wall: He spake also of (lectured on) beasts (zoology), and of fowl (ornithology), and of creeping things (entomology), and of fishes (ichthyology) " (I Kings 4: 33).

Using modern scientific terminology, Solomon was a specialist in botany, zoology, ornithology, entomolgy, and ichthyology.

4. Solomon was a great statesman:

" All the kings of the earth sought the presence of Solomon, to hear his wisdom, that God had put in his heart " (II Chron. 9: 23).

They desired to learn the principles of government which made him so successful in the administration of the affairs of his kingdom. The queen of Sheba came to Solomon with a doubting spirit, but returned greatly impressed by what she had heard and seen.

" She said to the king, It was a true report that I heard in mine own land of thy acts and of thy wisdom. Howbeit I believed not the words until I came, and mine eyes had seen it: and, behold, the half was not told me: thy wisdom and prosperity exceedeth the fame which I heard. Happy are thy men, happy are these thy servants, which stand continually before thee, and that hear thy wisdom " (I Kings 10: 6–8).

The capacity and extended influence of Solomon is briefly noted, as follows:

" God gave Solomon wisdom and understanding exceeding much, and largeness of heart, even as the sand that is on the seashore. And Solo-mon's wisdom excelled the wisdom of all the children of the east country, and all the wisdom of Egypt. For he was wiser than all men; . . . and his fame was in all nations round about. . . . And there came of all people to hear the wisdom of Solomon, from all kings of the earth, which had heard of his wisdom '' (I Kings 4: 29–34).

This is the man who was educated after the divine plan, and who wrote the greatest book in " the Greatest Book " on the subject of education, the book of Proverbs. In this book he has left this word for all those who desire to be truly educated: " The fear of the Lord is the beginning of wisdom: and the knowledge of the holy is understanding " (Prov. 9: 10).

Concerning the educational value of the book of Proverbs, we have the following testimony from noted scholars:

'' The book of Proverbs is pronounced by most Biblical scholars to be one of the greatest handbooks on right living ever published. It is preeminently an ideal educational book, teaching the whole duty of man. It declares that no one can be truly wise who is so utterly unwise as to disobey God or to be ignorant of His rules of government of the universe or of man. In its teaching, it is a complete outline of a perfect man. Coleridge says: ' The book of Proverbs is the best statesman's manual which was ever written, and adherence to the political economy and spirit of that collection of apothegms and essays would do more to eradicate from the people the causes of extravagance, debasement, and ruin than all the contributions on political economy of all other writers together.' '' [1]

Wisdom is the free gift of God, given liberally in answer to the prayer of faith; while the securing of knowledge is dependent upon our efforts, which will be blessed of Heaven if the motive actuating the endeavor is the honor and glory of God.

It was thus that the four Hebrew youth gained their education in the courts of Babylon: " As for these four children, God gave them knowledge and skill in all learning and wisdom " (Dan. 1:17).

In the following chapter, " Educational Development and Processes," consideration is given to the processes of learning and development employed by Hebrew educators in the education and training of children and youth.

[1] A. B. Davidson on " Proverbs " in *Bible Treasury*.

VI

EDUCATIONAL DEVELOPMENT AND PROCESSES

In the Eden School

ACCORDING to the Bible record, the first school of the human family was conducted in the Garden of Eden. The students were the parents of the human family. When created they were made " a little lower than the angels," and given dominion over all the creatures of the earth (Ps. 8: 4–8).

Many trees "pleasant to the sight," and "good for food" were planted in this garden by the Creator; and among them were two trees specifically mentioned by name: "The Tree of Life," and "The Tree of Knowledge of Good and Evil" (Gen. 2: 8, 9). The keepers of the garden were given permission to eat freely the fruit of all the trees except the fruit of the tree of knowledge of good and evil. Eating the fruit of this forbidden tree would result in death (Verses 16, 17).

The students of the Eden school occupied their time dressing and keeping the garden, and in the study of plant and animal life (Verses 15, 19, 20). The One who established the school visited them from time to time, undoubtedly giving instruction as to how the educational program was to be carried forward (Gen. 3: 8–10).

Just how long the Eden school continued the Biblical record does not state, but there came a day when the students yielded to the temptation to eat of the fruit of the tree of knowledge of good and evil. The Eden school was then closed and the entrance to the garden was guarded by angels (Gen. 3: 22–24).

Knowledge of Good and Evil

Adam and Eve in their study and occupation had gained knowledge only of the good, but from henceforth because of their own choice they and their posterity, in a world cursed because of their disobedience, have been compelled to study the good mingled with evil. Their characters, as well as the school environment, were greatly changed, and ever since the work of educating the children and youth has been a difficult and perplexing problem. Good and evil have ever struggled for the ascendancy, and this struggle was never greater than it is today as revealed in unbridled passion and appetite, producing lawlessness, crime and anarchy.

The conflict between good and evil, and the final triumph of good over evil was foreshadowed in the words God addressed to the tempter: "I will put enmity between thee and the woman, and between thy seed and her seed; it shall bruise thy head, and thou shalt bruise his heel" (Gen. 3: 15).

Education and Redemption

The Eden school has never been reopened, but it has been transferred to heaven (Rev. 22: 2, 14). There it will remain until evil is overcome with good, and then it will be returned to earth and resume its work. All this has been provided for in the plan of salvation. In order to restore the human family to their Eden home, the Son of God partook of the form and nature of humanity, living among men as a child, a youth, and a man for thirty-three years; finally dying a cruel death on the cross to atone for the transgression of our first parents and their posterity.

The principles of education governing the Eden school, the failure of our parents to co-operate with the Founder of the school, the change of school environment, and the plans devised for reopening and conducting the school according to the original charter—all of these must be carefully considered before we can comprehend what is involved in the work of education today in a world where still exists a knowledge of good and evil. This necessity is briefly but clearly stated by a modern educational writer:

"In order to understand what is comprehended in the work of education, we need to consider both the nature of man and the purpose of God in creating him. We need to consider also the change in man's condition through the coming in of a knowledge of evil, and God's plan for still fulfilling His glorious purpose in the education of the human race." [1]

Here are presented four themes that must be considered and understood, before "we can understand what is comprehended in the work of education":

1. The nature of man.
2. The purpose of the Creator in creating him.
3. The change in man's condition through the coming in of the knowledge of evil.
4. God's plan for still fulfilling His glorious purpose in the education of the human race.

Where shall we go to find a full and clear explanation of these four fundamental questions? There can be but one answer—To the Bible,—the Word of God. While the Bible is the great textbook concerning the plan of redemption, it is also the greatest textbook on the divine plan of education. Of the relation of the work of education to the work of redemption, the following is a clear statement:

"In the highest sense the work of education and the work of redemption are one, for in education, as in redemption, 'other foundation can no man lay than that is laid, which is Jesus Christ.' . . . Under changed conditions, true education is still conformed to the Creator's plan, the plan of the Eden school. . . .

"The great principles of education are unchanged. 'They stand fast forever and ever;' for they are the principles of the character of God.

[1] Ellen G. White, *Education*, pp. 14, 15 (Pacific Press Publishing Association).

To aid the student in comprehending these principles, and in entering into that relation with Christ which will make them a controlling power in the life, should be the teacher's first effort and his constant aim.''

" The Holy Scriptures are the perfect standard of truth, and as such should be given the highest place in education. To obtain an education worthy of the name, we must receive a knowledge of God, the Creator, and of Christ, the Redeemer, as they are revealed in the Sacred Word.''[2]

In order that the human family might understand the divine process of educational development, God not only gave us His written Word, the Bible, but to make it still clearer, He sent to the world His living Word—His Son—the Word made flesh—and here during childhood and youth He was educated according to the divine plan. In His education, the processes of educational development were clearly revealed: " The child grew, and waxed strong in spirit, filled with wisdom; and the grace of God was upon him " (Luke 2: 40).

Here we have brought to view three phases in His educational development, and Heaven's co-operation and approval:

1. The Physical: " The child grew."
2. The Spiritual: " Waxed strong in spirit."
3. The Intellectual: " Filled with wisdom."
4. Co-operation and Approval: " The grace (favor) of God was upon him."

What might properly be regarded as another phase of development—the social—is found in the expression, " Jesus increased . . . in favor with God and man " (Luke 2: 52). But, really, the social development is the result of the symmetrical development and proper blending of the physical, mental, and spiritual powers of the child, which brings him into a favored relation with both God and man.

" He showed consistency without obstinacy, benevolence without weakness, tenderness and sympathy without sentimentalism. He was highly social, yet He possessed a reserve that discouraged any familiarity.''[3]

The three phases in the educational process of development during the childhood and youth of Christ were:

1. The Physical	The Social	God	The Christ Education
2. The Mental	in favor	and	or
3. The Spiritual	with	Man	Christian Education

This was the Christ education, and this today is Christian education. According to the testimony previously given:

" As matters now stand, the development of mere intellect has failed. Our educational theory has developed a fatal weakness; in the moment of our greatest confidence in it, it has broken down, and the primitive instincts and practices of savagery have gained the supremacy.'' (See p. 17.)

It is very heartening to know that not a few educators are seeking

---

[2] *Ibid.*, pp. 30, 17.
[3] White, *Counsels to Teachers*, p. 262.

to become acquainted with the education which is according to the Bible; which develops the whole being, physically, mentally, and spiritually, and prepares the student for the joy of service in this world, and for the higher joy of wider service in the world to come. (See pp. 36–39.)

The thorough, comprehensive education of Jesus at the age of twelve was a wonder and astonishment to the rabbis: "And all that heard him were astonished at his understanding and answers" (Luke 2: 47).

No doubt Joseph and Mary were perfectly familiar with the Old Testament instruction to parents regarding the education of their children. Undoubtedly they were chosen to be the parental guides during the childhood and youth of Jesus, because of their faith and confidence in this instruction, and the certainty that they would faithfully carry it out. They had the encouragement of the wisest of human teachers: "Train up a child in the way he should go; and when he is old, he will not depart from it" (Prov. 22: 6). They were stimulated to be faithful and diligent in their instruction and training by the words of Moses, whose mother prepared him to be the mighty leader of Israel from Egyptian bondage to the promised land:

"And thou shalt love the Lord thy God with all thine heart, and with all thy soul, and with all thy might. And these words, which I command thee this day, shall be in thine heart; and thou shalt teach them diligently unto thy children, and shalt talk of them when thou sittest in thine house, and when thou walkest by the way, and when thou liest down, and when thou risest up. And thou shalt bind them for a sign upon thine hand, and they shall be as frontlets between thine eyes. And thou shalt write them upon the posts of thy house, and on thy gates" (Deut. 6: 5–9).

Jesus was a perfect specimen of the product of Hebrew education. The records of the Four Gospels show how great was His familiarity with the Old Testament of Scripture, and with the older testament of nature. His numerous appeals through these two testaments, as witnesses to the truths He uttered, are heard in the oft-repeated expressions: "It is written" and "the kingdom of heaven is like." In His early years He was a diligent student of the Word and works of God. Concerning Christ's knowledge displayed during His ministry we read: "Now about the midst of the feast Jesus went up into the temple and taught. And the Jews marveled, saying: How knoweth this man letters, having never learned?" (John 7: 14, 15).

Jesus did not attend the schools of His day because the system of education given to Israel had become so perverted and trammeled with tradition that He did not feel that He could waste His time with these nonessentials. But under the instruction of His parents and the greater teacher—the Holy Spirit—He was fully prepared for His life's work. The scholars could not understand how He had acquired so much wisdom and knowledge without attending the rabbinical college. Of His contact with the rabbis, one has written:

"Though He did not place Himself under the instruction of the rabbis, by becoming a student in their schools, yet He was often brought in contact with them, and the questions He asked, as if He were a learned, puzzled the wise men; for their practices did not harmonize with the Scripture, and they had not the wisdom that comes from God. Even to those who were displeased at His non-compliance with popular customs, His education seemed of a higher type than their own.'' [4]

The Bible in Education

Reference has previously been made to an article entitled " The Child Grew " by Lucia Barton (p. 37), urging a study of the developing child life of Jesus, as an aid to teachers in solving the problem of child education today.

A valuable book entitled *The Making of a Man,* written by M. T. Lamb, gives some very helpful thoughts concerning the early education and training of Jesus, and makes an application of principles and methods to present problems of child education. We here make brief quotations from his book as to the place of the Scriptures in the education of Jesus:

" Things hidden from the wise and prudent are revealed unto babes. It was so in this case. These learned doctors in Jerusalem had never before met such a boy, bright, clear-headed, and devout, who appeared to have their entire Sacred Scriptures at His tongue's end, and evidently had thought deeply and earnestly on many of its profoundest problems. No wonder they were astonished at His understanding and answers. The whole world may share with them their astonishment, for no school system in any period of the world's history has been able to produce another such boy at twelve years of age. Our public school system today, the boast of the ages, is unable to furnish any such specimen of developing intellect and practical everyday wisdom.'' [5]

The Bible and the Intellect

The relation that the Bible sustains to the developing intellect, Mr. Lamb states as follows:

" At the risk of repeating, we wish to make very clear and emphatic the position taken, that if our boys and girls were trained as Jesus was trained up to twelve years of age, they would be in every desirable respect greatly the superiors of the boys and girls trained under the best methods of the present day. They would be wiser, clearer headed, of better judgment, of keener intellects, of larger capacity in every way. That is to say, their intellects would be far better educated (drawn out), they could think more deeply, take broader views, and would be more matured. In addition, their moral improvement would keep pace with their intellectual progress, so that their development would be more symmetrical; while the growing desire to fit themselves for large usefulness (' I must be about My Father's business,' said Jesus when twelve years of age), and to know more of God, would add inspiration and zest to their studies so that their future progress would be still more helpful; and reading, writing,

---

[4] White, *Fundamentals of Christian Education,* p. 440.
[5] M. T. Lamb, *The Making of a Man,* p. 156 (Hazlett Harrison & Co.).

geography, mathematics, grammar, history, as well as the natural sciences, would all find their proper place in such a child's curriculum of study, and be more zealously and successfully pursued than under any of our present processes." [6]

Ancient Jewish authorities positively assert that parents devoted the first ten years of the child's education exclusively to the study of the Old Testament. No other branch of study was allowed. From five to ten years of age, a child's attention was held to Old Testament history, Bible biography, and simple lessons drawn therefrom. From ten to fifteen years of age, a more comprehensive study of Old Testament history, laws, and prophecies was carried on; and probably also the historical books written by the prophets were used to show how God, in dealing with Israel and their kings, rewarded them for their righteous deeds, but punished them for their sins. By the command of God, pillars and monuments were erected which would rouse the curiosity and interest of the children and youth, and lead them to ask questions as to their meaning. The parents were directed to give full and complete answers to these inquiries. (See Ex. 12: 25–27; Josh. 4: 4–7; Ps. 78: 3–7.)

Concerning the early period of education, Mr. Lamb says:

" From five to fifteen years of age, those years when the memory is most retentive, when the character is forming, when what is learned thoroughly enters into the whole after-life as a controlling force—those years of supreme value in the history of that soul—were given to a study of God as He has revealed Himself to us in His Word; God had the right of way, the first chance in the capture and control of that child." [7]

The Talmud on Education

The Old Testament Scriptures were studied in the Hebrew homes and schools. Attention was also given other Jewish writings, the most notable of which are the Babylonian and Jerusalem Talmuds; the former written after the destruction of the first temple, and the latter after the destruction of the second. Many able Hebrew and Jewish scholars have contributed to the voluminous writing of the Talmud, and while the stream of knowledge is not as clear and as pure as it was when men wrote " as they were moved by the Holy Ghost," yet some fragments of truth are found scattered throughout what is regarded as the source of authority in Hebrew and Jewish education. The author has already made it clear that he regards the Bible as the only source of truth and authority in education, and yet he freely admits that nuggets of truth are to be found scattered throughout the writings of scholars in ancient, medieval and modern times.

A very interesting and valuable work entitled *Pedagogics of the Talmud* appeared about a decade ago, written by Sir Hermann Gollancz, Goldsmith Professor of Hebrew in the University of London.

[6] *Ibid.*, pp. 161, 162.
[7] *Ibid.*, p. 147.

The purpose of the book is thus stated by the author in his Introduction:

" Our theme, however, in this essay is not education in general; our purpose is to deal with one aspect of it, namely, while tracing elements of pedagogic methods in the Talmud, to indicate in outline how, within limits, we might formulate a comparative study between the pedagogics of the Talmud and that of modern times. It can be shown how nearly all the modern theories on the subject of education are reflected in the pages of the Talmud and subsequent Hebrew literature; how the pedagogic principles of a Comenius (1671) and a Pestalozzi (1827) are there anticipated by more than a thousand years; and how in spite of the lapse of time, the statements of many rabbis on this head, as set forth in the Talmud, are almost identical with those put forth with an air of novelty in comparatively recent times by recognized authorities on the science of education.

" Indeed, comparing the rules of pedagogy of modern times with those scattered throughout Talmudic and rabbinic writings, we have come to the conclusion that even in the department of learning the truth holds, that that which is has already been ages ago; ' there is nothing new under the sun.' . . .

" I could scarcely have expected so strong a support for my contention regarding the value and right appreciation of the earliest contributions to the science of education, as that which I find in the following frank admission by Palmer, the evangelical Professor of Theology in Tübingen, and writer on pedagogy, in the early part of the last century: ' The want of the true historic sense is one of the chief causes why our pedagogues are so easily captivated by every new phase and catchword; and this absence of historic feeling argues at the same time a want of piety, and is an evidence of boastful and presumptuous self-conceit.' "

While " the want of the true historic sense " among modern educators is probably a just criticism, as quoted by Sir Hermann Gollancz, yet this same " absence of historic feeling " is manifest in his further claim:

" The pedagogues of the Talmud, if we may use the term, had no source of information from which to draw their deductions other than direct observation, that they made their inferences by penetrating into the depths of human nature, as each occasion presented itself. They had no earlier philosophic system upon which their theories might repose; they dealt simply with life's fresh evidences; in other words, with living examples." [8]

The Bible and Education

It is true that Talmudic pedagogics date back nearly 2,000 years, but the Abrahamic pedagogics antedate Talmudic pedagogics by nearly 2,000 years. The Jews said to Christ: "Abraham is our father" (John 8: 39), and of his teaching knowledge and ability God said: "For I know him (Abraham), that he will command his household after him, and they shall keep the way of the Lord, to do justice and judgment" (Gen. 18: 19). The pedagogics of Moses antedate the Talmud nearly

[8] Hermann Gollancz, *Pedagogics of the Talmud*, pp. 3–5 (Oxford University Press).

1,500 years, and that of Solomon 1,000 years. Sir Gollancz, truly, perhaps unconsciously, indicates the presence of true historic sense in making his first quotations from these two Masters of Pedagogy:

" These words, which I command thee this day, shall be in thine heart: and thou shalt teach them diligently unto thy children, and shalt talk of them when thou sittest in thine house and when thou walkest by the way, and when thou liest down, and when thou risest up. And thou shalt bind them for a sign upon thine hand, and they shall be as frontlets between thine eyes. And thou shalt write them upon the posts of thy house and on thy gates '' (Deut. 6: 6–9).

" And thou shalt show thy son in that day saying, This is done because of that which the Lord did unto me when I came forth out of Egypt '' (Ex. 13: 8).

" My son, hear the instruction of thy father, and forsake not the law of thy mother '' (Prov. 1: 8).

The farther we ascend the stream of knowledge, the clearer and purer will we find its flow. What has been written in the Talmud and subsequently by all scholars of ancient, medieval, and modern times, as far as it is true, is but a reflection of the oracles of God contained in the Old Testament Scriptures, and of the life and teaching of Him who was "greater than Solomon " and Moses. Only a few educators have recognized the Bible as the source of truth and authority in education. We quote from one of these educators:

" The institutions of human society find their best models in the Word of God. For those of instruction (education) in particular, there is no lack of precept and example. Lessons of great profit, even in this age of educational progress, may be found in the history of God's ancient people.

" The Lord reserved to Himself the education and instruction of Israel. His care was not restricted to their religious interests. Whatever affected their mental or physical well-being became also an object of divine solicitude, and came within the province of divine law.'' [9]

In the following chapter consideration is given to the principles and methods of teaching as revealed in the Old and New Testament Scriptures. We also give the views of ancient, medieval, and modern educators, who in their writings are not out of harmony with the only authoritative source of all wisdom and knowledge.

[9] Ellen G. White in *Review and Herald,* October 30, 1900.

VII

PRINCIPLES AND METHODS OF TEACHING

The Eden School

IN considering principles and methods of teaching it is well to recall the fact that education had been carried on outside of the Garden of Eden for nearly six thousand years, and that the change in man's character and environment necessarily called for some change in carrying out the educational program. The Creator and angels were man's first teachers and they held converse face to face. But when sin came into the world, the method of teaching and the character of the instruction were changed to meet the needs of sinful man.

As long as the Garden of Eden remained on earth, Adam and Eve and their posterity offered their sacrifices before the closed gate of Eden in the presence of the guarding angels. Cain and Abel there offered sacrifices to God. The first murder grew out of jealousy that sprang up in Cain's heart because his sacrifice was rejected and his brother Abel's accepted. The Lord personally spoke to Cain, reproving him for not offering an acceptable sacrifice. After he slew his brother Abel, the Lord again spoke to Cain, pronouncing a curse upon him and the ground he was to till (Gen. 4: 3–15).

Teachers of the Human Family

As sin increased, direct communication between man and his Maker decreased. Angels visited Abraham, Lot, and Jacob and others of the patriarchs, communicating to them messages from God and ministering to them in their needs (Gen. 18, 19). On Mount Sinai God spoke His ten-commandment law with an audible voice to ancient Israel, shortly after their deliverance by the hand of Moses from Egyptian bondage. The people were so terrified by the voice of God that they besought Moses: " Speak thou with us and we will hear; but let not God speak with us lest we die " (Ex. 20: 19). When Moses made known to the Lord the entreaty of Israel, their request was granted. He told the people: " The Lord heard the voice of your words when ye spake unto me, and the Lord said unto me, I have heard the voice of the words of this people which they have spoken unto thee; they have well said all that they have spoken." Then Moses expressed in God's own words His greatest desire for His chosen people: " O that there were such an heart in them, that they would fear me, and keep all my commandments always; that it might be well with them and with their children forever! " (Deut. 5: 28, 29).

Then the Lord revealed to Moses His plan for instructing and directing His people, how they should live in the land " flowing with milk and honey," toward which they were journeying: " Go say to them, Get to your tents again. But as for thee, stand thou here by me, and I will speak unto thee all the commandments and statutes, and the judgments, which thou shalt teach them, that they may do them in the land which I give them to possess it " (Deut. 5: 30, 31).

Forty days was Moses in the mount writing the statutes and laws for the instruction and guidance of Israel. This instruction is called the " Book of the Law of Moses," and it was placed " in the side of the ark," while the ten commandments spoken audibly, and graven on two tables of stone by the finger of God, were placed " in the ark " (Deut. 10: 1–5; 31: 24–26).

The ten-commandment law, and the instruction contained in the book of the laws of Moses (contained in the Pentateuch), were to be diligently taught by the parents to their children as we have already noted (Deut. 6: 4–9).

The priests and Levites in addition to their ministry in connection with tabernacle and temple were also to be teachers of the people. Their work of teaching throughout all the cities of Judah is briefly described in II Chronicles 17: 7–10. Ezra, the priest and scribe, was undoubtedly one of the greatest of teachers in Israel after their restoration from Babylonian captivity. His consecration to the teaching profession is briefly stated: " For Ezra had prepared his heart to seek the law of the Lord, and to do it and to teach in Israel statutes and judgments " (Ezra 7: 10). Artaxerxes, King of Persia, strongly supported Ezra's educational program: " And I, even I Artaxerxes, the king, do make a decree to all the treasurers which are beyond the river, that whatsoever Ezra the priest, the scribe of the law of the God of heaven, shall require of you, it be done speedily. . . . And thou Ezra, after the wisdom of thy God, that is in thine hand, set magistrates and judges, which may judge all the people that are beyond the river, all such as know the laws of thy God; and teach ye them that know them not " (Ezra 7: 21–25).

Speaking of the priest in his capacity as a teacher of the people, the Prophet Malachi, living after Ezra's time, said: " The law of truth was in his mouth, and iniquity was not found in his lips; he walked with me in peace and equity, and did turn many from their iniquity. For the priest's lips should keep knowledge, and they should seek the law at his mouth; for he is the messenger of the Lord of Hosts " (Mal. 2: 6, 7).

Prophets were another very highly respected class of teachers. Some of them had also the ability to foresee or foretell future events and were called " seers." Among the teaching prophets may be mentioned Samuel, Elisha, and Elijah. They conducted schools sometimes called the " schools of the prophets " and the students were called the " sons of the prophets." Several of these schools were established, and concerning the first school established at Ramah, whither David fled when pursued by King Saul, we read: " And Saul sent messengers to take David; and when they saw the company of people prophesying, and

Samuel standing as one appointed over them, the Spirit of God was upon the messengers, and they also prophesied" (I Sam. 19: 20). The number of students at each school probably was not large; for we read of only fifty sons of the prophets in the school at Jericho, and one hundred at another place (II Kings 2: 15–18; 4: 42–44).

The prophets served in three capacities:

1. They made known the will of God when important undertakings were being contemplated at the royal court.

2. They were leaders in religious and social reforms.

3. They were teachers in the schools, some of them writing historical and philosophical books that were studied in the schools.

The sages were another very important class of teachers, who are mentioned along with the priests and the prophets. The prophet Jeremiah speaks of a time when all three classes of teachers would be faithful in giving instruction and counsel to Israel: "The Law shall not perish from the priest, nor counsel from the wise, nor the word from the prophet" (Jer. 18: 18). The priests expounded the law, the prophets foretold future events and gave warning and instruction as to how the people were to relate themselves to critical situations as they arose; while the sages entered more into the problems of daily life giving counsel as to how to live in the home and the community. They were the most learned class of teachers, and were sympathetically in touch with the work of priests, prophets, and scribes, and helped the people to co-operate with them by giving heed to their messages. They were one with the people visiting from home to home, and their advice and counsel were given in short, pithy maxims or proverbs, which were drawn from history, literature, and everyday life. They were the philosophers in Israel. (See pages 195, 196.)

Moses and many of the prophets foretold the coming of the Messiah who would be the greatest of teachers and the Saviour of Israel: "I will raise them up a Prophet from among their brethren like unto thee (Moses), and I will put my words in his mouth; and he shall speak unto them all that I shall command him. And it shall come to pass, that whosoever will not hearken unto my words which he shall speak in my name, I will require it of him" (Deut. 18: 18, 19). This heaven-sent Teacher, the Son of God, and His divine credentials were recognized by Nicodemus, a teacher and a member of the Jewish Sanhedrim, and also by many others who heard Him:

" Rabbi, we know that thou art a teacher come from God " (John 3: 2; 12: 42). " All bare him witness, and wondered at the gracious words that proceeded out of his mouth " (Luke 4: 22). " They were astonished at his doctrine; for he taught them as one that had authority, and not as the Scribes " (Mark 1: 22).

At the close of His three and one-half years of teaching, preaching, and healing ministry, Christ assured His disciples that He would send in His place a teacher from heaven, who would ever be with them in their work. This Teacher, the Holy Spirit of Truth, would bring to mind the things that Christ had taught them and guide them in the way of all truth. He would convince the world of sin, of righteousness, and of judgment (John 14: 26; 16: 7–13).

As we rename these teachers, we shall see that the Hebrew people, the Israel of God, the Jews scattered among the nations, have always been provided with able, competent instructors:

Summary of Teachers

1. *God the Creator.* He was instructor of Adam and Eve in Eden, and He continued to instruct them in modified ways outside of Eden.

2. *Angels or Ministering Spirits.* Angels taught and ministered in Eden and have continued their ministry outside of Eden.

3. *Patriarchs or Parents.* Since the fall of Adam and Eve the parents have the first responsibility in teaching their children.

4. *Priests and Levites.* They were ordained to be teachers of parents and their children in spiritual and temporal things.

5. *Sages.* They were teachers in the home and community giving counsel in proverbs and maxims.

6. *Prophets and Seers.* They were leaders and teachers, in religious, social, and political reforms.

7. *Christ the Sent of God.* God gave to the human family His Son to show the way of truth and life in a world filled with a knowledge of good and evil. As a student and teacher, He illustrated the true principles and methods of education.

8. *The Holy Spirit of Truth.* Christ prayed to His Father that the Holy Spirit might be sent to the world to continue the work for the human family which He had carried on during His three and one-half years of ministry. His request was granted (John 14: 15–17, 26).

Restatement of Principles

It is plain to be seen from the Hebrew educators engaged in the work of instructing the children and youth, that there was close co-operation with the Creator and Provider of the human family. Loyalty to God and a dependence upon Him for wisdom and knowledge, to direct them in their efforts to separate the evil from the good, characterized all their instruction. To foster in their students respect and reverence for God and His holy law, and a hatred and abhorrence for sin and all evil, was the constant aim and purpose of the teachers of Hebrew education. With this end in view, the students were encouraged in the exercise of faith that they might have divine wisdom not only to discern between good and evil, but also to be diligent in their efforts to gain knowledge and ability to enable them to " prove all things, and hold fast that which is good " (I Thess. 5: 21).

Teachers of Hebrew education developed symmetrically and harmoniously the physical, mental, and spiritual powers, as revealed in the education of the child Jesus, trained by His earthly parents. This is possible only as earthly teachers unite in partnership with heavenly teachers in all their work. This divine partnership is expressed in the prayer of Manoah and his wife regarding the promised child: " O my Lord, teach us what we shall do unto the child that shall be born. . . . How shall we order (train) the child; and how shall we do unto him? " (Judges 13: 8, 12). Again this divine partnership is earnestly sought and formed by Solomon, who prayed: " Give, therefore, thy servant an understanding heart . . . that I may discern between good and bad, for who is able to judge this thy so great a people? " The Lord was pleased with his request, and responded: " Behold I have done according to thy words; lo, I have given thee a wise and understanding heart " (I Kings 3: 9–12).

What Hebrew Teachers Taught

In other chapters consideration will be given to what was taught by Hebrew educators. Already we have learned that Moses was forty days on Mount Sinai with God who gave him his ten-commandment law graven in stone, and also statutes and judgments which he wrote in a book called " The Book of the Law of Moses." These are found in the Pentateuch, which includes the first five books of the Bible— " Genesis," " Exodus," " Leviticus," " Numbers," and " Deuteronomy."

In addition to the writings of the law we have in the Bible the writings of the prophets. Isaiah speaking of the importance of both these writings said: " To the law and to the testimony (writings of the prophets); if they speak not according to this word, it is because there is no light in them " (Isa. 8: 20). Christ said: " Think not that I am come to destroy the law or the prophets; I am not come to destroy, but to fulfill " (Matt. 5: 17). Again when giving the golden rule, He said: " Therefore all things whatsoever ye would that men should do unto you, do ye even so unto them, for this is the law and the prophets " (Matt. 7: 12).

In addition to the writings of the law and the prophets, we have in the Old Testament the biographical, historical, and poetical books. All of these were studied in the schools of the prophets. In connection with these, and necessary to an understanding of the Old Testament Scripture, there were studies in science, mathematics, language, music, physical and industrial training. All these will be given consideration later on. The remainder of this chapter will be devoted to a consideration of the qualifications of teachers and methods of teaching.

Spirit and Qualifications of Teachers

1. *Teachers of Truth.* Teachers being in partnership with the " God of all truth "; with His Son who is " the way and the truth "; with the holy " Spirit of Truth "; with angels who show " what is noted in the Scripture of truth," and diligent students of the Bible, which is the " Word of truth "—certainly will be teachers of truth, the whole truth, and nothing but the truth. Like the Master Teacher, the under teacher not only teaches the truth, but also lives the truth. This

gives power and authority to the truth taught and greatly influences the lives of those taught.

2. *Purity of Life.* " The wisdom that is from above is first pure " (Jas. 3: 17). Purity, modesty, virtue, are the first requisites to good teaching, and without these in the daily life of the teacher no progress can be made in character building. If the students are to develop purity, modesty, and virtue, these traits must shine forth in the daily life of the teacher. Only the pure in heart shall see God (Matt. 5: 8).

3. *Kindliness of Heart.* No one, whatever else his qualifications, is prepared to teach unless love is the constraining motive and power in his life. Without love you cannot feed the lambs or the sheep. This is particularly true in the teaching of the children. Jesus first said to Peter: " Feed my lambs," and then added " Feed my sheep " (John 21: 15–17). This was the evidence that Peter's heart was full of love for his Master. The Master Teacher is asking for this evidence of their love for Him from all His under teachers. He especially wants the lambs well cared for, as He recognizes that only good lambs will develop into good sheep. He tells how He regards those who are unloving in their attitude toward His little children: " Whoso shall offend one of these little ones which believe in me, it were better for him that a millstone were hanged about his neck, and that he were drowned in the depths of the sea " (Matt. 18: 6). In His busy life He took time to contact with the little children. It displeased Jesus when the disciples thought He was too busy to be annoyed by their presence, and He reproved them, saying: " Suffer the little children to come unto me, and forbid them not, for of such is the kingdom of heaven " (Mark 10: 14).

4. *Impartiality in Dealing.* When true love motivates the actions of the teacher, no partiality will be shown. Love will seek to find ways to help those who are dull and backward in their studies, ugly or disagreeable in their dispositions, homely and slovenly in their appearance, awkward and uncouth in their movements. Love will realize that all these conditions are the result of the lack of opportunity which is now provided by the school. While no partiality will be shown, yet, as directed by our unerring educational guide book: " Of some have compassion, making a difference . . . pulling them out of the fire; hating even the garment (not the pupil) spotted by the flesh " (Jude 22, 23). In this difficult and delicate work the teacher may have the wisdom that comes by faith, and also " the discerning of spirits " which is one of the gifts imparted by the Spirit of Truth,—the Holy Spirit (I Cor. 12: 8–10).

5. *Sincerity and Honesty.* The pupils should have a growing confidence in the teacher's sincerity and honesty. Children, especially, are quick to detect any elements of insincerity, dishonesty and hypocrisy. Bluffing and camouflaging are entirely out of place in any school, especially so on the part of the teachers. The best way to repress these undesirable traits in the pupils is the manifestation of the opposite

traits by the teacher. The following exhortations should be carefully heeded by teachers:

" Fear the Lord and serve him in sincerity and in truth " (Josh. 24: 14). "In all things shewing thyself a pattern of good works; in doctrine (teaching) shewing uncorruptness, gravity, sincerity " (Titus 2: 7). " The wisdom that is from above is . . . without partiality and without hypocrisy " (Jas. 3: 17).

6. *Thorough and Painstaking.* Diligence and perseverance characterize the work of every successful teacher. This spirit of earnest activity will not characterize the efforts of the pupils unless it is continually manifest on the part of the teacher. The degree of thorough painstaking effort exhibited by the pupils is a true reflection of the teacher's spirit and work. In Hebrew education diligence and perseverance were emphasized.

" And these words . . . shall be in thy heart; and thou shalt teach them *diligently* unto thy children " (Deut. 6: 6, 7). " Keep thy heart with all diligence; for out of it are the issues of life " (Prov. 4: 23).

7. *Order and Promptness.* A teacher may be diligent and painstaking, but lack the ability to direct himself and his pupil in a prompt and orderly way. Tardiness and disorder will demoralize any school. Here again the pupils will reflect the life and spirit of the teacher. Orderly procedure in the program, everybody and everything in place and on time, contributes largely to the success of any well conducted school. The following admonitions should be heeded:

" Let all things be done decently and in order " (I Cor. 14: 40). " To everything there is a season, and a time to every purpose under the heaven " (Eccl. 3: 1–10).

8. *Original and Resourceful.* The teacher should resolutely refuse to be a copyist or an imitator. He should think for himself and encourage his pupils to do so. It will increase the spirit of confidence in and loyalty to the teacher, if he can from time to time tell his pupils of new discoveries that he has made. They will bring new discoveries to the teacher. A modern educator has briefly emphasized the importance of originality and resourcefulness both on the part of the teacher and the student:

" Every human being, created in the image of God, is endowed with a power akin to that of the Creator,—individuality, power to think and to do. . . . It is the work of true education to develop this power; to train the youth to be thinkers, and not mere reflectors of other men's thought. Instead of confining their study to that which men have said or written, let students be directed to the . . . vast fields opened for research in nature and revelation. Let them contemplate the great facts of duty and destiny, and the mind will expand and strengthen. Instead of educated weaklings, institutions of learning may send forth men strong to think and to act, men who are masters and not slaves of circumstances, men who possess breadth of mind, clearness of thought, and the courage of their convictions." [1]

[1] White, *Education,* pp. 17–18.

This spirit of searching was manifest in the student and teaching life of Solomon (Prov. 2: 4; Eccl. 1: 13). The Holy Spirit aids in the work of research (I Cor. 2: 10). Christ urged the habit and spirit of research in the study of the Scriptures (John 5: 39).

9. *Pleasing and Ready Speech.* One of the greatest acquisitions of a teacher is a pleasing voice and ready speech. This talent he should seek to develop in every pupil. If the voice is rasping and disagreeable to listen to in other ways; if his speech is too rapid, or too slow and hesitating, his power and ability to communicate knowledge is greatly handicapped, and the entire school suffers a serious loss. Then again the disagreeable discordant voice is a constant source of annoyance and irritation to the pupils, producing restlessness and disorder. The teaching priests and Levites " read in the book in the law of God distinctly, and gave the sense and caused them to understand the reading " (Neh. 8: 8). Christ taught with a pleasant gracious voice (Ps. 45: 2; Luke 4: 22).

10. *Enthusiasm, Courage and Faith.* Enthusiasm is contagious. If it is in the heart of the teacher, it will be reflected in the life of the pupils. They should feel, "My teacher would rather teach than anything else in the world." In order that enthusiasm shall not wane, the courage of the teacher, even under the most forbidding and trying conditions, must not fail. In order that courage may continually burn and glow in the soul of the teacher, he must constantly exercise a strong, abiding faith in God; faith in the heavenly instruction and instructors provided; faith in the divine call to his heaven-appointed work. This honored privilege in an earthly school to prepare his students to enter the school above should bring continual joy and serve to stimulate to stronger endeavor. From the inspired authoritative Guide Book in education the teacher may daily have his enthusiasm renewed, his courage strengthened, and his faith increased.

The all-wise and loving Father of the whole family in heaven and in earth assures His children who live in a world filled with good and evil, of His guidance and protection:

" I will instruct thee and teach thee in the way which thou shalt go; I will guide thee with mine eye " (Ps. 32: 8). " I am the Lord thy God which teacheth thee to profit; which leadeth thee by the way that thou shouldest go " (Isa. 48: 17). In wonder Elihu exclaimed: " Behold, God exalteth by his power; who teacheth like him? " (Job 36: 22).

Methods in Hebrew Education

Only a brief reference will be made here to the methods followed in Hebrew education. These will be enlarged upon when consideration is given to the subjects taught. The following were the more important methods used in ancient Hebrew education:

1. *Use of Symbols.* The home was the center of education, the father and the mother were the principal teachers. The children were taught in connection with the daily activities of the home, and the

religious services both at home and in public ceremonies at various annual feasts. The symbols connected with the daily sacrifice, the Passover, the Feast of Tabernacles, etc., were used to awaken interest and to impress spiritual lessons on the mind and heart of the children.

2. *Direct Injunction.* This consisted in repeating the "thou shalts" and the "thou shalt nots" contained in the ten-commandment law spoken from Mount Sinai, and also those contained in the book of the laws of Moses written by him while forty days in the mount. They tell what is right and what is wrong. They tell what to do and what not to do. They were to do or refrain from doing because God had so commanded, whether they could understand the reason or not. "Thou shalt not steal," "Thou shalt not kill" (Ex. 20: 13, 15). "Ye shall keep my sabbaths, and reverence my sanctuary. I am the Lord" (Lev. 26: 2).

3. *Oral Instruction.* The method of teaching among the Hebrews was chiefly oral. The parents were commanded to teach their children the Decalogue, and the laws and statutes written by Moses: "And ye shall teach them your children, *speaking* of them when thou sittest in thine house, and when thou walkest by the way, when thou liest down and when thou risest up. And thou shalt write them upon the door posts of thine house and upon thy gates" (Deut. 11: 18–20).

4. *Teaching by Song.* Truth was impressed by the children singing the song of Miriam after the deliverance at the Red Sea; the battle song of Deborah after the victory over Sisera; and the lament of David over Jonathan and Saul. This method of teaching through song is well expressed in the following:

" As the people journeyed through the wilderness many precious lessons were fixed in their minds by means of song. At the deliverance from Pharaoh's army the whole host of Israel had joined in the song of triumph. Far over the desert and sea rang the joyous refrain, and the mountains re-echoed the accents of praise: ' Sing ye to Jehovah, for He hath triumphed gloriously.' Often on their journey was this song repeated, cheering the hearts, and kindling the faith of the pilgrim travelers. The commandments as given from Sinai, with the promises of God's favor and records of His wonderful works for their deliverance, were by divine direction, expressed in song, and were chanted to the sound of instrumental music, the people keeping step as their voices united in praise." [2]

5. *Biography and History.* A very interesting and impressive way of teaching was through biography and history. The first book of the Bible, Genesis, contains the story of creation; a description of the beautiful home of the first parents of the human family and the sad experience of losing it. Then follows the record of the long-lived patriarchs and the story of the destruction of the earth by the flood. After the account of the flood are interesting biographies of Abraham, Isaac, Jacob and Joseph, and their pilgrimage life, finally ending in their posterity settling in Egypt with Joseph ruler next to Pharaoh for

[2] *Ibid.,* p. 39.

nearly sixty years. This is followed by a history of their bondage, and final deliverance from Egypt; their forty years wandering in the wilderness; their struggles in establishing a home in the promised land of Canaan; and their growth and influence as a nation under the rule of David and Solomon. The story of these events, and the lessons to be learned from them, were often retold to the children, and had a gripping effect upon mind and heart, as they do when repeated today.

6. *Parable and Allegories.* One of the methods employed by the sacred writers for making clear and plain the truth to be impressed is that of parable teaching. Jothan's parable about the trees; Nathan's parable spoken to David about the rich man and the lamb are examples of parable teaching in the Old Testament. This was the method largely used by the Master Teacher as recorded in the Four Gospels of the New Testament. Bunyan's *Pilgrim's Progress* is undoubtedly the best modern work exemplifying the parable teaching method.

7. *Repetition in Learning.* Frequent repetition was a very much used method by Hebrew teachers. "For precept must be upon precept, precept upon precept; line upon line, line upon line; here a little and there a little" (Isa. 28: 10). The admonition to the Hebrew parent and teacher was, "Thou shalt teach them diligently." The Hebrew word, *veshinantom,* means to teach by repetition through constant digging. The parallelism employed in the writing of Psalms and Proverbs was used to fix the idea in the memory; and acrostics served a similar purpose. In Psalm 119: 13 we have an allusion to the learner repeating the words from the mouth of the teacher: "With my *lips* have I declared all the judgment of thy *mouth.*"

8. *Memory Method.* As already stated, the laws were committed to memory. This is attested to by Josephus who says: "For it is a good thing that those laws should be graven in their souls and preserved in their *memories* so that it may not be possible to blot them out" (*Antiquities,* VI: 4, 8–12). Jesus frequently quoted the Scripture, saying, "It is written," "It is written." Some Bible scholars are inclined to think that Jesus before He began His ministry had committed to memory the whole of the Old Testament Scriptures.

9. *The Art of Questioning.* The Hebrew education plan was so arranged that it constantly provoked questions from the learner. As the children and youth saw the symbols used and the various forms of divine service they would ask: "What mean ye by this service?" (Ex. 12: 26), "What mean ye by these stones?" (Josh. 4: 6). Moses refers to this method of teaching: "Remember the days of old, consider the years of many generations, ask thy father, and he will shew thee; thy elders and they will tell thee" (Deut. 32: 7). This plan of instruction was not only to benefit the children but also the grandchildren (Ps. 78: 4–6). The purpose of this instruction is clearly stated: "That they (the children) might set their hope in God, and not forget the works of God, but keep his commandments" (Verse 7).

10. *Disciplinary Method.* It may seem questionable to regard dis-

cipline as a method of teaching. It was not employed in the Eden school. When the school was removed just outside of the gate of Eden the disciplinary method (a blessing in disguise) was introduced into the school. The presence of thorns and thistles, and the sweat and toil necessary to the earning of a livelihood were measures of discipline introduced into the school now conducted under changed conditions. Our first parents had partaken of the fruit of the tree of knowledge of good and evil, and so good and evil were everywhere present. Their daily program required them to choose between the evil and the good, and to strive earnestly to overcome evil with good. That was the Hebrew education program, and that should be the educational program today. The principles and methods of discipline must be understood and mastered if teachers succeed in their high and holy calling.

In closing this chapter on the Principles and Methods of Teaching, we urge teachers and educators to carefully study the principles and methods of the Master Teacher.

" As the highest preparation for your work, I point you to the words, the life, the methods of the Prince of teachers. I bid you consider Him. Here is your true ideal. Behold it, dwell upon it, until the Spirit of the divine Teacher takes possession of your heart and life." [3]

" In the presence of such a Teacher, of such opportunity for divine education, what worse than folly is it to seek an education apart from Him, —to seek to be wise apart from Wisdom; to be true while rejecting truth; to seek illumination apart from the Light, and existence without the life; to turn from the Fountain of living water, and hew out broken cisterns, that can hold no water." [4]

" They (teachers) must study Christ's lessons and the character of His teaching. They must see its freedom from formalism and tradition, and appreciate the originality, the authority, the spirituality, the tenderness, the benevolence, and the practicability of His teaching."

[3] White, *Counsels to Teachers,* p. 18 (Pacific Press).
[4] White, *Education,* p. 83.

VIII

PRINCIPLES AND METHODS OF DISCIPLINE

Principles of Discipline

THE methods of discipline must be based on right principles of discipline if they are to be successfully applied. The following principles of Hebrew discipline necessarily grow out of the changed conditions that came into the world on account of the first parents of the human family partaking of the fruit of the tree of knowledge of good and evil.

1. *Disloyalty and Disobedience.* The partaking of the forbidden fruit indicated a spirit of *disloyalty* which resulted in an act of disobedience. Man's relation of loyalty and obedience to his Maker was changed. To vividly and solemnly impress this change of relationship between God and man upon the transgressors, the whole face of nature was changed. It seemingly rose up in rebellion against man, and the dominion and control given him was weakened. Thorns and thistles interfered with his cultivation of plants, and even the soil refused to yield its former abundance. The animal creation quarreled with their master. All this was a constant reminder to man of his transgression; and he saw in it a reflection of his own rebellious attitude and spirit toward his Maker.

Thus man was punished or disciplined for his transgression during his lifetime, and his pilgrimage on earth closed in death and the grave. The death of the Son of God on the cross atoned for man's transgression, and provided for his resurrection and return to his Eden home, provided he voluntarily submitted to the Creator's program of discipline, and exercised implicit faith in the plan devised for his salvation.

2. *All are Transgressors.* " All have sinned and come short of the glory of God," says the inspired record of man's creation and history (Rom. 3: 23). "As by one man sin entered into the world, and death by sin; so death passed upon all men, for that all have sinned " (Rom. 5: 12). Our first parents became sinners by deliberate transgression; their posterity by inheritance. Their children have been and still are born into the world with parental dispositions and tendencies to evil, and therefore are sinners by nature, and not by choice. Children are born with a sinful nature, and it expresses itself in infancy notwithstanding the protests and denials of some modern educators. The Psalmist David strongly affirms it:

" Behold I was shapen in iniquity and in sin did my mother conceive me " (Ps. 51: 15). " The wicked are estranged from the womb; they go astray as soon as they are born " (Ps. 58: 3). God, speaking of man's

72

inherited tendencies to evil at the time of the flood, said: " The imagination of man's heart is evil from his youth " (Gen. 8: 21).

3. *Discipline of Transgressors.* Discipline originated, and was first applied after Adam and Eve were expelled from the Garden of Eden. The spirit and purpose of God's program of discipline of transgressors of His laws are clearly stated by the Apostle Paul:

" My son, despise not thou the chastening of the Lord, nor faint when thou art rebuked of him; for whom the Lord loveth he chasteneth, and scourgeth every son whom he receiveth. . . . Now no chastening for the present seemeth to be joyous, but grievous, nevertheless afterward it yieldeth the peaceable fruit of righteousness unto them who are exercised thereby " (Heb. 12: 5–11).

The best example of the true spirit and purpose of divine discipline was revealed in the School of the Twelve conducted for three and one-half years by the Master Teacher. His discipline was so kind and impartial that when told that one of them should betray Him, none suspicioned the other, and all in unison exclaimed, " Lord is it I? " Christ was faithful in counseling, instructing, and reproving them, as pride, covetousness, and a vindictive spirit would crop out from time to time. Eleven remained loyal and true to their Master, and were commissioned by Him to carry on the work He had begun.

His reproof was mingled with encouragement: " Neither do I condemn thee; go and sin no more " (John 8: 11). " Behold thou art made whole; sin no more, lest a worse thing come unto thee " (John 5: 14). Even the woes pronounced on the Scribes, Pharisees and lawyers, were uttered in love and compassion in a last effort to save souls from ruin. Weeping He made His final appeal: " O Jerusalem, Jerusalem, thou that killest the prophets and stonest them which are sent unto thee; how often would I have gathered thy children together even as a hen gathereth her chickens under her wings, and ye would not " (Matt. 23: 37).

The Holy Spirit that reproves the transgressor for sin is also called the " Comforter " (John 16: 7–11). The holy angels minister to those who are heirs of salvation, and speak " good words, and comfortable words," as they endeavor to guide and direct in the way of truth and holiness " (Zech. 1: 13).

While the Bible, the Holy Word of God, given to the human family as their only guide book, contains reproof, correction, and rebuke; yet it is through " patience and comfort of the Scripture " that erring, faulty humanity finds hope (Rom. 15: 4).

The purpose and spirit of heavenly discipline is to obtain in all earthly discipline. Earthly teachers, like the heavenly, will exercise a spirit of love, mercy and patience in all their dealings with those whom they instruct. In the Talmud education is repeatedly called a " heavenly work " (Erub. 13a). The apostle Paul writing to Timothy enjoins upon him the spirit of a true teacher: " Foolish and unlearned questions avoid, knowing that they do gender strifes. And the servant of the Lord must not strive, but be gentle unto all men, apt to teach, patient, in meekness instructing those that oppose themselves . . . that they may recover themselves out of the snare of the devil " (II Tim. 2: 23–26).

The fifth commandment of the decalogue requires children to honor their parents, that their days on earth may be prolonged. The apostle Paul, in connection with his reference to the fifth commandment, speaks directly to the children: " Children, obey your parents in the Lord, for this is right " (Eph. 6: 1). Immediately following he gave counsel to the father—the head of the family—as to a wrong attitude toward his children, and urges that they be properly instructed: " And ye fathers provoke not your children to wrath; but bring them up in the nurture and admonition of the Lord " (Verse 4). Speaking again directly to the children, Paul indicates that obedience in all things will be very pleasing to the Lord: " Children obey your parents in *all things;* for this is *well pleasing* unto the Lord " (Col. 3: 20). Speaking again to the fathers, Paul tells how a provoking attitude will affect the children: " Fathers, provoke not your children to anger lest they be discouraged " (Verse 21).

Methods of Discipline

The spirit and purpose of Hebrew educational discipline is made very clear by the above quotations taken from our educational guide book; but it yet remains to study the disciplinary methods used by the Hebrews in the home and in the school. The following were the principal methods employed by parents and teachers:

1. *Discipline of Authority.* The first mention of the exercise of commandatory or authoritory discipline is in connection with the home of the patriarch Abraham: " I know him (Abraham) that he will *command* his household after him, and they shall keep the way of the Lord, to do justice and judgment " (Gen. 18: 19). Abraham responded to authoritative discipline when God commanded him: " Take now thy son, thine only son, Isaac, whom thou lovest, . . . and offer him for a . . . burnt offering " (Gen. 22: 2). Note that Abraham loved Isaac. Love prompted the commands of Abraham to his household, and love responded in obedience even though the reasons for the commands were not understood.

God loved Abraham, and love for God caused him to prepare to offer his son, even though the reason for so doing he did not understand. This is the discipline Hebrew parents exercised in love for God and their children until they arrived to the age of moral responsibility. At times Jesus exercised this authority. In the temple He said to the priests and rabbi: " Take these things hence; make not my Father's house a house of merchandise " (John 2: 16). Love prompted the command: but while they obeyed, love did not prompt obedience. He was asked: " By what authority doest thou these things, and who gave thee this authority? " (Matt. 21: 23). He did not answer their query, for they had rejected Him as being the Son of God. Of His teaching we read: "The people were astonished at his doctrine, for he taught them as one having authority and not as the Scribes " (Matt. 7: 28, 29). What gave Christ power and authority in His ministry was the truth He taught and lived. Truth learned, and lived, is the only source of power and authority. Teachers of truth, who are livers of truth, are the greatest of our educational needs today.

Parents especially are called upon to exercise the discipline of authority, because they deal with the children during those years of irresponsibility when they must be as God to their children. The exercise of this authority is sadly lacking in many homes today, and the children, even while still in infancy, exercise control over their parents. This same situation exists in many schools, and lawlessness, crime and anarchy are manifested in the lives of students while still in their teens.

2. *Discipline of Exhortation and Appeal.* Many times the discipline of entreaty and appeal is sufficient. It should always be administered first. This is used most in the book of Proverbs and Ecclesiastes, most of which were written by Solomon. The endearing address, " My son " was used by teachers as well as by parents, and students in the schools of the prophets were called " the sons of the prophets." Elisha called after Elijah as he was ascending heavenward: " My father, my father." In the Talmud we read: " He who instructs his neighbor's child is as though he had given him birth " (Sanh. 19b; 99b).

Undoubtedly Solomon was exhorting and entreating his own son, Rehoboam, in the first three chapters of the book of Proverbs, beginning with the words: " My son, hear the instruction of thy father and forsake not the law of thy mother, for they shall be an ornament of grace unto thy head, and chains about thy neck. My son, if sinners entice thee, consent thou not " (Prov. 1: 8-10).

Solomon then in the fourth chapter refers to the instruction given to him by David his father: " I was my father's son, tender and only beloved in the sight of my mother. He taught me also and said unto me, Let thine heart retain my words; keep my commandments and live. . . . Hear, O my son, and receive my sayings; and the years of thy life shall be many " (Prov. 4: 3, 4, 10).

Just how much of the instruction in this book, consisting largely of the discipline of entreaty and appeal, was given personally by David to Solomon, and by Solomon to Rehoboam, we do not know. But Solomon exhorts all children to receive and appreciate the instruction of the father: " Hear, ye children, the instruction of the father, and attend to know understanding " (Prov. 4: 1). He encourages parents to be faithful in instructing their children by assuring them their efforts will not be in vain: " Train up a child in the way he should go, and when he is old, he will not depart from it " (Prov. 22: 6).

3. *Discipline of Reproof and Rebuke.* This mode of discipline, as already noted, was used by Christ, but always mingled with pity and

love. The apostle Paul used this method when Elymas the sorcerer opposed him in his work: " Then Saul (who also is called Paul), filled with the Holy Ghost, set his eyes upon him, and said: ' O full of all subtilty and all mischief, thou child of the devil, thou enemy of all righteousness, wilt thou not cease to pervert the right ways of the Lord?'" (Acts 13: 9, 10). Note that when Paul administered this rebuke he was "filled with the Holy Ghost." This great Teacher of Truth was aiding him in vindicating the truth, and the result was that truth prevailed. It is unsafe to administer rebuke unless aided by heavenly teachers. It is the most difficult of all disciplines, and yet it must not be neglected. Paul charged Timothy to " reprove, rebuke, exhort, with all longsuffering " (II Tim. 4: 2).

Solomon encouraged the discipline of reproof, but it must be administered with discrimination and with discretion: " He that reproveth a scorner getteth to himself shame; and he that rebuketh a wicked man getteth himself a blot. Reprove not a scorner lest he hate thee; rebuke a wise man and he will love thee " (Prov. 9: 7, 8).

A word of counsel is given by Solomon to those who are reproved:

" He that regardeth reproof is prudent " (Prov. 15: 5). " He that regardeth reproof shall be honored " (Prov. 13: 18). " He that refuseth reproof erreth " (Prov. 10: 17). " He that hateth reproof is brutish " (Prov. 12: 1). " He that hateth reproof shall die " (Prov. 15: 10).

The psalmist David expresses his appreciation of reproof: " Let the righteous smite me; it shall be a kindness; let him reprove me; it shall be an excellent oil which shall not break my head " (Ps. 141: 5).

4. *Discipline of Expulsion and Separation.* Another mode of discipline is suggested by Solomon to be administered to those who scorn at reproof and will not listen to rebuke. It is the discipline of expulsion and separation from those who are open to counsel and reproof: " Cast out the scorner and contention shall go out; yea, strife and reproach shall cease " (Prov. 22: 10).

Christ at times used this disciplinary measure with those who scorned and derided Him in His efforts to bless and help others: " And they laughed him to scorn. But when he had put them all out he taketh the father and the mother of the damsel and them that were with him, and entereth in where the damsel was lying, and he took the damsel by the hand and said unto her . . . Damsel, I say unto thee, arise. And straightway the damsel arose and walked " (Mark 5: 40–42).

Expulsion or dismissal, temporary or permanent, may at times have to be resorted to in order to save the school from demoralization and ruin. When this is the situation there should be no hesitation. Prompt, decisive action should be taken, as the Lord commanded Joshua: " Get thee up, wherefore liest thou thus upon thy face? . . . There is an accursed thing in the midst of thee; . . . thou canst not stand before thine enemies until ye take away the accursed thing from among you " (Josh. 7: 10–13). It was not the time for prayer, but for action; and until Achan was removed from the camp no progress could be made.

Teachers must be sure that prayer and personal effort have preceded the taking of such drastic measures of permanent expulsion, or even temporary dismissal. They may by faith claim divine wisdom and discernment to know when and how to proceed in such times of crisis.

5. *Discipline of Punishment.* Discipline that carries with it no penalty or punishment of the transgressor for the violation of rules and regulations is of little or no value. Punishments are of value only as they enable the transgressor to refrain from violating the rules and regulations adopted for the good of the family, school, church or government. Disciplinary punishments in the home and the school may be divided into two classes:

(1) Individual Punishments and (2) Social Punishments. Brief consideration of each of these classes follows:

(1) *Individual Punishments.* These include those that were related only to the individual receiving the punishment. In the home life the children would learn of violations of commands given by God which were committed by those older in years. These laws and commands had to do with the sanctuary service; the relation of one to another in the home, and in the community. If one had failed in paying his tithe, one-fifth must be added to it (Lev. 27: 31). If one had in any way become defiled or unclean, he must remain in seclusion from one to seven days (Lev. 11: 13–28; Num. 19: 11, 16).

Punishment of the body—corporal punishment—was authorized by divine law, even to the extent of capital punishment, of a disobedient, rebellious son. The parents were permitted to make their complaint but it rested with the elders of the city to decide whether this extreme measure should be taken or less severe punishment administered (Deut. 21: 18–21). Corporal punishment was considered a duty resting upon the parents when counsel, warning and reproof failed:

" He that spareth the rod hateth his son; but he that loveth him chasteneth him betimes " (Prov. 13: 24). " Chasten thy son while yet there is hope, and let not thy soul spare for his crying " (Prov. 19: 18). " Withhold not correction from the child; for if thou beatest him with the rod, he shall not die " (Prov. 23: 13).

There was no restriction as to the age of the child when corporal punishment was to be administered. The Talmud prohibits it before the child reaches eleven years of age, at which time it fixed the age of responsibility. It would seem that the restriction as to time would have been indicated by divine law if it were to be made. Corporal punishment—the use of the rod—or other means to cause bodily pain and suffering can be recognized by the child before the mental and spiritual faculties begin to function. The child will refrain from crying or manifesting its ugly or disagreeable traits if it knows that such conduct will be followed by some form of punishment that gives bodily pain.

While corporal punishment is often cruelly and unwisely administered, yet its right use is fully sanctioned or approved in the Scrip-

tures. The disapproval or entire abandonment of corporal punishment
is not producing the desirable attitudes and relations between parents
and children; between teachers and pupils that existed even when corporal punishment was at times unwisely administered. There is not
the respect, loyalty and obedience that were manifest under this form
of discipline.

Corporal punishment was not considered as necessary for all children,
and was to be used only when other measures failed; and it was always
to be administered in love. The following counsel regarding corporal
punishment, by a modern educator, is worthy of consideration:

" One of the first lessons a child needs to learn is the lesson of obedience.
Before he is old enough to reason, he may be taught to obey. By gentle,
persistent effort, the habit should be established. Thus, to a great degree,
may be prevented those later conflicts between will and authority that do
so much to create alienation and bitterness toward parents and teachers, and
too often resistance of all authority, human and divine." [1]

" The work of ' breaking the will ' is contrary to the principles of
Christ. The will of the child must be directed and guided. Save all the
strength of the will, for the human being needs it all; but give it proper
direction. Treat it wisely and tenderly, as a sacred treasure. Do not
hammer it in pieces; but by precept and true example wisely fashion and
mould it until the child comes to years of responsibility.

" The mother may ask, ' Shall I never punish my child？ ' Whipping
may be necessary when other resorts fail; yet she should not use the rod
if it is possible to avoid doing so. But if milder measures prove insuf-
ficient, punishment that will bring the child to its senses should in love
be administered. Frequently one such correction will be enough for a lifetime, to show the child that he does not hold the lines of control." [2]

(2) *Social Punishments.* These were necessitated because of wrong
relations in the social life of the community. The children in the home
and the student in the school learned of the wrong relations and the
punishments administered, and were thus taught early in life to recognize right standards of conduct and the punishment that was inflicted
on those who failed to properly relate themselves to others living in the
community.

Those found guilty of stealing were required to restore double: " For
all manner of trespass, whether it be for ox, for ass, for sheep, for
raiment, or for any manner of lost thing which another challengeth to
be his, the cause of both parties shall come before the judges; and
whom the judges condemn, he shall pay double unto his neighbor "
(Ex. 22: 9).

For the following transgressions the individual was cut off from
Israel: (1) The eating of blood (Lev. 17: 10). (2) The offering of
sacrifices away from the tabernacle (Lev. 17: 1–5). (3) Those not
observing the annual day of atonement (Lev. 23: 26–30). (4) Those
that consult with wizards (Lev. 20: 6).

[1] White, *Education*, p. 287.
[2] White, *Counsels to Teachers*, p. 116.

The death penalty was visited upon those guilty of the following: (1) The sin of Blasphemy (Lev. 24: 16). (2) Rebellion and Stubbornness (Deut. 21: 18–21). (3) The sin of Adultery (Lev. 20: 10–14).

The visitation of various punishments, depending upon the character of the transgressions committed, must have made a deep impression upon the children and youth and served to keep ever in their minds and hearts the high moral standards of living.

Education and Conduct

The apostle James, the philosopher of the New Testament, gives a pen picture of one who is truly educated. Before drawing this picture, he asks and answers this all-important question: " Who is a wise man and endued with knowledge among you? " (Jas. 3: 13). In other words this is his question: " Who is an *educated man?* " In answering this question he declares that an educated man will " show out of a good conversation (conduct) his works with meekness of wisdom." In short, a man's education is determined by his conduct rather than by his knowledge.

The apostle James then proceeds to speak of evil conduct, where there is " bitter envying and strife " and boldly declares:

" This wisdom (education) descendeth not from above, but is earthly, sensual, devilish. For where envying and strife is, there is confusion and every evil work. But the wisdom (education) that is from above is first pure, then peaceable, gentle, and easy to be entreated, full of mercy and good fruits, without partiality and without hypocrisy " (Jas. 3: 15–17).

Notice that false and true education are characterized by the apostle in terms of conduct rather than in terms of knowledge:

False Education: 1. " Earthly." 2. " Sensual." 3. " Devilish." 4. " Bitter envying." 5. " Strife in your hearts." 6. " Confusion." 7. " Every evil work."

True Education: 1. " From above " (Heavenly). 2. " Pure." 3. " Peaceable." 4. " Gentle, and easy to be entreated." 5. " Full of mercy and good fruits." 6. " Without partiality." 7. " Without hypocrisy."

The foregoing answer from the Scriptures to the question, " Who is an educated man? " is somewhat out of harmony with the generally accepted idea, that a man's education is to be determined by the amount of knowledge accumulated while in school pursuing various courses of study, and attested to by the diploma received or the degree conferred. Knowledge is important, but the wisdom by faith which enables one to use rightly the knowledge gained is far more important.

We now pass to Part III of this book, " Hebrew Educational Practice," where consideration is given to instruction in the home, and school, from the time of the patriarchs to the exile. The principles and methods of teaching and discipline just considered will be applied to the student and the various subjects taught, beginning with the most important subject, " The Holy Scriptures."

PART THREE

HEBREW EDUCATIONAL PRACTICE

IX

EDUCATION IN THE HOME

Antediluvian Education

FROM the time the school was removed from Eden to the time of the Flood was a period of about 1,500 years. Very little is revealed in the Scriptures concerning the educational practice during the Antediluvian age. As far as one can gather from the reading of Biblical history (and we have no other) of the antediluvians, education centered in the family. The tragic death of Abel caused by his brother Cain was a very unpromising beginning in family education. In fact for the time being this tragedy closed the Adam family school, as Cain and his family were by command of God driven to "the land of Nod on the east of Eden" (Gen. 4: 12–16). Another son was born into Adam's family, and Eve called his name Seth, "For God, said she, hath appointed me another seed instead of Abel whom Cain slew" (Gen. 4: 25).

The family of Adam and Eve must have grown to large numbers during his long life of 930 years for we read: "And the days of Adam after he had begotten Seth were 800 years, and he begat sons and daughters" (Gen. 5: 4, 5).

Adam's family was divided in two parts: One division—Cain and his descendants—lived in the land of Nod east of Eden; while Seth and his brothers and sisters with their descendants lived in Eden near the Garden of Eden. Cain and his descendants undoubtedly maintained the attitude that had been manifested by the father which led him to take the life of his brother. Concerning Seth and his son and the others dwelling in Eden we read: "And to Seth, to him also there was born a son; and he called his name Enos; then began men to call upon the name of the Lord" (Gen. 4: 26). So the earth was peopled by two classes which lived separately for some time. One class was the ungodly descendants of Cain, and the other class was the godly descendants of Seth and his brothers, and sisters born during the years of Adam and Eve.

Seth and his descendants undoubtedly, like Abel, lived a pastoral life, raising stock, and probably also tilled the ground, which occupation Cain largely abandoned when he removed from Eden. Abandoning largely the tilling of the soil, which, like the keeping of flocks, is most favorable to physical, intellectual, and spiritual development, Cain occupied his time in the building of the first city ever built, and called it after the name of his firstborn son—Enoch (Gen. 4: 17). Some of Cain's descendants, like their progenitor, followed mechanical, instead of agricultural occupations. They manufactured musical instruments, and became artificers in brass and iron. We read of some who dwelt in tents and kept cattle. The dwellers in Nod were an intelligent and progressive class of people; but were lacking in moral power. Bigamy was first practiced among them, and it was followed by polygamy (Gen. 4: 17–22).

It seems that after some time had elapsed the two classes or divisions of Adam's family began to mingle and associate together, and as a result polygamy and other gross sins became common among the antediluvians. Wickedness became so great and violent that God decided to destroy all the human race, except Noah and his family, with whom He would repeople the earth (Gen. 6: 1–8).

The antediluvians were not an ignorant barbarous people, but they were giants not only physically but also intellectually. Concerning their development after the descendants of Seth united with the descendants of Cain, we read: " There were giants in those days; and also after that when the sons of God (Seth's descendants) came in unto the daughters of men (Cain's descendants) and they bare children to them, the same became mighty men which were men of old, men of renown " (Gen. 6: 4). The family schools of the ten patriarchs whose names are recorded in Genesis 5 must have been great seats of learning. All these heads of families, except Enoch (who was transferred to the University of the Universe), lived from over a half to nearly a full millennium of years. Seven of these patriarchal educators lived contemporaneously for hundreds of years, and the combined influence of their knowledge and skill must have resulted in wonderful discoveries and achievement. A modern educator gives the following evaluation of antediluvian education:

" Men living before the flood lived many hundreds of years, and when one hundred years old were considered but youths. Those long-lived men had sound minds in sound bodies. Their mental and physical strength was so great that the present feeble generation can bear no comparison to them. Those ancients had nearly one thousand years in which to acquire knowledge. They came upon the stage of action from the ages of sixty to one hundred years, about the time those who now live the longest have acted their part in their little short lifetime and have passed off the stage."

" Adam had learned from the Creator the history of creation; he himself witnessed the events for nine centuries, and he imparted his knowledge to his descendants. The antediluvians were without books, they had no written records; but with their great physical and mental vigor they had strong memories, able to grasp and retain that which was communicated to them, and in turn to transmit it unimpaired to their posterity. And for hundreds of years there were seven generations living upon the earth contemporaneously, having the opportunity of consulting together, and profiting each by the knowledge and experience of all. The advantages enjoyed by men of that age to gain a knowledge of God through His works has never been equaled since.'' 1

The antediluvians were destroyed and the face of the earth so disfigured that we find no trace of their civilization, and must depend solely on the Scripture record for any knowledge of their achievements. In the course of time the descendants of Noah and his sons, Shem, Ham, and Japheth, multiplied; and for fear that the earth again might be visited by a flood, they erected a tower for their protection. Before it was completed, God confused the language of the people so that they were not able to complete the structure, and the tower has since been known as the " Tower of Babel." The Creator had placed the rainbow in the clouds as a guarantee that He would not again destroy the earth by a flood, but idolatry was substituted in place of the worship of the true God, and wickedness greatly increased in the earth. Because of continued wickedness and transgression, the length of life was greatly shortened. Shem, one of the three sons of Noah, lived only 600 years. Seven generations later, Terah, the father of Abraham, lived only 205 years. Undoubtedly there was a gradual decrease of intellectual as well as physical and spiritual power. On account of the confusion of tongues the people widely scattered throughout the earth (Gen. 11).

Patriarchal Education

After the Flood education still centered in the family, thus continuing the plan of patriarchal education. About 500 years after the Flood God found a righteous man named Abram (afterward named Abraham), a descendant of Shem, whom He called to leave his country and his kindred and go on a special mission. In order that the magnitude and importance of his mission may be better comprehended, we here give the call that came to Abraham from the Lord:

" Get thee out of thy country and from thy kindred and from thy father's house, unto a land that I will show thee; and I will make of thee a great nation, and I will bless thee and make thy name great; and thou shalt be a blessing; and I will bless them that bless thee, and curse him that curseth thee, and in thee shall all families of the earth be blessed " (Gen. 12: 1-3).

The following is the record of Abraham's response to the call of God:

" So Abram departed as the Lord had spoken unto him; and Lot went with him; and Abram was seventy and five years old when he departed out of Haran. And Abram took Sarai his wife, and Lot, his brother's son, and all their substance that they had gathered, and the souls they had gotten in Haran, and they went forth to go into the land of Canaan " (Verses 4, 5).

The School of Abraham. Abraham was called by God to leave city

---

1 White, *Principles of True Science*, pp. 39, 38 (Washington College Press).

surroundings and conditions and go into the country; and his nephew Lot went with him. They went back to the life that was most favorable to educational progress and the development of character—the pastoral life—living in tents and caring for their flocks and herds. This life was a constant reminder to Abraham and his household of their pilgrimage life on earth. The Apostle Paul speaks of this aspect of Abraham's traveling school:

" By faith Abraham when he was called to go out into a place which he should after receive for an inheritance, obeyed; and he went out, not knowing whither he went. By faith he sojourned in the land of promise, as in a strange country, dwelling in tabernacles with Abraham, Isaac, and Jacob, the heirs with him of the same promise; for he looked for a city which hath foundations, whose builder and maker is God " (Heb. 11: 8–10).

Abraham's ability to educate and instruct his household is indicated by the following testimony from the One who called him to carry out the divine educational program: " I know him, that he will command his children and his household after him, and they shall keep the way of the Lord, to do justice and judgment " (Gen. 18: 19).

Abraham's school enrollment must have reached nearly 1,000 students —men, women, and children; for he had 318 trained, armed men who were fit for battle (Gen. 14: 14).

Abraham had great influence with the rulers and people wherever he went. Many times kings and princes received him with honors, and sent him on his way laden with gifts and words of blessing and good will (Gen. 19, 20, 21). As a result of the educational principles and practice of this traveling school held in tents and tabernacles, Abraham's family grew finally to be a great nation, and through it all the nations of the earth have been blessed.

The School of Lot. Lot and his family and servants for a time were in the school of Abraham; but a feud between Abraham and Lot's herdsmen made a separation necessary. Abraham asked Lot to choose a location for his family, and his servants to feed their flocks and herds; and Lot chose the well watered plain of Jordan, and pitched his tents toward the city of Sodom. It was not long before he sat in the gate of the city as one of its rulers. The wicked influences of the city weaned his family away from God's plan of living; and away from the principles of truth they had been taught (Gen. 13: 1–13; 19: 1–38). Lot's school broke up in confusion and disaster to himself and his family when Sodom was destroyed because " pride, fullness of bread, and abundance of idleness was in her, and in her daughters, neither did she strengthen the hands of the poor and needy " (Ezek. 16: 49).

A National School. The descendants of the patriarchs—Abraham, Isaac, and Jacob—went down into Egypt to live when Joseph, next to the youngest of the twelve sons of Jacob, stood next to Pharaoh as ruler of Egypt. He had received his training up to seventeen years of age in the home of Jacob and Rachel, and then suddenly and unexpectedly, because of the jealousy of his brothers, he was sold a slave into Egypt. There he became a servant in the household of Potiphar, the captain of Pharaoh's guard, and later, because of faithful, efficient service, he was given entire charge of the household. Refusing to yield to the temptations of the mistress of the household, he was cast into prison, where he was honored and appointed assistant warden because of efficient, sympathetic service. He remained in the prison several years, and was transferred to the royal palace because of a true interpretation of the dreams of two of Pharaoh's officers, and also the dreams of the king which the wise men of the royal court had been unable to interpret. He was honored and appointed prime minister of Egypt, which position he held for sixty years. Concerning his position and influence we read that Pharaoh "made him Lord of his house and ruler of all his substance; to bind his princes at his pleasure, and to teach his senators wisdom" (Ps. 105: 21, 22).

During these years his people greatly multiplied and prospered, but a king arose who knew not Joseph, and for four hundred years they suffered under grievous bondage, after which they were miraculously delivered. Then for forty years Israel as a nation was under training in the wilderness school conducted by God Himself, through Moses, their visible leader and teacher. During these forty years they were being trained as to how they should live in the "Promised Land," so that they would be an example of right living to the nations surrounding them. Education in the home, such as was given by Jacob and Rachel to their children, was constantly emphasized in the instruction given by Moses: "These words which I command thee this day shall be in thy heart and thou shalt teach them diligently unto thy children, and shalt talk of them when thou sittest in thine house, and when thou walkest by the way, and when thou liest down, and when thou risest up" (Deut. 6: 6, 7). Joseph's life of uprightness and fidelity under the severest trials was probably referred to, and the reward that follows faithful training in the home. Moses undoubtedly referred to the influence of his mother's training on his own life during the brief twelve years he was permitted to remain at home, and how that training helped him to refuse "to be called the son of Pharaoh's daughter; choosing rather to suffer affliction with the people of God, than to enjoy the pleasures of sin for a season; esteeming the reproach of Christ greater riches than the treasures in Egypt: for he had respect unto the recompense of the reward" (Heb. 11: 24–26).

In the wilderness school the children of Israel were separated from the confused artificial life of the city. In the manna God provided their daily food. In addition to the care of the flocks and herds they scrupulously maintained sanitary conditions throughout the camp. During the year spent at Sinai they were engaged in the construction of the tabernacle and its furniture which provided the facilities for worship.

Israel as a nation was in school for forty years learning how to live when they should finally arrive in their new home, the land of Canaan.

They might have learned in much less time, but their 400 years of bondage life in Egypt made it difficult for them to respond to the high ideals of home life which were placed before them. Their condition on leaving Egypt is well described by a modern writer:

" When brought out of Egypt there were among the Israelites few prepared to be workers together with Him in the training of their children. The parents themselves needed instruction and discipline. Victims of life-long slavery, they were ignorant, untrained, degraded." [2]

The divine plan of education in Eden centered in the family. This plan as adapted to man's condition after the fall still centered in the family. The family was still to be the school and the parents the teachers. Concerning this plan of family or home education in the days of the patriarchs who lived just following the close of the Eden school, the writer just quoted above says:

" The education centering in the family was that which prevailed in the days of the patriarchs. For the schools thus established, God provided the conditions most favorable for the development of character. The people who were under His direction still pursued the plan of life that He had appointed in the beginning. Those who departed from God built for themselves cities, and, congregating in them, gloried in the splendor, the luxury, and the vice that makes the cities today the world's pride and its curse. But the men who held fast God's principles of life dwelt among the fields and hills. They were tillers of the soil and keepers of flocks and herds, and in this free, independent life, with its opportunities for labor, and study, and meditation, they learned of God, and taught their children of His works and ways. This was the method of education that God desired to establish in Israel." [3]

Instruction in the Home

Every Hebrew mother hoped to be the mother of the promised Messiah; and therefore special diligence was exercised by the parents in the training of the boys of the family. The interest in one family regarding the training of a promised son is expressed in the following questions asked of the angel who brought the good news: " How shall we order (train) the child, and what shall be his work? " (Judges 13: 12, margin).

Solomon speaks of the solicitous care of his father and mother for him when a child and how his faithful father taught him right principles to govern his life and conduct (Prov. 4: 1-7).

The book of Proverbs, written by Solomon, is largely an appeal to children and youth to choose the good and to refuse to do those things which are evil. Solomon had great confidence in the power and influence of right early training: " Train up a child in the way he should go; and when he is old he will not depart from it " (Prov. 22: 6). A certain definite plan of education and training is indicated by the ex-

[2] White, *Education*, p. 34.
[3] *Ibid.*, pp. 33, 34.

pression "the way." This way called "the way" was followed in the training of Joseph, Moses, Daniel, Esther, John the Baptist, Jesus, Timothy and many other Bible characters that we cannot take time or space to mention. A later chapter will be devoted to a close detailed examination of some of the student product of Hebrew education; for the final justification of any system of education is determined by the character of its product. The Master Teacher said: "Wisdom (education) is justified of her children" (Matt. 11: 19).

The home was the principal educational institution among the ancient Hebrews. No formal schools were conducted until the days of Samuel the Prophet. The home was the center of learning, and the father and mother were the principal teachers. They were assisted sometimes by others associated with the family called "nursing fathers" and "nursing mothers." This instruction was never entrusted to the lips of a stranger (Num. 11: 12; Isa. 49: 23).

The Talmud states that a child comes to the age of responsibility to the law of Jehovah at thirteen. Some scholars think that Moses was twelve years of age when he went to live in Pharaoh's daughter's home; and that Samuel was of the same age when the voice of God spoke to him at night. Jesus was twelve years of age when His parents took Him to the temple at Jerusalem, where He tarried unbeknown to His parents and astonished the teachers of Israel with His wisdom and knowledge (Luke 2: 42-48).

During the entire period of Hebrew history the family was regarded as the fundamental educational institution. The father and mother were held responsible for both the education and the conduct of their offspring. The father was the leading instructor and disciplinarian, but the mother earnestly co-operated with him in these vital matters.

There were many injunctions given to parents to love their children and to exercise patience toward them in their faults. The instruction of Elijah was designed to "turn the hearts of the fathers to the children, and the heart of the children to their fathers" (Mal. 4: 6). Jacob manifested fatherly love toward his children, and especially so toward the two younger members of his family—Joseph and Benjamin (Gen. 37: 3; 42: 4; 43: 1-7). David's patience and forbearance with Absolom expressed a father's love and tender pity (II Sam. 18: 5). Wishing to picture the love and pity of Jehovah for Israel he does so by referring to earthly fathers: "Like as a father pitieth his children, so Jehovah pitieth them that fear him" (Ps. 103: 13). Jehovah represents His love by that of a mother for her child (Isa. 49: 15, 16). Christ in the parable of the prodigal son represented the love of His Heavenly Father by that of an earthly father toward a wayward son (Luke 15: 12-32). The Apostle Paul, after urging children to be obedient to their parents, then gives a word of caution and admonition to fathers in their dealing with them: "Children, obey your parents in all things, for this is well pleasing unto the Lord. Fathers, provoke not your children to anger, lest they be discouraged" (Col. 3: 20, 21).

What Was Taught in the Home

Religion. The most important work of parents in the home school was that of teaching religion, and for many centuries this responsibility rested entirely upon the home. Concerning the early religious influence and instruction in the home we quote the following from Doctor Swift:

" The religious education of the child really began with the rites of infancy already described by which he was marked as belonging to a race (nation) set apart unto Jehovah. As he grew older, this ideal was gradually built up within his consciousness by the words and actions of those about him. Even before the child could speak, he began unconsciously to receive lessons of reverence and love of the law. Long before he could understand language his attention was attracted by members of the family pausing before the doorway, touching reverently the *mezuzah*, a small shining cylinder of wood or metal, kissing the hand that touched it, and then passing on (*Jewish Encyclopedia*, VIII 532a). Later on he would learn that the mezuzah was placed upon the doorway in obedience to the divine command: ' Thou shalt write them (the laws) upon the door posts of thy house and upon thy gates ' (Deut. 5: 4). Within the cylinder, written on a small piece of parchment, were two passages: Deuteronomy 6: 4–9 and 11: 13–20. About this time also the child must have begun to notice the phylacteries and bright twisted threads hanging from the four corners of his father's simlah.

" As soon as children began to speak their parents began to teach them Bible verses. . . .

" There was scarcely a question childish lips could frame for which the answer was not waiting in the sacred writings. The story of Adam and Eve (Gen. 2: 7) answered the child's question, ' Who made me and what am I made of? ' ' Why don't all people speak the same language? ' was answered by the story of the tower of Babel (Gen. 11: 1–9). And when he asked who made the sea and the stars his father recited the majestic poem of the creation: ' In the beginning God created the heaven and the earth ' (Gen. 1: 1; 2: 3). No matter what the question, in this last analysis, and in its final effect upon the child the answer was always, ' God.' It was God who formed man out of the dust of the earth—it was God who confused the tongues of men—it was God who divided the waters from the land and placed the sun, moon and stars in the sky—it was God who wrote the laws with His finger on tables of stone, and who had laid down the hundred regulations governing every day and hour. In this atmosphere, pervaded by a continuous sense of the reality, holiness, purity, and dominion of Jehovah the religious consciousness of the child was awakened, stimulated, and nurtured.

" In the home, as in the temple and in the synagogue, prayer was a conspicuous and important channel of religious expression. The life of every member of the family was a life of prayer. Before and after meals a prayer of thanksgiving was offered (Matt. 15: 36; Acts 27: 35). Besides this, prayers were offered three times each day, morning, afternoon, and evening (Ps. 55: 7; Dan. 6: 10). One of the first things taught to children was to pray.'' [4]

[4] F. H. Swift, *Education in Ancient Israel*, pp. 62–65 (Open Court Pub. Co.).

The religious festivals were also occasions for giving religious instruction. Concerning their educational value and significance Doctor Swift says:

" Every religious festival offered parents an opportunity for giving impressive religious instruction. Many festivals were definitely set aside as seasons for instruction in natural history and religion (Neh. 8: 18). Within the home the parents in obedience to the divine command explained to the children the origin of the festival and the meaning of each symbolic act " (Ex. 14: 2–14; Ps. 78: 1–8).

Morals. Religion and morals were inseparably connected. Jehovah whom His people worshiped was revealed through the prophets as a being who was righteous, pure, and holy; and His worshipers must be pure, honest, merciful, and holy in character. All the moral virtues were emphasized in the home training and instruction. Absolute obedience to parents was regarded as the primary virtue of childhood, and children were taught to manifest a special respect and deference to their parents during old age:

" Hearken unto thy father that begat thee; and despise not thy mother when she is old " (Prov. 23: 22). " My son, help thy father in his age, and grieve him not as long as he liveth " (Ecclesiasticus 3: 12).

I have added " faith" to Doctor Swift's list of moral virtues taught to the Hebrew children, which he suggests were presented in part as follows:

" They were presented in part through proverbs, moral precepts, psalms, and prayers, in part through biographies and historical narratives, in part through symbolic rites, customs, festivals already described. It must suffice here to name briefly the more important of these virtues, bearing in mind they ' were taught line upon line, precept upon precept, (here a little and there a little) in season and out of season.' "

1. Obedience	11. Thrift
2. Reverence	12. Prudence
3. Brotherly love	13. Patriotism
4. Charity	14. Patience
5. Compassion	15. Meekness
6. Hospitality	16. Loyalty
7. Temperance	17. Diligence
8. Chastity	18. Perseverance
9. Truthfulness	19. Mercy
10. Industry	20. Faith [5]

Manners. There can be no question but that good manners were emphasized in the home instruction. There are many exhortations and lessons in narrative form contained in the Scriptures, indicating proper attitudes toward and relations with others. But all of these outward forms were pervaded with the spirit of religion and morals, without which the most polished manners are empty and shallow. The spirit

[5] *Ibid.*, p. 67.

which prompts and pervades the act is of more importance than the act itself. If simplicity, kindness, and sincerity are lacking, we have only "the form without the power." The love and fear of God in the heart is to motivate and color all the acts and deeds done to others; and these will be noted and rewarded by the Father of all. The following are a few of many instances that might be noted:

"Thou shalt rise up before the hoary head, and honor the face of the old man, and fear thy God; I am the Lord" (Lev. 19: 32). "For whosoever shall give you a cup of water to drink in my name, because ye belong to Christ, verily I say unto you he shall not lose his reward" (Mark 9: 41). "Blessed are the merciful, for they shall obtain mercy" (Matt. 5: 7). "Blessed are the peacemakers, for they shall be called the children of God" (Matt. 5: 9).

All spirit of boasting and conceit are condemned:

"Let another man praise thee and not thine own mouth" (Prov. 27: 2). "Be not wise in thine own eyes; fear the Lord and depart from evil" (Prov. 3: 7).

The manner of conversation received attention:

"A whisperer separateth chief friends" (Prov. 16: 28). "In the multitude of words there wanteth not sin; but he that refraineth his lips is wise" (Prov. 10: 19). "A fool uttereth all his mind; but a wise man keepeth it in till afterward" (Prov. 29: 11).

Stinging and bitter words are not to be uttered: "A soft answer turneth away wrath; but grievous words stir up anger" (Prov. 15: 1).

In the book of Proverbs much wholesome advice is given regarding the value of proper conversation, and the evils of perverse speech.

"A wholesome tongue is a tree of life; but perverseness therein is a breach in the spirit" (Prov. 15: 4). "A word fitly spoken is like apples of gold in pictures of silver" (Prov. 25: 11).

The wisdom, laws, and righteousness of God are themes for frequent conversation.

"And my tongue shall speak of thy righteousness and of thy praise all the day long" (Ps. 35: 28). "The mouth of the righteous speaketh wisdom, and his tongue talketh of judgment" (Ps. 37: 30). "O how love I thy law! it is my meditation all the day" (Ps. 119: 97).

Tact is a sign (or indication) of good breeding and culture, but unbridled curiosity is linked with irreverence and disobedience. Undoubtedly the story of Lot's wife (Gen. 19: 26) and of the 70,000 slain for looking into the ark (I Sam. 6: 19) were used by parents in teaching their children to restrain their curiosity.

Table manners were given consideration. Gluttony, indulged in by the children, brought reproach upon the parents.

"He that is a companion of gluttonous men shameth his father" (Prov. 28: 7, margin). "Put a knife to thy throat if thou be a man given to appetite" (Prov. 23: 2).

The above admonitions would seem to indicate that it were better to be dead than to live a life of gluttony. A prayer for victory over a gluttonous appetite is recorded, in which are mentioned the dangers that result from an unrestrained appetite:

" Feed me with food of my allowance; lest I be full and deny thee, and say, Who is the Lord? or lest I be poor and steal and take the name of my God in vain " (Prov. 30: 8, 9, margin).

Specific rules of the table are given in one of the wisdom books:

" Eat, as becometh a man, those things which are set before thee and devour not lest thou be hated. Leave off for manners' sake; and be not insatiable lest thou offend. When thou sittest among many, reach not thine hand out first of all. A very little is sufficient for a man well nurtured. Sound sleep cometh of moderate eating; he riseth and his wits are with him " (Ecclesiasticus 31: 16–21).

The generous, kind, and just treatment of neighbors was strongly emphasized.

" Thou shalt love thy neighbor as thyself " (Lev. 19: 18). " Say not unto thy neighbor: Go and come again, and tomorrow I will give, when thou hast it by thee " (Prov. 3: 28).

Hospitality was considered a religious obligation and the stories of how Abraham and Lot " entertained angels unawares " must have often been repeated to the children (Gen. 18: 3–18 and Chap. 19).

Health and Service. One is impressed by the repeated statements in the Scriptures concerning the healthy physical appearance of Hebrew children and youth.

Joseph is " well-favored " (Gen. 39: 6).

Moses is a " proper child " (Heb. 11: 23).

David " was ruddy and withal of a beautiful countenance and goodly to look to " (I Sam. 16: 12).

Daniel and his three companions, " children in whom was no blemish, but well favored " (Dan. 1: 4).

Esther, " the maid was fair of form, good of countenance " (Esther 2: 7, margin).

The strength of body resulting from good health was early applied in useful labor in and about the home:

Joseph, when only a lad of seventeen in Potiphar's household, was so skilful in his work that he was made steward (Gen. 39: 2–6).

Samuel as a boy was useful and skilful in his service in the tabernacle (I Sam. 2: 18, 26; 3: 19).

David in his youth was strong and skilful with his hands in using the sling or playing the harp, or in protecting his flocks from the bear and the lion (I Sam. 16: 18; 17: 34, 35, 40).

Nehemiah was so trained that he was able to serve wine or mortar as the occasion demanded (Neh. 2: 1, 17; 4: 6, 15–23).

Daniel and his three companions while still in their teens had been so taught, that they were "skilful in wisdom, and cunning in knowledge" (Dan. 1: 4).

Industrial Education. Concerning industrial education in the Hebrew home we quote from Doctor Swift:

" Industrial occupation which had arisen during the Native period continued after the Exile. That every boy learned some handicraft seems evident from the fact that the most highly educated of all classes, the scribes and rabbis, supported themselves, if necessary, by plying some trade. It was left for the Talmud to direct every father, regardless of his social position, to teach his son a trade (Babylonian Talmud " Tract Kiddushin" 30 b.). But here as in many other instances, it seems probable that the Talmud merely formulated as law what had been common practice for centuries, perhaps from time immemorial. . . .

" It seems reasonable to assume that in most cases he (the son) followed his father's occupation, and acquired his earliest training by assisting his father or elder brothers in shop or market place. As he grew older he would assist more and more until at length he would enter upon a regular apprenticeship." 6

These views of industrial education and training are sustained in the Scriptures. We have a concrete example of a girl so educated and trained in the excellent woman administering the affairs of her household with great skill and wisdom (Prov. 31: 10–31). We have also the concrete example of industrial education being carried forward in the school by students and teachers, with Elisha the Prophet supervising the work of establishing the school in a more favorable location (II Kings 6: 1–7).

From our study of Hebrew education in the home, we have found conclusive evidence that the parents made a real business of educating and training their children while under their care. We have also found that the home educational program was broad and comprehensive, resulting in a thorough and symmetrical development of the physical, mental and spiritual powers of the child. In the next chapter we shall consider the educational program as carried out in the Hebrew schools.

6 Swift, *Education in Ancient Israel*, pp. 60–61.

X

EDUCATION IN THE SCHOOL

The Schools of the Prophets

FORMAL education evidently was not introduced until the time of Samuel the prophet. Previous to this time, educational effort was blended with the activities of the home and with social and religious functions. The indirect rather than the direct method of education obtained, until Samuel established the system of schools called the "schools of the prophets." These were not to take the place of home education, but rather to aid and supplement the work of parents. Many parents were neglectful of their duty and these schools were a means of supplying, in a measure, the training and instruction which the children failed to obtain at home.

Samuel established two of these schools, one at Ramah, his home, and the other at Kirjath-jearim, where the ark remained for so many years after it was returned by the Philistines. Other schools were established during the reigns of David and Solomon, and the prosperity of Israel during their reigns was in a large measure due to the thorough, efficient training of young men, who became wise counselors in the affairs of the nation.

In the days of Elijah and Elisha there were several of these schools, and they served as mighty barriers against the spirit of worldliness and apostasy that threatened the very existence of the nation as the chosen people of God.

Schools Established by Samuel. The Scripture record seems to indicate that Samuel was principal of the school at Ramah where he lived; for it speaks of "the company of the prophets . . . and Samuel standing as appointed over them" (I Sam. 19: 20). The students in these schools were later spoken of as "sons of the prophets" (II Kings 2: 3, 5, 7, 15) because for the most part prophets were their teachers.

The purpose of these schools and the character of the students enrolled are clearly stated by a modern writer on Hebrew education:

"These schools were intended to serve as a barrier against the widespreading corruption, to provide for the mental and spiritual welfare of the youth, and to promote the prosperity of the nation by furnishing it with men qualified to act in the fear of God as leaders and counselors. To this end Samuel gathered companies of young men who were pious, intelligent and studious."[1]

Concerning the influence of these schools the above writer adds:

[1] White, *Education*, pp. 46, 47.

" These schools proved to be one of the means most effective in promoting that righteousness which ' exalteth a nation.' In no small degree they aided in laying the foundation of that marvelous prosperity which distinguished the reigns of David and Solomon.''

Schools Established by Elijah and Elisha. Following the reigns of David and Solomon these schools fell into decay; but they were revived by Elijah and Elisha. Mention is made of their establishment at Bethel, Gilgal, Jericho, and Jordan. We have in II Kings 6 the record of the removal of one of these schools from an unfavorable location to Jordan. A token of divine approval of the enterprise was shown by the floating of the axe-head which had fallen into the river.

Elijah visited the schools he had established just before he was translated, and then left them to the fostering care of Elisha, his successor. Elisha's ministry in behalf of these schools was very valuable. At Jericho with salt he purified the spring that was the source of their water supply (II Kings 2: 19–22). At Gilgal he used meal to neutralize the effect of a poisonous plant in some cooked pottage provided for one hundred students (II Kings 4: 38–44).

The work of Elijah and Elisha in connection with these schools and their influence throughout the nation are described by the above writer:

" The Schools of the Prophets, established by Samuel, had fallen into decay during the years of Israel's apostasy. Elijah re-established these schools, making provision for young men to gain an education that would lead them to magnify the law and make it honorable. Three of these schools, one at Gilgal, one at Bethel, and one at Jericho, are mentioned in the record. Just before Elijah was taken to heaven he and Elisha visited these centers of training. The lessons that the prophet of God had given them on former visits he now repeated. Especially did he instruct them concerning their high privilege of loyally maintaining their allegiance to the God of heaven. He also impressed upon their minds the importance of letting simplicity mark every feature of their education. Only in this way could they receive the mold of heaven and go forth to work in the ways of the Lord.

" The heart of Elijah was cheered as he saw what was being accomplished by means of these schools. The work of reformation was not complete, but he could see throughout the kingdom a verification of the word of the Lord, ' Yet I have left me seven thousand in Israel, all the knees which have not bowed unto Baal.' '' [2]

The leading prophet of the time (as Samuel, Elijah, and Elisha) had general charge of these schools, and directed the work of education throughout the nation. Under them were a large number of priests, prophets, sages, and Levites, who constituted the teachers of the nation. It was unfortunate when the king did not co-operate with the prophet, as was the case with King Ahab in his relation to Elijah. We have an example of united co-operation on the part of King Jehoshaphat who sent his princes along with the Levites " to teach in the

[2] White, *Prophets and Kings,* pp. 224–225 (Pacific Press).

cities of Judah." The record says: "And they taught in (the cities of) Judah, and had the book of the law of the Lord with them, and went about throughout all the cities of Judah, and taught the people" (II Chron. 17: 9).

The influence of that national educational movement is thus described:

" And the fear of the Lord fell upon all the kingdoms of the lands that were round about Judah, so that they made no war against Jehoshaphat. Also some of the Philistines brought Jehoshaphat presents and tribute silver; and the Arabians brought him flocks, seven thousand and seven hundred rams, and seven thousand and seven hundred he goats " (Verses 10, 11).

Great industrial activity and financial prosperity throughout the nation resulted from the movement:

" And Jehoshaphat waxed great exceedingly; and he built in Judah castles and cities of store, and he had much business in the cities of Judah " (Verses 12, 13).

Subjects Taught in the Schools. The subjects of study in the schools of the prophets, while not definitely named, can be gathered from the Scripture narrative describing the life-activities of the people. We venture to name the following lists of subjects, which we classify under principal and subordinate subjects:

Principal Subjects.

1. *The Sacred Scriptures.* These include the ten commandments, and the writings of Moses, now known as the Pentateuch.

2. *Sacred History.* There were fourteen volumes of sacred history, written for the most part by prophets, mentioned in the Bible. These volumes have not been preserved, but they must have been carefully studied, as they contained valuable lessons for the youth, drawn by the prophet writers from the dealings of God with His people and with the kings that ruled over them.

3. *Sacred Poetry.* This included the book of Job, and the poetic selections in the Pentateuch in the earlier schools established during the reign of Samuel; and the books of Psalms, Proverbs, Ecclesiastes, and the Song of Solomon in the later schools established by Elijah and Elisha. Undoubtedly further poetic material for study was contained in the fourteen volumes of sacred history mentioned in Chapter XV.

4. *Sacred Music.* Both vocal and instrumental music occupied a large place in the social and religious life of Israel. When Saul was returning from seeking his father's asses, he met a company from one of the schools of the prophets, playing and singing (I Sam. 10: 5). Both David and Solomon organized vocal and instrumental talent in connection with religious services. David says, " Four thousand praised the Lord with instruments which I made . . . to praise the Lord therewith " (I Chron. 23: 5). Out of these four thousand there were 288 spoken of as being " cunning " in music—especially trained and gifted.

Solomon composed 1,005 songs (I Kings 4: 32). Of his interest in music he says: " I gat me men singers and women singers, and the delights of the sons of men, as musical instruments, and that of all sorts " (Eccl. 2: 8).

5. *Sacred Science.* To the ancient Hebrews, not only God's word, but also God's works were holy and sacred. " The Lord is righteous in all his ways, and holy in all his works " (Ps. 145: 17). There can be no doubt that science was given a large place in the education of the Hebrew children and youth. The writings of David, Solomon, and other Bible writers are full of appreciative utterances regarding the operations of God in nature. It would seem that the students in the schools of the prophets studied directly the book of nature rather than books that had been written about nature.

6. *Physical and Industrial Education.* The general tenor of the Old Testament teaching indicates that the Hebrew youth developed strong healthy bodies and also gained a practical knowledge of industrial employments. Even the professionalist had served an apprenticeship at some trade. Priest, prophet, and sage were able to turn their hands as well as their hearts and minds to service wherever the circumstances required it.

When we read the description of the virtuous, industrious, and illustrious house-mistress, and learn how economically and efficiently she ministered to the interest of her household and the poor and needy in the community, we are assured that the Hebrew girls received a thorough training in household affairs. These and other principal subjects will be given further study and consideration. (See Prov. 31: 10-31.)

Subordinate Subjects.

1. *Writing.* The art of writing was well developed in Israel. The art of printing was unknown, but the scribes were a professional class, highly efficient and highly respected for their invaluable service. The " ready writer " and " ready scribe " are familiar terms to the Bible student (Ezra 7: 6; Ps. 45: 1).

2. *Reading.* This was also a highly developed art, used constantly in religious services, in the reading of the law. The perfection reached in this art is indicated by the following passage of Scripture: " They read in the book of the law of God distinctly, and gave the sense, and caused them to understand the reading " (Neh. 8: 8).

3. *Mathematics.* Mathematics must have been thoroughly studied, for God gave His people difficult tasks to perform, which were outlined in minutely detailed specifications, involving extent, volume, proportion, and symmetry, as in the building of the tabernacle and the temple. They must have been given a thorough training in business mathematics, for they were a strong and successful people in commercial enterprises, taking the lead of the nations around them.

From the educational practice cited above, it is certainly evident that the ancient Hebrews gave earnest thought and attention to matters of education.

The Teachers in Israel

The standing and qualifications of these Hebrew educators and their methods of instruction have been commented on by students of Hebrew education. Concerning the priests and Levites we give the following from Doctor Swift:

" Through their declaration of the will of Jehovah, discovered by the use of the sacred lot or some other means . . . they created and disseminated conceptions of Jehovah. They organized and directed public festivals, many of which were little less than dramatized lessons in religion and history. They taught to the individuals, resorting to them in private, and to the multitude publicly assembled in the temple or in the open, forms of worship. They collected and transmitted (at first orally, later by writing) laws, rites, ceremonies, . . . and history (Mal. 2: 7). They compiled, edited and transmitted this literature. They put much of it in forms easy to grasp, and remember, and taught it to the people. Through their literary efforts they began the compilation of that great body of literature which still remains the world's unsurpassed text for religious and moral instruction." [3]

Of the prophets we are told:

" The Hebrew prophets were not primarily nor chiefly foretellers of the future. Their importance is due to the part they played in public affairs and to their service as public teachers. Their rise to the position of public leaders in Israel is contemporaneous with the rise of the monarchy. Among the causes which explain their entrance into the arena of public affairs, there may be mentioned: (1) the need of seers at the royal court to declare the will of Jehovah when important undertakings were being contemplated and upon other occasions; (2) the need of religious reform; (3) the need of social reform.

" Religious and social abuses (e. g., idolatry and the increasing oppression of the poor), combined with a constant fear of outside foes, resulted in bringing together devout men, endowed with a greater vision, yearning for reform and moved by religious and patriotic zeal. . . . Such bands went by the name of prophets or ' sons of the prophets.' They appear to have lived in communities, frequently in the vicinity of some famous sanctuary as Bethel and Gilgal. Some prophets, such as Samuel and Elisha, were intimately associated with such communities." [4]

Speaking of the instructors in the schools of the prophets we are told:

" The instructors were not only versed in divine truth, but had themselves enjoyed communion with God, and had received the special endowment of His Spirit. They had the respect and confidence of the people, both for learning and for piety." [5]

[3] Swift, *Education in Ancient Israel*, p. 34.
[4] *Ibid.*, p. 35.
[5] White, *Education*, p. 46.

The leading prophets, as Samuel, Elijah, and Elisha, were not confined to the work of supervising these schools under their care, but went here and there throughout the kingdom as the situations demanded their wisdom and counsel:

" The prophets were wandering teachers. In their own eyes and the eyes of the people, they were Jehovah's divinely commissioned messengers. Wherever there was opportunity to make known His will, wherever there was need of protest against evils or encouragement in righteousness, thither they betook themselves.'' [6]

Comparing the Hebrew teacher with those of other nations Doctor Swift continues:

" It may be seriously doubted whether any nation has ever produced a group of religious and moral teachers comparable with the prophets of ancient Israel. Through their spoken public addresses and writings they became the creators of national religious and social ideals, critics and inspirers of public policies, denunciators of social wrongs, preachers of individual and social righteousness, and the source and channel of an ever loftier conception of Jehovah and of the mission of Israel. In fulfilling each of these capacities, they were acting as public teachers. In every national crisis they were at hand to denounce, to encourage, to comfort and always to instruct. They were the public conscience of Israel, the soul of its religion, the creators of public opinion, its most conspicuous, its most revered, its most convincing teachers.'' [7]

The remaining chapters of this section are devoted to a consideration of the principal subjects taught in the Hebrew schools, special thought being given to the principles and methods of instruction.

[6] Swift, *Education in Ancient Israel*, p. 37.
[7] *Ibid.*, p. 38.

XI

THE HOLY SCRIPTURES

The Inspired Word of God

THE collection of thirty-nine books composing the Old Testament Scriptures were regarded by the Hebrews and Jews as the inspired Word of God. These books were classified into three divisions: (1) The Law; (2) The Psalms; (3) The Prophets. All these writings were regarded as divine revelations and are spoken of as being the "oracles of God," which were committed to Israel. The first division—The Law—was spoken and written at Mount Sinai. The commitment of these holy oracles is referred to by Stephen and the Apostle Paul:

" This is he that was in the church in the wilderness with the angel which spake to him in the Mount Sinai, and with our fathers; who received the lively oracles to give unto us " (Acts 7: 38). " What advantage then hath the Jew? . . . Much every way; chiefly because unto them were committed the oracles of God " (Rom. 3: 1, 2).

To the historical, prophetical, and poetical portions of the Sacred Scriptures which were given later, from time to time, there is frequent reference throughout the Bible. How the Holy Scriptures were written is clearly stated by the Apostle Peter:

" Knowing this first, that no prophecy of the Scripture is of any private interpretation. For the prophecy came not in old time by the will of man; but holy men of God spake as they were moved by the Holy Ghost " (II Peter 2: 21).

The apostle Paul affirms that the Holy Scriptures were given by inspiration of God, and also indicates the purposes for which they were given:

" All scripture is given by inspiration of God, and is profitable for doctrine, for reproof, for correction, for instruction in righteousness; that the man of God may be perfect, thoroughly furnished unto all good works " (II Tim. 3: 16, 17).

Paul speaks of the comparative nobility of two of his churches in the study of the Scriptures:

" And the brethren immediately sent away Paul and Silas by night unto Berea. . . . These (the Bereans) were more noble than those in Thessalonica, in that they received the Word with all readiness of mind, and searched the Scriptures daily, whether these things were so " (Acts 17: 10, 11).

Christ strongly emphasized the importance of searching the Scriptures:

" Ye do err, not knowing the Scriptures, nor the power of God "
(Matt. 22: 29). " O fools and slow of heart to believe all that the
prophets have spoken " (Luke 24: 25). " Search the Scriptures, for in
them ye think ye have eternal life, and they are they which testify of
me " (John 5: 39).

Characteristics of the Word of God

The Word of God works effectually in those who believe; and produces in their lives its own characteristics. But it must be received
as the Word of God and not the word of men. This is the testimony
of the Apostle Paul: " When ye received the Word of God which ye
heard of us, ye received it not as the word of men, but as it is in
truth, the Word of God, which effectually worketh in you that believe " (I Thess. 2: 13).

The following character elements are produced in the lives of those
who have implicit faith in the Word of God and accept it as their
guide and counselor:

1. *Pureness.* " The words of the Lord are pure words, as silver
tried in a furnace of earth, purified seven times " (Ps. 12: 6). " Thy
word is very pure, therefore thy servant loveth it " (Ps. 119: 140).
" Every word of God is pure; he is a shield to them that put their
trust in him " (Prov. 30: 5). " The commandment of the Lord is
pure enlightening the eyes " (Ps. 19: 8).

2. *Cleanliness.* " Ye are clean through the word which I have
spoken unto you " (John 15: 3). " The fear of the Lord is clean enduring forever " (Ps. 19: 9).

3. *Sweetness.* " How sweet are thy words unto my taste! Yea,
sweeter than honey to my mouth " (Ps. 119: 103). " Then did I eat
it and it was in my mouth as honey for sweetness " (Ezek. 3: 3).

4. *Righteousness.* " Thy testimonies that thou hast commanded
are righteousness and very faithful " (Ps. 119: 138, margin). " The
statutes of the Lord are right rejoicing the heart " (Ps. 19: 8). " My
tongue shall speak of thy word; for all thy commandments are
righteousness " (Ps. 119: 172).

5. *Sureness.* " The testimony of the Lord is sure making wise the
simple " (Ps. 19: 7). " Thy testimonies are very sure " (Ps. 93: 5).
" We have a more sure word of prophecy whereunto ye do well that
ye take heed " (II Peter 1: 19).

6. *Truthfulness.* " The judgments of the Lord are true and
righteous altogether " (Ps. 19: 9). " Thou art near, O Lord; and
all thy commandments are truth " (Ps. 119: 151). " Thy righteousness is an everlasting righteousness, and thy law is the truth " (Ps.
119: 142).

" Sanctify them through thy truth, thy Word is truth " (John
17: 17).

7. *Holiness.* " The law is holy, and the commandment holy, and just,
and good " (Rom. 7: 12). " Which he had promised afore by his prophets

in the Holy Scriptures" (Rom. 1: 2). "And that from a child thou
hast known the Holy Scriptures" (II Tim. 3: 15).

8. *Justness.* "The law is holy, the commandment holy, just and
good" (Rom. 7: 12). "Just and true are thy ways, thou king of
saints" (Rev. 15: 3).

8. *Goodness.* "The law is holy, and the commandment holy, and just,
and good" (Rom. 7: 12). "Turn away my reproach which I fear; for
thy judgments are good" (Ps. 119: 39). "Good is the word of the
Lord which thou hast spoken" (II Kings 20: 19).

10. *Life.* "The Word of God is living and powerful" (Heb. 4: 12,
margin). "The words I speak unto you, they are spirit and they are
life" (John 6: 63). "Who (Christ) hath abolished death and brought
life and immortality to light through the gospel" (II Tim. 1: 10).

11. *Power.* "The Word of God is living and powerful" (Heb.
4: 12, margin). The gospel "is the power of God unto salvation"
(Rom. 1: 16). "And they were astonished at his doctrine and his
word was with power" (Luke 4: 32). "Upholding all things by the
word of his power" (Heb. 1: 3).

12. *Perfection.* "The law of the Lord is perfect, converting the
soul" (Ps. 19: 7). "Whoso looketh into the perfect law of liberty,
. . . this man shall be blessed in his deed" (Jas. 1: 25). "All scripture is given by inspiration of God . . . that the man of God may be
perfect, perfected unto all good works" (II Tim. 3: 16, 17, margin).

As we partake of food, the food elements are digested and assimilated and build up the various tissues of the body. Good foods containing all the necessary elements are essential to the building of
strong bodies. So in the building of good strong character we are to
eat, digest and assimilate the Word of God, and the character elements
noted above and many others will appear in the life and character
of the growing child. The prophet Jeremiah speaks of his experience
in eating the word of God: "Thy words were found and I did eat
them; and they were unto me the joy and the rejoicing of my heart"
(Jer. 15: 16).

The Apostle Paul recognized the character building power of the
Word of God: "And now, brethren, I commend you to God and to
the word of his grace which is able to build you up and to give you
an inheritance among all them which are sanctified" (Acts 20: 32).

The Bible, as already noted (see pages 29, 30) is the greatest educating book in the world, and we now give consideration to the study
of the Holy Scriptures in Hebrew homes and schools.

Study of the Scriptures in the Home

We have quoted several times the words of Moses spoken to Israel
urging faithfulness and diligence in teaching their children the laws
and statutes given at Sinai (Deut. 6: 4-9; 11: 18-21). (See pages
67, 84.) We have also considered quite fully the principles and
methods of teaching and discipline in the home. In this chapter we

wish to consider further the place of the Scriptures in home education, and the results of its study and teaching.

In Patriarchal Homes. There must have been a diligent study and practice of the Scriptures in the patriarchal homes that educated and trained Joseph, Moses, Samuel, David, Solomon, Isaiah, Daniel, Esther, and many others receiving honorable mention in Holy Writ. Further consideration will be given to these in the chapter dealing with the product of Hebrew education. (See page 207.) The patriarchal home of Lot and of Eli failed in giving the training that was necessary to keep their children from yielding to evil influences and practices. Only two of Lot's children escaped the destruction of Sodom. When Lot entreated the rest of his children to flee from Sodom, the record says: " He seemed as one that mocked " (Gen. 19: 14). Concerning Eli's lack of control of his children we have the sad record: " His sons made themselves vile and he restrained them not " (I Sam. 3: 13).

In the Home of Timothy. Direct reference is made by the Apostle Paul to Timothy's early study of the holy Scriptures under the instruction of his mother Eunice, and his grandmother Lois: " Continue thou in the things which thou hast learned, and hast been assured of, knowing of whom thou hast learned them; and that from a child thou hast known the holy Scriptures, which are able to make thee wise unto salvation through faith which is in Christ Jesus " (II Tim. 3: 14, 15).

Paul recalls to his mind the character of Timothy's early teachers and which he sees reflected in his service: " I call to remembrance the unfeigned faith that is in thee, which dwelt first in thy grandmother Lois, and in thy mother Eunice; and I am persuaded that in thee also " (II Tim. 1: 5).

The following comment on the early home education of Timothy will be encouraging to parents:

" Timothy's father was a Greek and his mother a Jewess. From a child he had known the Scriptures. The piety that he saw in his home life was sound and sensible. The faith of his mother and his grandmother in the sacred oracles was to him a constant reminder of the blessing in doing God's will. The Word of God was the rule by which these two godly women had guided Timothy. The spiritual power of the lessons that he had received from them kept him pure in speech, and unsullied by the evil influences with which he was surrounded. Thus his home instructors had co-operated with God in preparing him to bear burdens.

" Paul saw that Timothy was faithful, steadfast, and true, and he chose him as a companion in labor and travel. Those who had taught Timothy in his childhood were rewarded by seeing the son of their care linked in close fellowship with the great apostle. Timothy was a mere youth when he was chosen by God to be a teacher; but his principles had been so established by his early education, that he was fitted to take his place as Paul's helper. And though young, he bore his responsibilities with Christian meekness.'' . . .

'' As the lessons of the Bible are wrought into the daily life, they have a deep and lasting influence upon the character. These lessons Timothy learned and practiced. He had no specially brilliant talents, but his work was valuable because he had used his God-given abilities in the Master's service. His knowledge of experimental piety distinguished him from other believers and gave him influence.'' [1]

In the Home of Jesus. Probably in no home in all Israel was there more faithful teaching than in the home of Jesus at Nazareth, where He lived for nearly thirty years before beginning His three and one-half years ministry. We have already given brief study to His early life (see pages 54–58); but wish to give further consideration to His study of the Holy Scriptures.

His knowledge of the Scriptures at twelve years of age was a great surprise and marvel to the rabbis, and from what we can learn in the gospel records, the Scriptures were His only textbook during His childhood days. That He also was a diligent student of nature, is abundantly proven by His parables. He also was a keen observer of human life and many of His parables are based on life experiences.

Education of the children was strongly emphasized by the Jews and abundant provision was made for schools in connection with the synagogues. Books were provided for the children. We have already considered the Jewish primer prepared by Rabbi Akkibah (see pages 30, 31), who was a leading educator in Christ's day, and perished at the time of the destruction of the Temple, A. D. 70. It is not probable that Mary or Joseph used the educational books of the day in the education and training of Jesus; or that He attended the synagogue schools. When older in years He did not attend the higher schools taught by the rabbis as a preparation for His mission (John 7: 14). His knowledge of the Scriptures was superior to theirs and they were displeased at His nonconformity to their educational program. This situation is well described by a modern educator:

'' From its earliest years, the Jewish child was surrounded with the requirements of the rabbis. Rigid rules were prescribed for every act, down to the smallest details of life. Under the synagogue teachers the youth were instructed in the countless regulations which as orthodox Israelites they were expected to observe. But Jesus did not interest Himself in these matters. From childhood He acted independently of the rabbinical laws. . . .

'' In every gentle and submissive way Jesus tried to please those with whom He came in contact. Because He was so gentle and unobtrusive, the scribes and elders supposed that He would be easily influenced by their teaching. They urged Him to receive the maxims and traditions that had been handed down from the ancient rabbis, but He asked for their authority in Holy Writ. He would hear every word that proceeds from the mouth of God; but He could not obey the inventions of men. Jesus

[1] E. G. White, *Acts of the Apostles*, pp. 203–205 (Pacific Press).

seemed to know the Scriptures from beginning to end, and He presented them in their true import. The rabbis were ashamed to be instructed by a child. They claimed that it was their office to explain the Scriptures, and that it was His place to accept their interpretation. They were indignant that He should stand in opposition to their word.'' [2]

Not only did they oppose Him before He started on His mission; but during His three and one-half years of ministry they continued to oppose and antagonize with increasing hatred and violence, until at last they crucified Him on the cross.

Knowledge Outside of the Scriptures

The question may properly be raised as to the knowledge that Jesus had of the "three R's," or what are now termed the "common branches" of education. In the reading of the Four Gospels we conclude that He was taught at home by His parents the following common branches of learning:

1. *Reading.* Before He began His ministry He read in the synagogue one Sabbath morning the Scripture lesson from the book Isaiah. The reading was very impressive "and the eyes of all them that were in the synagogue were fastened upon him" (Luke 4: 16-20).

2. *Writing and Spelling.* His writing in the sand of the sins of those who accused one of their neighbors was so plain and legible that it was quickly read by the accusers, who fled before He finished the writing (John 8: 1-11).

3. *Arithmetic and Accounting.* Numbers were frequently used by Jesus in His parable teaching, and in some instances arithmetical problems were given which had to be solved in order that His instruction might be fully comprehended. When Peter questioned Jesus as to how many times he should forgive the trespasser, he was thinking within the limits of the 12's of the multiplication table—the 7's. Jesus' greater mercy and forgiving spirit were expressed in His knowledge of a larger multiplication table: "I say not unto thee until seven times, but until seventy times seven" (Matt. 18: 21, 22).

A number of His parables had to do with accounting, which showed a keen, accurate knowledge of the debit and credit principles as they should be applied in business dealings with others.

4. *History and Government.* Jesus through the study of the Old Testament Scriptures became well acquainted with the history of His people and the nations with whom they had dealings down through the centuries. When questioned as to the individual's relation to government, He replied: "Render therefore unto Cæsar the things that are Cæsar's; and unto God the things that are God's" (Matt. 22: 21).

5. *Industry and Trades.* Jesus lived a life of industry and learned from Joseph the carpenter's trade. In His parables He mentions various trades and occupations indicating a sympathetic knowledge of

[2] E. G. White, *Desire of Ages,* pp. 84-85 (Pacific Press).

the problems the farmer, the shepherd and the merchantmen had to solve in performing their arduous duties.

6. *Nature and Science.* Jesus undoubtedly was a very diligent student of nature and science, and studied them for the purpose of making clear and plain the spiritual truths He came to reveal.

The following quotations from modern educators give us their view of how Jesus during the years He lived in Nazareth gathered information in various lines, along with the knowledge He gained from His study of the Holy Scriptures:

" His discourses indicate some practical knowledge of various trades and professions of His day. He knew something of farming, gardening, and fruit growing, the methods of the shepherd, and the characteristics of sheep. He knew men, not simply theoretically, but practically. He had probed to the bottom the shallow pretenses and the hypocrisy of the scribes and Pharisees. He had undoubtedly become familiar with the history of His own nation outside of the records found in the Old Testament. He attended with His parents the regular services of the synagogue on the Sabbath day, and listened to the discourses there. He was evidently a lover of nature, and studied the flowers and the grasses and the various fruits that flourished in Palestine. By constant contact with men and things about Him, His bright, quick intellect could not help but constantly absorb knowledge from a multitude of sources outside of His daily study of God's Word.

" But all these things were incidental, they were secondary considerations, and were not allowed to interfere at all with His great life-work, and the preparation therefor by a constant and complete absorption of God's Word as it existed in His day. And our present contention is, not that God's Word shall take the place or in any way supersede the usual branches of study either in the common school or the college or the university, unless these other branches of study are allowed to crowd God's Word out of its primal place, but that it should be at the head of all . . . the real inspiration to all these other branches of study." [3]

" The question asked during the Saviour's ministry, ' How knoweth this man letters having never learned? ' (John 7: 15) does not indicate that Jesus was unable to read, but merely that He had not received a rabbinical education. Since He gained knowledge as we may do, His intimate acquaintance with the Scriptures shows how diligently His early years were given to the study of God's Word. And spread out before Him was the great library of God's created works. He who had made all things studied the lessons which His own hand had written in earth, sea, and sky. Apart from the unholy ways of the world, He gathered stores of scientific knowledge from nature. He studied the life of plants and animals, and the life of man. From His earliest years He was possessed of one purpose; He lived to bless others. For this He found resources in nature; new ideas of ways and means (of blessing others) flashed into His mind as He studied plant life and animal life. Continually He was seeking to draw from the things seen illustrations by which to present the living oracles of God." [4]

[3] Lamb, *The Making of a Man*, pp. 167, 168.
[4] White, *Desire of Ages*, p. 70.

"Among the great teachers of the world, Christ is remarkable for His habitual use of illustrations drawn from the external world, especially the scenes and objects of the region He moved in. The plants, the animals, the landscape and skies of Galilee were a treasury He constantly drew from. . . .

"These allusions to nature give us an insight into a beautiful feature of the character of the Saviour. He must have been a close observer of the external world. The boy of Nazareth had a keen eye for the changing seasons, the starry heavens, the glowing sunsets. He loved the rocks and hills about Nazareth, and doubtless knew every nook, every hidden dell with its murmuring brook. From the neighboring height He had often looked over the great rich plain, with its waving cornfields and bright river threading between. He saw Carmel like a crouching lion grandly framing in the picture on the South and West, and Tabor and Gilboa towards the East, while snow-crowned Hermon guarded the North. Great events had taken place in that scene of which Joseph and Mary often told him. . . .

"Christ was a mountain boy, and a mountain boy never ceases to love the hills. So in after life, Christ always sought the mountains when He wished to rest or pray or speak to His disciples alone. Other teachers preferred the forum or the porch. He is the teacher of the mountain, which by its elevation, its stability, its bright light and open air was the fit symbol of His doctrine. The forum and the porch are gone. The mountain remains, and the Sermon on the Mount bids fair to outlast the mountain itself. Discourses on these solitary heights, far away from all that could interrupt by sound or sight, must have seemed like voices from heaven.

"And when again He retired thither to pray alone, He had a closet fit for the Son of God. The canopy above was lighted by the silent stars; the earth beneath was out of sight and hearing. Both place and time seemed made for communion with the Creator of all. . . . Christ was not lonely on the mountain. His Father and the holy angels were with Him."[5]

Christ's Training and Modern Education

We close this consideration of Hebrew home education with a comparison of the education given to Jesus with that given to the child under the systems of modern education. We quote again from Mr. Lamb:

"At the risk of repeating, we wish to make very clear and emphatic the position taken, that if our boys and girls were trained as Jesus was trained up to twelve years of age, they would be in every desirable respect greatly the superiors of the boys and girls trained under the best methods of the present day. They would be wiser, clearer-headed, of better judgment, of keener intellects, of larger capacity in every way. That is to say, their intellects would be far better educated, ' drawn out,' they could think more deeply, take broader views, and would be more matured. In addition, their moral improvement would keep pace with their intellectual progress, so that their development would be more symmetrical; while the growing desire to fit themselves for large usefulness (' I must be

[5] F. H. Smith, *Christ and Science*, pp. 149–155 (Fleming H. Revell Co.)

about My Father's business,' said Jesus when twelve years of age), and to know more of God, would add inspiration and zest to their studies so that their future progress would be still more helpful; and reading, writing, geography, mathematics, grammar, history, as well as the natural sciences, would all find their proper place in such a child's curriculum of study, and be more zealously and successfully pursued than under any of our present processes.'' 6

'' We would not be misunderstood in stating the case so strongly. We do not mean that children should not be permitted to go to school, or to be taught the ordinary branches of study—reading, writing, arithmetic, geography, grammar, and history—to become familiar with the anatomy and physiology and hygiene of their own bodies, and, if the opportunity presents, to study all the natural sciences, every branch of human learning that may be useful in fitting them for the various occupations of human industry.''

'' But all of these things were incidental, they were secondary considerations, and *were not allowed to interfere at all with His great life-work, and the preparation therefor,* by a constant and complete absorption of God's word as it existed in His day. And our present contention is not that God's word shall take the place, or in any way supersede the usual branches of study, either in the common school or the college or the university . . . but that it shall be at the head of all—the real inspiration to all these other branches of study.'' 7

Study of the Scriptures in the Schools

The study of the Scriptures carried on in the home was undoubtedly given a large and probably the chief place in the schools of the prophets first established by Samuel and which were continued through the reigns of David and Solomon. The Scriptures then consisted of the Pentateuch and portions of what later became the book of the Psalms, many of which were written by David. When these schools were later revived by Elijah and Elisha during the reigns of kings Ahab and Jehoshaphat it is probable that the students were privileged to study the writings now contained in the books of the Bible—" Job," " Proverbs " and " Ecclesiastes," the two latter books being written by Solomon, and the former by Moses. It is probable that the book of Job was studied in the schools established by Samuel, since both the Pentateuch and the book of Job were completed by Moses before his death, which occurred just before Israel crossed the Jordan into the land of Canaan. The writings composing the Pentateuch consist largely of biographical, judicial, and historical material, in prose style, while Job, Proverbs, and Ecclesiastes are philosophical writings in poetical style, dealing with the philosophy of life. The material contained in the Bible books: " Joshua," " Judges," " Books of Samuel," " The Kings," and " The Chronicles," must have been accessible for study in the earlier schools of the prophets, for Joshua and Samuel, the authors of the first four books,

6 Lamb, *The Making of a Man*, pp. 161–162 (Hazlett Harrison & Co.).
7 *Ibid.*, pp. 166–168.

died before Israel had become a well established nation ruled by David and Solomon. The four remaining books containing the Chronicles of the kings of Israel were the national records kept of the events as they transpired. While these records were made by scribes or recorders, and kept in the royal palace, yet undoubtedly David and Solomon had them duplicated so they could be used by the prophets and priests in the schools. From these records lessons could be drawn showing the results that followed from obeying and disobeying the righteous laws, and statutes God had given to Israel to promote the prosperity and happiness of His chosen people.

Another source of instruction were historical books written by prophets, which have not been preserved, but which indicate that sacred history was one of the principal studies in the schools of the prophets. Fourteen volumes of sacred history are mentioned in the Old Testament Scriptures with the names of the authors, and the field covered by each of these writers. These will be considered in the chapter on " History and Prophecy."

Other Studies in the Schools of the Prophets

From what has just been said regarding the study of the Scriptures, we can gather some idea of what other subjects were taught in the schools of the prophets. We place the study of the Scriptures as the first and most important, and then add others which the Scriptural record seems to justify as being a part of the curriculum of the schools of the prophets.

1. *The Sacred Scriptures.* The study of the sacred Scriptures received the main emphasis, and seems to have been regarded as the basis or foundation of all the other subjects taught in the school.

2. *Sacred History.* The Pentateuch and the books following, up to and including the book of Esther, are largely biographical and historical in content. In these books, fourteen volumes of historical works written by prophets are cited, but these have not been preserved along with the sacred Scriptures. They were used as textbooks in the study of history and prophecy in the schools of the prophets.

3. *Sacred Literature.* Four of the books of Scripture, " Job," " The Psalms," " Proverbs," and " Ecclesiastes " are written in poetical style, the highest form of literary expression. Throughout the Scriptures are many poetical fragments. Much of the prose of the Scriptures approaches the high poetical plane. It would seem that not only the exalted beautiful truths of the Scriptures were studied and taught in these schools; but also the beautiful exalted forms of language in which truth is framed were given earnest, thoughtful consideration.

4. *Sacred Music.* There can be no question but what sacred music was taught and studied; for one book of the Scriptures is entirely devoted to sacred music. It was the Hebrew hymnal or psalter. In addition to the words of music, the accompanying instru-

ments for various songs are mentioned. Music, vocal and instrumental, was an integral part of the worship connected with the sanctuary and temple, and therefore must have been one of the principal studies in the schools of the prophets.

After the exile Nehemiah and Ezra endeavored to restore the former glory of Israel in its physical, intellectual, and spiritual achievements. They frequently made reference to the former days and solemnly entreated the people to follow God's program fully and to forsake those evils that brought to them the seventy years of bondage and servitude.

Nehemiah gave his time and energy mainly to the mechanical and industrial program for the rebuilding of the once beautiful city that had been laid waste by their enemies. Ezra devoted his time and energy to the intellectual and spiritual restoration of his people. He more than any other educator—both a priest and scribe—arduously worked to restore the sacred writings, and to multiply copies so that his people could have them for study and meditation.

Concerning Ezra's work as an educator, a modern writer says:

" Ezra endeavored to gain a heart preparation for the work he believed was before him. He sought God earnestly that he might be a wise teacher in Israel. As he learned to yield mind and will to divine control, there were brought into his life the principles of true sanctification, which in later years had a moulding influence, not only upon the youth who sought his instruction, but upon all others associated with him. . . .

" The efforts of Ezra to revive an interest in the study of the Scriptures were given permanency by his painstaking, lifelong work of preserving and multiplying the Sacred Writings. He gathered all the copies of the law that he could find, and had these transcribed and distributed. The pure Word, thus multiplied and placed in the hands of many people, gave knowledge that was of inestimable value.

" Ezra's faith that God would do a mighty work for His people led him to tell Artaxerxes of his desire to return to Jerusalem to revive an interest in the study of God's word, and to assist his brethren in restoring the holy city. As Ezra declared his perfect trust in the God of Israel, as One abundantly able to protect and care for His people, the king was deeply impressed. He well understood that the Israelites were returning to Jerusalem that they might serve Jehovah; yet so great was the king's confidence in the integrity of Ezra, that he showed him marked favor, granting his request, and bestowing on him rich gifts for the temple service. He made him a special representative of the Medo-Persian kingdom and conferred on him extensive powers for the carrying out of the purposes in his heart." [8]

Undoubtedly Ezra was the greatest educator during post-exile times. He started a program of education which developed through the years in the establishment of synagogue schools for the children, and advanced schools taught by the scribes, sages, and the rabbis. Many renowned Jewish educators did a large work in preparing edu-

[8] White, *Prophets and Kings*, pp. 608, 610 (Pacific Press).

cational literature. They prepared historical, philosophical, and literary works—the Babylonian and Jerusalem Talmuds being a miscellaneous collection of the knowledge and wisdom of Jewish scholars, covering about a thousand years following the destruction of Solomon's Temple by Nebuchadnezzar, King of Babylon (606 B. C.). Some of these scholars endeavored to pattern their writings after books contained in the Scriptures. This collection of books is called the "Apocrypha"; and despite many efforts, these books have never been admitted into the canon of Sacred Scriptures. Among these books may be mentioned "Ecclesiasticus" by Jesus Ben Sira, often called the "wisdom book." It is composed largely of proverbs and wise sayings after the order of the books in the Scriptures named "Proverbs" and "Ecclesiastes." Biographical and historical books were written—the "Book of Enoch" and the "Book of Jasher" being an attempt to give a Scriptural flavor and authority to these writings. Whatever gems of truth these later Jewish writings contain, they are but faint glimmering reflections of the oracles of God as given to Moses and other holy men of old who wrote as they were moved by the Holy Ghost. There is such a cunning mixture of truth and error that the instruction and counsel contained in them has never been generally regarded as consistent and safe to follow. The commandments and precepts of these teachers of Israel were disapproved by Christ: "Woe unto you, ye blind guides . . . which strain at a gnat and swallow a camel" (Matt. 23: 16, 24). "In vain do they worship me, teaching for doctrines the commandments of men" (Matt. 15: 9).

The Holy Scriptures—the Bible—is and ever will be the greatest educational book. All other books should be pervaded by its great principles. All subjects of instruction will find in the Bible their foundation principles. No student can safely and most profitably investigate any field of knowledge without entering that field through the gateway of the Bible. It magnifies and glorifies the field of study, and gives the student a clearer and truer conception of the principles and methods of investigation than can be gained by confining one's efforts to the fallible writings of men.

In this chapter our theme has been the Word of God. In the next chapter our theme is the works of God. The first is the study of the Bible; the second is the study of science. The Bible gives us a knowledge of what God has said; and science gives us a knowledge of what God has made. The book of revelation and the book of creation have one and the same Author, and their study together certainly cannot be regarded as unnatural and unpedagogical, but rather as promising more fruitful returns to the diligent and thoughtful student.

XII

NATURE AND SCIENCE

The Word and Works of God

IN the previous chapter it has been shown that the Holy Scriptures occupied the chief place in Hebrew education. They were regarded as the revelation of God's thoughts expressed in human language. While this book of revelation was held in highest esteem and reverence and studied with great diligence, yet the book of creation was also sacredly regarded and faithfully studied. The book of revelation was what God had *said*. The book of creation was what God had *made*. One was the *word* of God; the other the *works* of God. And further, the works of God came into existence as the direct result of the power of the word of God.

Since God is the author of both creation and revelation, there will be no contradiction between them. Their testimony will agree, and each will shed light upon the other. Today these two books are usually spoken of as the Bible and Science, and naturally we should expect perfect agreement in the testimony of the theologian and the scientist.

A study of the first chapter of the Bible (Gen. 1) makes plain the relation of the word of God to the works of God. In this chapter occur several times the two expressions " God said," and " God made." In addition to these the expression " it was so," and " it was good " are repeated several times, emphatically affirming that the commands of the Creator were fully and effectively carried out, as declared by the psalmist David:

" By the word of the Lord were the heavens made, and all the host of them by the breath of his mouth. . . . For he spake and it was done; he commanded and it stood fast " (Ps. 33: 6-9).

The " it was so " and the " it was good," and finally " it was very good " may have been included in the record of creation to be a constant rebuke to the skeptic and doubter. The apostle Paul emphasizes the proper attitude of the theologian and scientist: " Yea, let God be true and every man a liar," who disagrees with what God has said (Rom. 3: 4).

We have in the first two chapters of the Bible the record of the creation of the heavens and the earth. Without this revelation from the Creator, man would have no sure foundation upon which to build a system of natural science. In the study of the natural sciences the student is dealing with what God has made, and there is open to him a revelation of His knowledge, wisdom, love, and power. After our first parents partook of the fruit of the tree of knowledge of good and evil, they were not able, in their study of the book of creation, to clearly discern between truth and error. For this reason God wrote His second book—the book of revelation.

When the patriarch Job questioned the wisdom and knowledge of God in His dealings with him, his own knowledge and wisdom were challenged: "Where wast thou when I laid the foundations of the earth? Declare if thou hast understanding. Who hath laid the measures thereof, if thou knowest? or who hath stretched the line upon it? Whereupon are the foundations thereof fastened? or who laid the corner stone thereof; when the morning stars sang together, and all the sons of God shouted for joy?" (Job 38: 4–7). To God's challenge Job humbly replied: "Behold I am vile, what shall I answer thee? I will lay mine hand upon my mouth. Once have I spoken, but I will not answer; yea, twice; but I will proceed no further" (Job 40: 4, 5). After a few more searching questions, Job acknowleged his ignorance and repented of his unbecoming attitude toward his Creator: "I uttered that I understood not; things too wonderful for me which I knew not. . . . Wherefore I abhor myself and repent in dust and ashes" (Job 42: 2–6).

The student of God's works as well as of God's word must be humble and teachable. He must recognize that in the study of science he is becoming acquainted with the thoughts of God. The eminent scientist Agassiz long ago said: "Scientific systems are in truth but translations into human language of the thoughts of the Creator."

With this agrees the celebrated astronomer Kepler, who on discovering laws regulating planetary motions, exclaimed: "O God, I think thy thoughts after thee."

A modern writer, in defining science, gives expression to the same idea: "All true science is but an interpretation of the handwriting of God in the material world."

Vital Questions Answered

The knowledge gained regarding the works of creation is termed "science." The student and teacher of science may find in the first chapter of Genesis, and elsewhere in the Bible, answers to some important questions regarding the Creator and His creation—answers which cannot be found elsewhere in the writings of scientists and philosophers. Among these are the following questions:

1. Who created the world and the universe?
Answer. "God" (Gen. 1: 1).
2. When were they created?
Ans. "In the beginning" (Ibid.).
3. How were they created?
Ans. "By the word of God" (Ps. 33: 6–9).
4. How long a period of time was employed in creating this world?
Ans. "Six days" (Ex. 20: 11).

5. What forms of matter, energy, and life were brought into existence during the creation week?

Ans. Light, heat, air, water, land, plants, animals, and man (Gen. 1; Ex. 20: 8–11).

6. Whom did God associate with Himself in the work of creation?

Ans. Christ, His Son (Gen. 1: 26; Heb. 1: 3).

7. What was God's purpose in creating the earth?

Ans. That it might be inhabited by intelligent beings in whom He would find pleasure (Isa. 45: 18; Rev. 4: 11).

Correct answers to these questions are essential to an intelligent study of the works of creation; for they help one to understand better the relation of God to His creation. Without this primal Bible foundation the truths of science are often distorted and misinterpreted, and may be used to curse and destroy mankind, instead of being a blessing, as the Creator intended.

Some Students of Nature

Some of the greatest Bible characters lived a shepherd life during their early years and were close students of nature. Among these may be mentioned Joseph, David and Moses. Moses was not fitted to be the mighty leader of his people out of slavery from Egypt, until he had served as shepherd in the valley and among the mountains of the land of Midian. John the Baptist was in the deserts until the day of his showing unto Israel (Luke 1: 80; Matt. 3: 1, 2). This study of the word of God and the works of God made these men mighty leaders and teachers of God's chosen people.

The psalms written by David reveal how his spirit was atune to the things of nature, and the inspiration and uplift that came to his soul as he diligently studied and pondered the wonderful truths revealed in God's book of creation: " I meditate on all thy works; I muse on the work of thy hands. I stretch forth my hands unto thee; my soul thirsteth after thee, as a thirsty land " (Ps. 143: 5, 6).

To find and to know God through the study of His works was far more to David than a mere knowledge of and acquaintance with the wonderful things in nature. As he saw God working mightily without, this gave him assurance that He would work mightily within. This gladdened his heart, and he gave utterance to his triumphant experience: " Thou, Lord, hast made me glad through thy work: I will triumph in the works of thy hands " (Ps. 92: 4).

David's study of science did not lead him into infidelity and skepticism, but into communion and fellowship with God. He testified that "the Lord is righteous in all his ways and holy in all his works " (Ps. 145: 17), and that the wicked shall be destroyed " because they regard not the works of the Lord, nor the operations of his hands " (Ps. 28: 5).

Solomon, like David his father, had a keen interest in the study of natural science. Of his devotion to this study he says: " And I gave my heart to seek and search out by wisdom concerning all things that are done under heaven " (Eccl. 1: 13).

In addition to being a great musician and writer, Solomon was a noted science lecturer: " He spake of (lectured on) trees from the cedar tree that is in Lebanon even unto the hyssop that springeth out of the wall; he spake also of beasts, and of fowl and of creeping things and of fishes " (I Kings 4: 33).

Summing up his knowledge of science in present-day terminology it embraced the following subjects:

1. Plant Life—Botany.
2. Animal Life:
   (1) " Beasts "—Zoology.
   (2) " Fowl "—Ornithology.
   (3) " Creeping Things "—(insects)—Entomology.
   (4) " Fishes "—Ichthyology.

Concerning the influence of this noted biologist the Scriptures declare: " There came of all people to hear the wisdom of Solomon from all the kings of the earth, which had heard his wisdom " (Verse 34).

Of Daniel and his three companions, who, until they were about eighteen years of age, were educated in the schools of Israel, it is said that they passed the entrance requirements into the University of Babylon with the following recorded standing: " Children in whom was no blemish, but well favored, and skilful in all wisdom, cunning in knowledge and understanding science and such as had ability in them to stand in the king's palace " (Dan. 1: 4).

Christ and Science

As already noted (pages 104, 105) Christ was a diligent student of nature and had a broad knowledge of the science of creation, but He did not seek to impart it, as His mission was to impart a knowledge of the science of salvation. Speaking of His purpose in coming to our world, He said: " The thief cometh not, but for to steal and to kill and to destroy; I am come that they might have life, and that they might have it more abundantly " (John 10: 10). " The Son of Man is come to seek and to save that which was lost " (Luke 19: 10).

From a study of Christ's parables, a modern educator has concluded that His knowledge of science was far in advance of His time, but that He made use of it only to make clear the principles of the kingdom of heaven:

" Christ might have opened to men the deepest truths of science. He might have unlocked mysteries that have required centuries of toil and study to penetrate. He might have made suggestions in scientific lines that would have afforded food for thought and stimulus for invention to the close of time. But He did not do this. He said nothing to gratify curiosity, or to satisfy men's ambitions by opening doors to worldly greatness. In all His teaching, Christ brought the minds of men in contact with the Infinite Mind. He did not direct the people to study men's

theories about God, His Word or His works. He taught them to behold
God as manifested in His works, in His Word, and by His providences.'' [1]

Christ's hearers were to behold Him and their heavenly Father at
work in the rising sun and the falling rain: "He maketh his sun to
rise on the evil and the good, and sendeth his rain on the just and on
the unjust" (Matt. 5: 45). These were day by day a manifestation
of His love and mercy.

God's care for the birds was to be a constant reminder of His care
for His children: "Behold the fowls of the air; for they sow not,
neither do they reap, nor gather into barns; yet your heavenly
Father feedeth them. Are ye not much better than they?" (Matt.
6: 26). God feeds the birds; and He will not neglect to feed His
children. He will not only feed, but He will also clothe them: "And
why take ye thought for raiment? Consider the lilies of the field,
how they grow; they toil not, neither do they spin; and yet I say
unto you, that Solomon in all his glory was not arrayed like one of
these. Wherefore, if God so clothe the grass of the field, which today
is, and tomorrow is cast into the oven, shall he not much more clothe
you, O ye of little faith?" (Matt. 6: 28–30).

Human life was to be radiant as the light and as preserving as the
salt: "Ye are the light of the world," and, "Ye are the salt of the
earth" (Matt. 5: 13, 14).

Christ had knowledge of both the animate and the inanimate world.
Life and energy in all its diversified manifestations, material things
possessed with varied qualities and properties, were all used to reveal
truth. He had created all these things, and He used them to illustrate
and magnify the principles of the kingdom. This method of teaching
by object lessons is well stated by a modern educator:

"So wide was Christ's view of truth, so extended His teaching that
every phase of nature was employed in illustrating truth. The scenes
upon which the eye daily rests were all connected with some spiritual truth,
so that nature is clothed with the parables of the Master." [2]

"The words of Christ placed the teachings of nature in a new aspect,
and made them a new revelation. He could speak of the things which
His own hands had made; for they had qualities and properties that were
peculiarly His own. In nature, as in the sacred pages of the Old Testament Scriptures, divine momentous truths are revealed, and in His teaching Jesus laid these open before the people bound up with the beauty
of natural things." [3]

"A greater than Solomon is here" (Matt. 12: 42). Both Solomon
and Christ followed the Hebrew method in the study and teaching
of nature and science. That method now, as well as in ages past, will
result in wide knowledge and strong character. Today the knowledge
side is being stressed and the character side is being neglected, so

---

[1] White, *Principles of True Science,* p. 560 (Washington College Press).
[2] White, *Christ's Object Lessons,* p. 20.
[3] White, *Counsels to Teachers,* pp. 178, 179.

that what should prove a blessing is proving to be a curse. Modern inventions and facilities, instead of being used entirely to bless and uplift the bodies, minds, and souls of men, are being largely used to degrade and destroy body, mind and soul. A return to the Hebrew aims and methods of science study and teaching is much needed today.

Paul and Science

Christ revealed Himself to Saul (afterward called Paul) while on his way to Damascus to persecute the Christians. He immediately preached Christ and fled into the deserts of Arabia to escape death. There in the desert school he remained three years a student of the word and works of God (Gal. 1: 15–18). This apostle of " much learning," after getting a vision of Him in whom are hid all the treasures of wisdom and knowledge, gave the following admonition and exhortation:

" Beware lest any man spoil you through philosophy and vain deceit, after the tradition of men, after the rudiments of this world, and not after Christ " (Col. 2: 8). " O Timothy, keep that which is committed to thy trust, avoiding profane and vain babblings, and opposition of science falsely so called; which some professing have erred concerning the faith " (I Tim. 6: 20, 21).

The apostle Paul warns against any philosophy, or any science that has no Christ in it; " in whom are hid all the treasures of wisdom and knowledge, . . . and ye are complete in him " (Col. 2: 3, 10). He even enters into the highest seats of science and philosophy at Athens, and meets human science with divine philosophy, declaring that Jehovah is the unknown God whom His hearers have ignorantly worshiped. Then in words quoted from a poet of their own, he pictures Him as a father whose children they are: " For we also are his offspring " (Acts 17: 28).

What were the results of Paul's attack against Greek science and philosophy in Athens, their chief seat of learning? " Some mocked, and others said, We will hear thee again of this matter. So Paul departed from among them. Howbeit certain men clave unto him and believed, among the which was Dionysius the Areopagite, and a woman named Damaris, and others with them " (Acts 17: 32-34).

Paul, probably reflecting on his experience at Athens, wrote the following:

" For the Jews require a sign, and the Greeks seek after wisdom: but we preach Christ crucified, unto the Jews a stumbling block, and unto the Greeks foolishness; but unto them which are called, both Jews and Greeks, Christ the power of God, and the wisdom of God. Because the foolishness of God is wiser than men; and the weakness of God is stronger than men. For ye see your calling, brethren, how that not many wise men after the flesh, not many mighty, not many noble, are called: but God hath chosen the foolish things of the world to confound the wise; and God hath chosen the weak things of the world to confound the things which are mighty; and base things of the world, and things which are despised, hath God chosen, yea, and things which are not, to bring to nought things that are: that no flesh shall glory in his presence '' (I Cor. 1: 22–29).

Even Christ, the Master Teacher, was not able to reach many of the learned among His own people. Nicodemus and Joseph of Arimathea were two of the few that believed on Him and who ministered to Him in His last hours, providing a place of burial.

Fortified Against False Science

While the Bible is not a book devoted to science, yet it is the only true basis and foundation of science study. Not only does it furnish the only true answers to the questions previously raised and answered, but it also provides the only safe and positive protection and safeguard against the many false theories which are strongly advocated in the science instruction given in many of the schools of learning. Some of these false theories are: The theory of evolution. The nebular theory. The eternity of matter. The inherent energy in matter. The spontaneous generation of life. The mechanistic philosophy of life.

Evolution Theory. Contrary to the theory of evolution, the Bible teaches that man was brought into being by a separate, distinct, creative act, instead of being the result of a long, serial development of animal life, requiring ages to develop from the minutest and simplest form of protoplasmic being.

'' And God said, Let us make man in our image, after our likeness '' (Gen. 1: 26). '' And the Lord God formed man of the dust of the ground, and breathed into his nostrils the breath of life, and man became a living soul '' (Gen. 2: 7). '' Which was the son of Enos, which was the son of Seth, which was the son of Adam, which was the son of God '' (Luke 3: 38).

A modern educator speaks plainly against the low pedigree evolution assigns to man, and exalts his heavenly ancestry:

'' Shall we, for the privilege of tracing our descent from germs and mollusks and apes, consent to cast away that statement of Holy Writ, so grand in its simplicity, ' God created man in His own image, in the image of God created He him '? Shall we reject that genealogical record—prouder than any treasured in the courts of kings—' which was the son of Adam, which was the son of God '? ''[4]

Nebular Theory. The earth and myriads of worlds in space are not the result of cooling fiery mists and vapors, but they stood forth in all their majesty and glory at the command of Jehovah, their Creator and Upholder (Ps. 33: 6–9).

Even though finite man cannot understand how matter was created, yet "through faith we understand that the worlds were framed by the word of God, so that things which are seen were not made of things which do appear" (Heb. 11: 3).

[4] White, *Education,* p. 130.

Matter and Energy. The theory that nature is self-acting and self-directing, that it possesses an inherent energy and power which act independent of the Creator is not sustained by the Scriptures. Some regard nature as God, and that all the operations of nature are self-originated and self-controlled. Many definitions of scientific terms are couched in language that conveys that idea. For example: " Physics is that branch of science which treats of matter and motion and the laws which govern them." " Gravity is that force attracting two bodies directly according to the product of their masses and indirectly according to the square of their mean distance."

The law does govern, but the Creator governs according to the law He has made for each particular thing. The force does not attract of itself, but the Creator employs or delegates power or force, which acts according to His will or law, in the fulfilling of His purpose. As a celebrated scientist said of gravity: " It is the delegated power of the Almighty acting according to His will." If the student would think that back of the law, back of the force is God, the Creator and Upholder of all, governing all things according to the pleasure and purpose of His will, then the Scriptural accusation would not apply: " God is not in all his thoughts " (Ps. 10: 4).

The impersonal idea in our common speech is expressed so frequently regarding the familiar phenomena of nature about us. For example: " It snows." " It rains." In the Holy Scriptures the personal idea is always expressed:

" He giveth snow like wool; he scattereth the hoar frost like ashes " (Ps. 147: 16). " He maketh his sun to rise on the evil and on the good, and sendeth rain on the just and on the unjust " (Matt. 5: 45). " He giveth to the beast his food and to the young ravens which cry " (Ps. 147: 9). " Behold the fowls of the air. . . . Your heavenly Father feedeth them " (Matt. 6: 26).

This consciousness of the continual presence of the Creator, upholding and sustaining all things by His power, wisdom, and love, is the greatest reward and satisfaction that comes to the student of science. Sir Isaac Newton, probably the most celebrated of all scientists, was a diligent student not only of the works of God, but also the word of God. He wrote books on both—the *Principia,* containing the results of his scientific investigations, and books on the prophecies of Daniel and the Revelation, the results of his study of prophetic portions of the Scriptures. His consciousness of the divine presence of God in his works, and the realization of this presence to aid him in his study are expressed in his own words:

" I can take my telescope, and look millions of millions of miles into space; but I can lay it aside and go into my room, shut the door, get on my knees in earnest prayer, and see more of heaven, and get closer to God than I can assisted by all the telescopes and material agencies of earth."

Pasteur, like Newton, found prayer a valuable aid as he worked in his laboratory. He said: "Posterity will one day laugh at the foolishness of the modern materialistic philosophy. The more I study nature the more I stand amazed at the works of the Creator. I pray while I am engaged in my work at the laboratory."

Life. The theory of spontaneous generation has been disproved by Pasteur and other scientists. Recently, however, the theory has been revived, and claims are made that it is possible for the skilled scientist to produce life. This is contrary to the plain teaching of Scripture. This is the prerogative of God alone, and this power He gave to His Son:

" With thee is the fountain of life " (Ps. 36: 9). " Who knoweth not in all these that the hand of the Lord hath wrought this? In whose hand is the life of every living thing, and the breath of all mankind " (Job 12: 9, 10, margin). " For as the Father hath life in himself; so hath he given to the Son to have life in himself " (John 5: 26).

Freedom of Man. The mechanistic philosophy had no place in Hebrew philosophy or science. The divine right of freedom of choice is repeatedly stated throughout both Testaments of Scripture. While the divine counsel urges man to choose the good, and reject the evil— to walk in the way of life instead of the way that leads to death—yet there is no compulsion, no forcing of the will.

After the parents of the human family had partaken of the fruit of the tree of knowledge of good and evil, the Creator gave them an encouraging promise. Speaking to Satan He said: "I will put enmity between thee and the woman, and between thy seed and her seed" (Gen. 3: 15). This implanted enmity did not destroy the power of choice; for Cain chose to do evil, while Abel chose to do good.

Moses and Joshua, two of the greatest leaders of Israel, recognized man's power of choice:

" I have set before you life and death, blessing and cursing; therefore choose life, that both thou and thy seed may live " (Deut. 30: 19). " If it seem evil unto you to serve the Lord, choose you this day whom you will serve " (Josh. 24: 15).

The prophets, Elijah and Isaiah, urged the people to make a choice between life and death:

" And Elijah came unto all the people and said, ' How long halt you between two opinions? If the Lord be God follow him; but if Baal, then follow him " (I Kings 18: 21). " If ye be willing and obedient, ye shall eat of the good of the land; but if ye refuse and rebel, ye shall be devoured by the sword; for the mouth of the Lord hath spoken it " (Isa. 1: 19, 20).

Christ and the apostles called upon their hearers to choose life, and forsake the ways that lead unto death:

" Jesus stood and cried, saying: ' If any man thirst let him come unto me and drink ' " (John 7: 37). " Strive to enter in at the straight gate " (Luke 13: 24). " Whosoever will, let him partake of the water of life freely " (Rev. 22: 17).

The only constraining power that the apostle Paul mentions, is that of love: "The love of Christ constraineth us" (II Cor. 5: 14).

The mechanistic theory which regards man as a mere machine with no power of choice; and concludes that all his behavior is wholly the result of molecular reactions determined by physical laws, is strongly opposed by some philosophers and scientists. Doctor Arthur Compton, in his recent work on *The Freedom of Man*, declares that the laboratory of the physicist does not support the mechanistic theory. He writes:

" Chapter II gives in some detail my reasons for believing that this simplified behavior fails as a complete description of our actions. In some reflex actions and habitual acts we may behave as automata; but where deliberation occurs we feel that we choose our own course. In fact a certain freedom of choice may, it seems to me, be considered as an experimental fact with which we must reconcile our theories. Because the mechanist's basic hypothesis leaves no room for such freedom, I see no alternative other than to reject the hypothesis as inadequate.

" On the other hand, if freedom of choice is admitted, it follows by the same line of reasoning that one's thoughts are not wholly the result of molecular reactions determined by physical laws. For if they were, one's thoughts would be fixed by physical conditions, and his choice would be made for him." [5]

The mechanistic philosophy of life is a fascinating theory to many, because it eliminates all sense of human responsibility. Those accepting it excuse questionable conduct by arguing that man is a mere machine and its maker is responsible for the way it functions. Moral restraints are tabooed, conscience is seared, and iniquity abounds.

The prophet Isaiah graphically describes the results which follow in the wake of the mechanistic philosophy of life: "And behold joy and gladness, slaying oxen, and killing of sheep, eating flesh, and drinking wine; let us eat and drink for tomorrow we die" (Isa. 22: 13).

Doctor Walter Albion Squires in his book, *The Pedagogy of Jesus in the Twilight of Today*, gives an enlightening analysis of the mechanistic philosophy and the fruitage it bears:

" On applying this principle we discover that mechanistic interpretation eliminates all thought of human responsibility. If conduct is mechanically determined, human responsibility is a myth. All our conceptions of it are meaningless ' epiphenomena ' which rise like a mist over a stream of events flowing ever onward under the relentless stress of mechanical law. If this interpretation of life and conduct is true no human being is ever blameworthy. The explanation wipes out all moral distinction between the life nobly lived and the life spent in debauchery and crime; both are inevitable and fatalistic events in the cosmic process." [6]

[5] A. Compton, *The Freedom of Man*, p. 129 (Yale University Press).
[6] W. A. Squires, *The Pedagogy of Jesus in the Twilight of Today*, pp. 175, 176 (Harper & Brothers).

Doctor L. P. Jacks in his recent book, *The Revolt Against Mechanism*, indicates that true faith and religion are divine creative forces rising against the tyrannies of mechanism in philosophy, science, and other systems of knowledge—religious or secular. Concerning the outlook for the triumph of faith and religion he says:

" If I am right in these interpretations the reason should be clear why the interests of religion are on the side of the creative forces now rising in revolt against the tyrannies of mechanism. Religion has everything to hope from their success and everything to fear from their failure. On the whole I think the omens are favorable, though a long way will have to be traveled, and many hard battles fought before victory is achieved." [7]

Those who take the Bible as their guide in the study of nature and science will not be deceived by the false theories of agnostics and skeptics. Beside the Scriptures of truth they have the guidance of the Holy Spirit of truth. Christ assured His followers that after His ascension He would send them this heavenly teacher: "I will pray the Father, and he shall give you another Comforter, . . . even the Spirit of truth" (John 14: 16, 17). "When he, the Spirit of truth, is come, he will guide you into all truth" (John 16: 13).

It is to be regretted that many students and teachers of nature and science do not recognize this heavenly provision, and place themselves under the guidance of this wonderful teacher of truth. Throughout the Scriptures He is spoken of as the Holy Spirit, the Holy Ghost, the Comforter, the Spirit of truth, and the Spirit of God. He is one of the heavenly Trinity consisting of the Father, the Son, and the Holy Ghost (Matt. 28: 19; I John 5: 7). The first mention of the Spirit of God is in the first chapter of the Bible in connection with the story of creation. The Spirit of God was an active agent in creation. "The Spirit of God moved upon the face of the waters" (Gen. 1: 2). Job, in speaking of the creative acts of God, says: "By his spirit he hath garnished the heavens" (Job 26: 13). In just what ways the Spirit of God co-operated in the work of creation, we do not know, but He was a powerful moving agency working with the Father and the Son.

When sin came into the world and marred God's beautiful creation, then it was necessary for another book—the book of revelation—to be written, that sinful man might understand why the earth's beauty was marred. The Spirit of God was the moving agency that God employed in the writing of this book—the holy Scriptures, the Bible. "Holy men of God spake as they were moved by the Holy Ghost" (I Peter 1: 21). The Spirit of God then had an active part in the writing of God's two books. This active agency in writing the books of creation and revelation, the Holy Spirit, has full deep knowledge of creation and revelation and is a safe guide to man in his study of both books. David, while studying the marvels of creation, cried out:

[7] L. P. Jacks, *The Revolt Against Mechanism*, p. 74 (Macmillan Co.).

"O Lord, how great are thy works, and thy thoughts are very deep" (Ps. 92: 5). The apostle Paul in the study of the book of revelation exclaimed, "O the depth of the riches both of the wisdom and knowledge of God! How unsearchable (by man) are his judgments, and his way past finding out" (Rom. 11: 33). But Paul tells how the depths of wisdom and knowledge of God both in creation and revelation can be fathomed and searched out. "God hath revealed them unto us by his Spirit; for the Spirit searcheth all things, yea, the deep things of God." The Spirit of God not only aids us in study and research, but it also aids us in praying to God, so that we shall know what to ask for, and rightly appreciate and use what is given. "Likewise the Spirit also helpeth our infirmities; for we know not what we should pray for as we ought, but the Spirit itself maketh intercession for us with groanings which cannot be uttered" (Rom. 8: 26).

How befitting that Newton should lay aside his telescope and go into his room and pray that he might have a deeper and clearer understanding than what could be revealed by the telescope alone. How becoming that Pasteur should pray as he worked in the laboratory for the presence and aid of the Spirit of truth who guides the earnest seeker after truth: "The Spirit searcheth all things; yea the deep things of God" (I Cor. 2: 10).

Prayer and the aid of the Holy Spirit are divine agencies essential to the discovery of truth both in creation and revelation. The scientist as well as the theologian is to study both books and they are to be true yoke fellows working together to find and to make known truth. There will be unity and harmony in their efforts, since the two books are in perfect agreement and shed light on each other. Creation has been marred and scarred by the curse of sin, and does not therefore reveal as clearly the thoughts of God as does the book of revelation.

Defenders of True Science

There is much controversy between scientists and theologians. It is unfortunate that the children and youth of this generation are exposed to this conflict between science and religion in the schools and in the Church. By some of these controversialists the Bible is belittled and science extolled. Others take the opposite view, exalting the Bible and belittling science. Both of the positions are wrong and both are leading a multitude of sincere unsuspecting youth into the fog-banks and quagmires of infidelity and skepticism.

It is only when the book of creation and the book of revelation are studied together and each recognized as an expression of the thoughts of the Creator and Upholder of all things, that our children and youth will develop into men and women having faith in God and in one another.

It is heartening as we scan the records of science-history to find the names of men who like Newton have studied both of God's books and found them mutually helpful in assisting them to climb the rugged heights up to the mountain peaks of knowledge. During the ascents of these giddy heights, faith and confidence in God have not only been maintained, but increased as revealed in lives of humble fruitful service in behalf of their fellows.

We shall give the testimonies of a few scientists, in their own words, as to the spirit and motive that actuated them in their arduous study and research.

Sir Isaac Newton in a letter to his friend, Doctor Bentley, wrote:

" When I wrote my treatise about our (solar) system, I had an eye upon such principles as might work with considering men for the belief of a Deity; and nothing can rejoice me more than to find it useful for that purpose. But if I have done the public any service this way, it is due to nothing but industry and patient thought."

Newton discovered the law of universal gravitation, and in another letter to Doctor Bentley he says that it takes gravity and God to operate the planets of the solar system in their rotations and revolutions about their center—the sun. He wrote:

" In my former letter, I represented that the diurnal rotations of the planets could not be derived from gravity, but required a Divine arm to impress them. And though gravity might give the planets a motion of descent toward the sun, either directly or with some little obliquity, yet the transverse motions by which they revolve in their several orbs required the Divine arm to impress them according to the tangents of their orbs." [8]

In this same letter Newton says that the law of universal gravitation refutes the hypothesis that matter at first was evenly distributed through space as now advocated by those who propose the " nebular theory." He wrote:

" I would now add, that the hypothesis of matter being at first evenly spread through the heavens is, in my opinion, inconsistent with the hypothesis of innate gravity, without a supernatural power to reconcile them; and therefore it infers a Deity. For if there be innate gravity, it is impossible now for the matter of the earth and all the planets and stars to fly up from them and become evenly spread throughout all the heavens, without a supernatural power; and that which can never be hereafter without a supernatural power, could never be heretofore without the same power." [9]

The scientific spirit and method of the celebrated astronomer Kepler who discovered the three planetary laws are indicated by the following words from his own pen:

" I beseech my reader that, not unmindful of the divine goodness bestowed upon man, he do with me praise and celebrate the wisdom and greatness of the Creator, which I open to him from a more inward explication of the form of the world, from a searching of causes, from a detection

[8] *Isaac Newton Opera*, Vol. IV, pp. 229, 441; translated by Samuel Horsley.
[9] *Ibid.*, p. 441.

of errors of vision; and that thus, not only in the firmness and stability of the earth, he perceive with gratitude the preservation of all living things in nature, as the gift of God, but also that in its motion, so recondite, so admirable, he acknowledge the wisdom of the Creator." [10]

Copernicus, who advocated the astronomical system bearing his name, and which in the main features is now the basis of astronomical calculations regarding the solar system, speaks of its admirable structure and arrangement as follows:

" Who in this fair temple would place this lamp in any other or better place than there whence it may illuminate the whole. We find then under this ordination an admirable symmetry of the world, and a certain harmonious connection of the motions and magnitude of the orbs, such as in any other way cannot be found. Thus the progressions and regressions of the planets all arise from the same cause, the motion of the earth. And that no such movements are seen in the fixed stars argues their immense distance from us, which causes the apparent magnitude of the earth's annual course to become evanescent. So great, in short, is this divine fabric of the great and good God."

Speaking of the philosopher, he says:

" I know that the thoughts of a philosopher are far removed from the judgment of the vulgar (common people); since it is his study to search out truth in all things as far as it is permitted by God to human reason."

Coming closer to our day we find eminent scientists who have fearlessly expressed their faith in a Divine, Supreme Being who was the designer and creator of all things. We give the testimonies of the following:

Pascal, who made remarkable discoveries in the study of fluids and hydrostatics, said that it was difficult " to convince obstinate atheists " of the existence of a Divine Creator of all things, from nature alone, and therefore he did not attempt it. These are his words:

" I do not undertake to prove this, not only because I do not feel myself sufficiently strong to find in nature that which shall convince obstinate atheists, but because such knowledge without Jesus Christ is useless and sterile." " Nature has perfections in order to show that she is in the image of God, and defects in order to show that she is only His image." [11]

The " sterility " of a knowledge of nature " without Jesus Christ," and also the cause of the " defects " and antagonistic forces in nature are more fully and truly expressed by a modern educator:

" Even a child, as he comes in contact with nature, will see cause for perplexity. He can but recognize the working of antagonistic forces. It is here that nature needs an interpreter. Looking upon the evil manifest even in the natural world, all have the same sorrowful lesson to learn,— ' An enemy hath done this.'

" Only in the light that shines from Calvary can nature's teaching be read aright. Through the story of Bethlehem and the cross let it be

[10] *Bridgewater Treatises,* Wm. Whewell, Treatise III, p. 314.
[11] *Ibid.,* p. 313, 317, 318.

shown how good is to conquer evil, and how every blessing that comes to us is a gift of redemption."[12]

Boyle, who made great discoveries in the field of mechanics, wrote several tracts on nature and science; among them were *Inquiry into the Final Causes of Natural Things; Free Inquiry into the Vulgar (Common) Notions of Nature;* and *The High Veneration Man's Intellect Owes to God.*

We give one or two extracts from his writings:

" In almost all ages and countries the generality of philosophers and contemplative men were persuaded of the existence of a Deity from the consideration of the phenomena of the universe; whose fabric and conduct they rationally concluded could not justly be ascribed either to chance or to any other cause than a Divine Being.

" Though I am willing to grant that some impressions of God's wisdom are so conspicuous that even a superficial philosopher may thence infer that the Author of such works must be a wise agent, yet how wise an agent He has in these works expressed Himself to be, none but the experimental philosopher can well discern. And 'tis not by a slight survey, but by a diligent and skilful scrutiny of the works of God, that a man must be, by a rational and affective conviction, engaged to acknowledge that the Author of nature is ' wonderful in counsel and excellent in working ' " (Isa. 28: 29).[13]

If space permitted we could give similar testimonies from Faraday, Black, Dalton, and other eminent scientists who have recognized the Creator in their study of His works. It is to be regretted that a few who have believed in the God of creation and revelation, and who have made wonderful discoveries of truths which have enlightened mankind, have, in the hour of test for their faith and belief, proven untrue either by recanting or modifying their views to avoid persecution. This was true of the scientist Galileo, and of Erasmus the theologian.

Boyle's statement: " In almost all ages and countries . . . philosophers are persuaded of the existence of a Deity from the consideration of phenomena of the universe," does not hold true in our day. It is indeed regrettable that just the reverse situation exists. Newton in his study of creation said that God was a " necessity." A few eminent scientists of today make the same positive declaration, but there are others, equally, if not more eminent, who just as positively declare that they find in their study no necessity of a God. The influence of their writings and teachings in colleges and universities is making agnosticism and infidelity popular with the youth of our country. Now even whole nations are accepting infidelity as their religion.

While the Hebrew nation does not exist, and as a people they are scattered among the nations of earth, still they firmly and persistently

[12] White, *Education,* p. 101.
[13] *Bridgewater Treatises,* Wm. Whewell, Treatise III, p. 319.

hold to the faith of their fathers: "In the beginning God created the heaven and the earth."

Science Methods and Literature

In this chapter we shall not deal with methods of nature and science study and teaching, nor with literature to be used therewith, except as it may be helpful in developing more fully the spiritual phase which is so generally neglected. Science and nature textbooks, reference books, and laboratory facilities have been greatly multiplied and increased so that these may be provided without difficulty; except for the limitations of necessary funds with which to procure them.

Nature or Science study with Hebrew teachers and students was carried on mainly in the great out-of-doors laboratory. This afforded the opportunity to observe and study not only the works, but also the workings of the Creator without the encumbrance of artificial conditions and surroundings. In the very presence of God at work in His great laboratory, the soul of the student was awed and his spirit invigorated as the marvelous mysteries of creation were opened to his inquiring mind. No germs of infidelity and skepticism tainted this heavenly atmosphere; but like David the shepherd on the hills of Syria, the heart cried out: "Many, O Lord my God, are thy wondrous works which thou hast done, and thy thoughts which are to us-ward" (Ps. 40: 5). This is the spirit that breathes in the Forest Hymn written by Bryant and in the writings of others who lived close to nature and nature's God.

The Scriptures repeatedly emphasize out-of-door study:

"Go to the ant, thou sluggard; consider her ways, and be wise" (Prov. 6: 6). "Lift up your eyes on high and behold (Him) who hath created these things, that bringeth out their host by number" (Isa. 40: 26). "Consider the lilies of the field, how they grow" (Matt. 6: 28). "Consider the ravens" (Luke 12: 24). "Behold the fowls of the air" (Matt. 6: 26).

The study of nature and the study of science is the study of the creation of God. The study of the simplest things in a simple way, by children, is called "nature study." The study of the same things, and others more complex, in a deeper and more orderly and systematic manner, by the youth, is called the study of "science."

We make the following suggestion regarding the study of nature, and the study of science:

Nature Study.

1. Nature study with the children should be largely out of doors, where the things studied will be observed in their natural surroundings. The following are a few of the out-of-door studies that require close, keen observations, which should be carefully and neatly recorded:
   (1) The Birds Where I Live.
   (2) The Birds that Stay the Year Through.

(3) The Birds that Come and Go.

(4) Bird Nests and Food.

(5) The Farmer's Bird Friends and Enemies.

(6) How Insects Live and Multiply.

(7) The Farmer's Insect Friends and Enemies.

(8) My Flower Neighbors.

(9) My Tree Neighbors.

(10) How Trees and Flowers Grow and Seed.

(11) The Weather from Day to Day During the Four Seasons.

(12) How the Weather Affects Plants and Animals.

2. Textbooks on nature may serve as a help but they may be a hindrance. The book of nature is to be studied far more than any books on nature.

3. The Bible is the most important book to be used in the study of nature. Without it the book of nature cannot be understood, and many false ideas will be taught; such as evolution, and the nebular theory of matter.

4. Other books used in Nature Study should be carefully examined to see that they are free from all false theories of creation.

5. The teacher of Nature Study to be a success must be a lover of nature; for all children love it.

Science Study.

1. The science student should continue the out-of-door nature study plan, delving deeper into the topics mentioned above, and adding others such as the following:

(1) Observing and Mapping the Heavens During the Seasons.

(2) Observing the Movement of Planets and their Moons.

(3) Invisible Animal Life.

(4) Mimicry in Nature and Its Value.

(5) Invisible Plant Life.

(6) Parasitic Life in Plants.

(7) Parasitic Life in Animals.

(8) Flowerless Plants.

(9) Rocks and Erosion.

(10) Soil and its Fertilization.

(11) Plant Fertilization.

(12) Feeding and Care of Farm Animals.

The above topics require out-of-door study and observation, and the keeping of careful records. It will be necessary to supplement the out-of-door laboratory study and experiment. Gather materials and preserve some of them in cans, jars, bottles, or other suitable containers. But as far as possible the student should have observed these specimens for laboratory study in their natural surroundings, and had an active part in their collection before taking up their study in the science laboratory.

One student in a biological laboratory was studying fresh water hydra poured from a bottle, and another was studying the fresh water sponge taken from a jar. Both were asked the habitat of these two specimens being studied under the microscope, and both declared their utter ignorance, even supposing they might have no other home except the jar and bottle. Such ignorance is inexcusable. If they had been salt water specimens, partial ignorance as to habitat might have been justified, as they might have had no opportunity for personal observation; but even then they should have known that they were not fresh water animalculæ.

2. The Bible should be the student's greatest handbook in the study of science. It is God's revelation written after the book of creation, and sheds great light upon it, explaining the contradictions and antagonisms that are manifest on every hand. The Bible is the only book that gives the cause for this confusion, and enables the student to discover truth and steer clear of the "science falsely so called," the tendency and influence of which leads man to disown and deny his Creator.

3. All other books should be carefully selected, and only those chosen for study that are in harmony with the science revealed in the Word of God.

4. In the study of the different sciences, and the various topics in each science, the student should first become acquainted with what God has written in His Word—the Bible—regarding them, and this knowledge will be a chart and compass to guide him in the way of truth, as he considers the theories contained in the fallible writings of men.

5. A historical study of the life work of Newton, Kepler, Copernicus, Boyle, Dalton, Faraday and other celebrated scientists who studied creation in the light of revelation will serve to encourage and stimulate students and teachers to study science today with their purpose and spirit—to reveal and magnify the Creator and Upholder of all things.

6. The following books are recommended as helpful to teachers and students in the development of spiritual life and power in their study of the physical and biological sciences:

Bible Teaching in Nature; The Ministry of Nature; Two Worlds are Ours, by Hugh MacMillan. *Christ and Science,* by Smith. *Christ's Object Lessons,* by Ellen G. White. *The Bible and a Scientific Man,* by Doctor Howard Kelly. *Cyclopedia of Nature Teachings.*

XIII

PHYSICAL EDUCATION

Health and Work

E VER since man has earned his bread by the sweat of his face; contending against thorns and thistles, and battling against pests that would deprive him and his posterity of food; health and labor have had to reckon with each other. Health makes labor productive, and labor promotes health. " The sleep of the laboring man is sweet, whether he eat little or much " (Eccl. 5: 12). Their mutual reaction is helpful not only in physical and material results, but also in the development of mental and spiritual power.

" Abundance of idleness and fullness of bread " mingled with pride, as in Sodom (Ezek. 16: 49), unfits people for life; but abundance of labor and even a scarcity of food, with humility, result in the more abundant life.

It was on appetite that the parents of the human family were tested and failed; and their posterity down through the centuries have been tested on the same point, and with but few exceptions have failed. The Creator planted in the Garden of Eden " every tree that is pleasant to the sight and good for food " (Gen. 2: 9); and gave specific directions regarding man's diet: " And God said, Behold, I have given you every herb bearing seed, which is upon the face of all the earth, and every tree, in the which is the fruit of a tree yielding seed; to you it shall be for meat " (Gen. 1: 29). In other words, their diet was restricted to the vegetable kingdom. Adam and Eve's posterity have disregarded this instruction and are now freely eating from the animal kingdom. Just when this change in diet occurred, the Scriptures do not reveal; but from the words of Christ it seems probable that flesh food was introduced into man's diet by the antediluvians before the Flood: " In the days that were before the flood they were eating and drinking, marrying and giving in marriage until the day that Noe entered the ark " (Matt. 24: 38). Eating, drinking, and marrying were divine arrangements, but their perversion and abuse caused God to destroy all but one family by an overwhelming destructive flood. " And God saw that the wickedness of man was great in the earth and that every imagination of the thoughts of his heart was only evil continually. . . . The earth also was corrupt before God, and the earth was filled with violence. And God looked upon the earth, and, behold, it was corrupt, for all flesh had corrupted his way upon the earth " (Gen. 6: 5, 11, 12).

The sanctity of the marriage institution was corrupted and violated. Monogamy, God's plan of one wife, was first replaced by bigamy, and then by polygamy. The unbridled indulgence of appetite was followed by unrestrained control of passions culminating in Sodomy, for which "Sodom and Gomorrah and the cities about them in like manner giving themselves over to fornication, and going after strange flesh" were destroyed by fire and brimstone rained from heaven (Gen. 19: 24, 25; Jude 7).

The wickedness of man in the perversion of appetite and the unrestrained flow of passion have been punished by destructive flood and fire, but these evils exact fearful tolls from man during his life, by shortening its span, and by the infliction of pain and suffering resulting from the multitudinous forms of disease that stalk through the length and breadth of the earth.

Abraham, the father of the Hebrew nation, and through whom all nations of the earth have been blessed, witnessed the destruction of Sodom. Through his intercession the destroying angels rescued Lot and his family before the city was burned. Abraham and Lot knew of the great wickedness of the Sodomites, and of the diseases that afflicted the people. Of Lot the Scriptures declare: "That righteous man dwelling among them, in seeing and hearing, vexed his righteous soul from day to day with their unlawful deeds" (II Peter 2: 8). It would seem from Abraham and Lot's connection with the Sodomites, and other peoples among whom they sojourned, that they were respected and honored. Lot was a ruler in Sodom (Gen. 19: 1). Abraham was honored by Abimelech, king of Gerar, who desiring a covenant of peace said: "God is with thee in all thou doest; now therefore swear unto me here by God that thou wilt not deal falsely with me, nor my son, nor my son's son; but according to the kindness that I have done unto thee, thou shalt do unto me, and to the land wherein thou hast sojourned. And Abraham said, I will swear" (Gen. 21: 22–24).

Abraham was a blessing to the people wherever he sojourned, because he kept "the way of the Lord to do justice and judgment" (Gen. 18: 19).

In the course of time, Jacob, a grandson of Abraham, in a time of severe famine went down to Egypt and with him went eleven of his twelve sons and their families—in all seventy souls. Joseph, the twelfth son, was already in Egypt, a ruler, next to Pharaoh, and he arranged for his father and brothers and their families to sojourn there during the famine. Jacob met Pharaoh and pronounced a blessing upon him. For many years the posterity of Abraham, Isaac and Jacob prospered and multiplied under the rule of Joseph and Pharaoh. A nation was born under conditions of prosperity which on the death of Joseph and Pharaoh suffered great oppression and adversity:

" And the children of Israel were fruitful and increased abundantly and multiplied, and waxed exceeding mighty and the land was filled with them. Now there arose up a new king over Egypt who knew not Joseph. And he said unto his people, Behold, the people of the children of Israel are

more and mightier than we; come on, let us deal wisely with them; lest
they multiply and it come to pass, that when there falleth out any way,
they join also unto our enemies, and fight against us. . . . Therefore
they did set over them taskmasters to afflict them with their burdens.
And they built for Pharaoh treasure cities, Pithom and Raamses. But
the more they afflicted them, the more they multiplied and grew ''
(Ex. 1: 7–12).

The Egyptians for many years had observed the growth and development of Israel. Joseph from the time he was seventeen years
of age had grown to manhood in close connection with the royal
court. The first years of his exile were spent as a servant in the
household of Potiphar, captain of Pharaoh's guard. He served so
faithfully and efficiently that he was promoted and given complete
charge of his household, and the record says: " Joseph found grace
in his (Potiphar's) sight, and he served him; and he made him overseer in his house, and all that he had he put into his hand. . . . And
he left all that he had in Joseph's hand; and he knew not ought he
had save the bread which he did eat " (Gen. 39: 4–6). This testimony
certainly indicates industrial efficiency gained in the home of his father
Jacob. How about health and moral efficiency? The record continues: " And Joseph was a goodly person and well favored." This
testimony affirms that his countenance glowed with health and the
heart was pure. As a demonstration of the purity of his character
and his mastery over passion, the record shows how he withstood the
temptations of the mistress of the household. He preferred to suffer
the bondage of the prison for several years, rather than to enslave
his soul by the indulgence of passion (Gen. 39: 7–20).

Possessing this threefold efficiency—physical, industrial, and moral,
he advanced in spite of his unfavorable environment, and was appointed assistant warden of the prison to which he was unjustly
committed. This is the record of his promotion: " The Lord was
with Joseph, and shewed him mercy, and gave him favor in the
sight of the keeper of the prison. And the keeper of the prison committed to Joseph's hand all the prisoners that were in the prison,
and whatever they did there, he was the doer of it. The keeper of
the prison looked not to anything that was under his hand; because
the Lord was with him, and that which he did the Lord made it to
prosper " (Gen. 39: 21–23).

God is with those who refuse to have the powers of body, mind
and soul weakened and polluted by gluttony and impurity of thought
and action. So after years of faithful, patient, and efficient service
in the household of Potiphar and in the prison house, the door of
opportunity opened for wider service, the successful performance of
which demanded good health, industrial efficiency, and sound character. He was called from the prison house to the throne of Pharaoh
and appointed food commissioner of Egypt. His commission involved
a seven-years' program in food production, and the distribution of

it during the seven years of famine that followed.   Concerning Joseph's appointment and the carrying of it out the following is recorded:

" And Pharaoh said unto Joseph: ' See, I have set thee over all the land of Egypt. Thou shalt be over my house, and according unto thy word shall all my people be ruled; only in the throne will I be greater than thou ' " (Gen. 41: 41, 40).

Concerning Joseph's efforts in gathering and distributing food the record continues:

" Joseph went out from the presence of Pharaoh and went through all the land of Egypt. . . . He gathered up all the food of the seven years, which were in the land of Egypt; and laid up the food in the cities. . . . And Joseph gathered corn (wheat) as the sand of the sea, very much, until he left numbering, for it was without number. . . . And the seven years of dearth began to come . . . and the dearth was in all lands; but in all the land of Egypt there was bread. . . . And the famine was over all the face of the earth; and Joseph opened all the store-houses, and sold unto the Egyptians; and the famine waxed sore in the land of Egypt.   And all countries came into Egypt to Joseph to buy corn, because the famine was so sore in all lands " (Gen. 41: 46–57).

Health and Disease

Worse than the famine for Israel was the hard cruel bondage they suffered in later years under the cruel taskmasters.   But instead of diminishing in number under the rigorous labors, the population of Israel rapidly multiplied; which so infuriated Pharaoh, that " he charged all his people saying: Every son that is born ye shall cast into the river, and every daughter ye shall save alive " (Ex. 2: 22). But this severe measure the midwives did not carry out, for they " feared God, and did not as the King of Egypt commanded them, but saved the men children alive. . . . Therefore God dealt well with the midwives; and the people multiplied and waxed very mighty " (Ex. 2: 17, 20).

Although the taskmasters " made their lives bitter with hard bondage in mortar, and in brick and in all manner of service in the field " (Ex. 2: 14), still the children of Israel must have enjoyed good health even though they did not enjoy their rigorous labors.   God sympathized with them in their bondage, as the record states:

" And it came to pass in process of time, that the king of Egypt died; and the children of Israel sighed by reason of the bondage, and they cried and their cry came up to God by reason of their bondage. And God heard their groaning, and God remembered his covenant with Abraham, with Isaac, and Jacob, and God looked upon the children of Israel, and God had respect unto them " (Ex. 2: 23–25).

Moses, whom his sister Miriam watched when a babe, after the mother had placed the infant in the ark of bulrushes to save him from the fate of Pharaoh's decree, was chosen of God to lead Israel out of the land of bondage unto the land flowing with milk and honey. In their new home they would be privileged to live in freedom according to God's plan of life started in Eden; which, under changed conditions, caused by partaking of the tree of knowledge of good and evil, was carried out by the long-lived patriarchs who remained true and loyal to their Creator.

Although "Moses was learned in all the wisdom and learning of the Egyptians, and was mighty in word and deed" (Acts 7: 22), he failed in his first attempt to deliver Israel, made at the age of forty years. After forty years of caring for the sheep and lambs he was prepared, at the age of eighty, to be a wise, sympathetic and powerful leader of his people.

After Moses had led Israel through the Red Sea a three-days' journey into the wilderness, God gave to them an absolute guaranty of physical health on the following conditions:

" If thou wilt diligently hearken to the voice of the Lord thy God, and wilt do that which is right in his sight, and wilt give ear to his commandments, and keep all his statutes, I will put none of these diseases upon thee, which I have brought upon the Egyptians: for I am the Lord that healeth thee " (Ex. 15: 26). " The Lord will take away from thee all sickness and will put none of the evil diseases of Egypt, which thou knowest, upon thee " (Deut. 7: 15).

Israel's exemption from the diseases of the Egyptians and other nations was due to their living in harmony with the sanitary and moral laws given to them by God through Moses at Sinai. The regulations regarding proper food, cleanliness of body, sanitary homes and premises, must be strictly obeyed if they were to be immune from the diseases that ravaged the surrounding nations. Concerning this wonderfully complete code of sanitary laws we have the following comment by Hon. Albert J. Beveridge:

" We must note that the very first and most numerous of these (laws written by Moses) concern the health of the people. From the time of Moses until this day, the most perfect laws of hygiene ever developed were the health ordinances of the great Hebrew lawgiver."

" We sometimes wonder at the amazing vitality of the Jews,—their physical persistence as a people—but if you read the laws of Moses, and reflect that they have been observed rigidly even to this day, wonder begins to dissolve." [1]

Although the Israelites did not have the best of food, and were forced to hard labor, yet they had good health. Labor made their appetites keen, and they relished and assimilated their food, which would not have been possible if they had lived in idleness or leisure. Concerning their physical condition when God by Moses delivered them from Egypt it is recorded: "He brought them forth also with

[1] A. J. Beveridge, *The Bible as Good Reading*, pp. 71, 74 (Houghton Mifflin Co.).

silver and gold, and there was not a feeble person among their tribes" (Ps. 105: 37).

Among the three million in slavery, "not one feeble person"! That certainly denotes a high attainment of physical efficiency which ought to be studied by those who live in countries that enjoy liberty and freedom.

Health and disease are frequently spoken of in the Scriptures. Health is lauded, and disease is dreaded. Health is to be sought, and disease is to be shunned. Our English word "health" comes from the Anglo-Saxon word *haelan* whose root is *hāl*, meaning "whole." The word "heal" comes from the same root. Then, one who is healthy is whole. When one is healed he is "made whole." So Jesus asked the man waiting to be healed at the pool of Bethesda: "Wilt thou be made whole?" In response to his eager desire Jesus said unto him, "Rise, take up thy bed, and walk. And immediately he was made whole" (John 5: 6-9).

When one has health, his whole body and every organ in it functions perfectly. There is no pain or discomfort. The whole body is at *ease,* for there is no *disease* to weaken or interfere with its proper functioning.

Healthiness and Holiness

But while the body may be well, the mind and the soul may be sick. Jesus in His ministry to the sick sought to make men, women, and children "every whit whole." The first words He said to the one brought to Him lying on a bed, sick with the palsy, were: "Son, be of good cheer; thy sins be forgiven thee." Then He added: "Arise, take up thy bed and walk, and go unto thine house. And he arose and departed to his house" (Matt. 9: 1-7). On another occasion He healed a man on the Sabbath day and He was accused of profaning the Sabbath. He replied: "Are ye angry at me because I have made a man every whit whole on the Sabbath day?" (John 7: 23). The Great Physician did not consider His medical ministry complete unless He healed body, mind, and soul. He desired His followers to possess holiness of soul as well as healthiness of body. David refers to this holy ministry in behalf of body and soul: "Who forgiveth all thine iniquities; who healeth all thy diseases" (Ps. 103: 3).

Healthiness and holiness are frequently linked together in the Scriptures as though they were complements of each other. Not only do the words "health" and "whole" originate from the same Anglo-Saxon root *hāl,* but also the words "healthy" and "holy" and similar derivatives (healthful, healthsome, healthiness, and wholly, wholesome, holiness) come from the same root word.

In choosing Israel the Lord said to them: "If ye will obey my voice indeed and keep my covenant, then ye shall be a peculiar treasure to me above all people . . . a kingdom of priests and an holy nation" (Ex. 19: 5, 6). Many times God exhorted them: "Be ye holy, for I am holy," not only when speaking of the holy law, the holy Sabbath, the holy tithe, and the holy ark, but also when giving instruction to them regarding the kind of food they were to eat, the clothing they were to wear, and the sanitary regulations that were to be observed in keeping their bodies and the camp clean and wholesome.

After naming the list of clean animals that they were permitted to eat, and the unclean which they were forbidden to eat, follows this exhortation:

" Ye shall not make yourselves abominable with any creeping thing that creepeth, neither shall ye make yourselves unclean with them that ye should be defiled thereby. For I am the Lord your God; ye shall therefore sanctify yourselves, and ye shall be holy; for I am holy " (Lev. 12: 43, 44). " Ye shall therefore put difference between clean beasts and unclean, and between unclean fowls and clean; and ye shall not make your souls abominable by beast, or by fowl, or by any manner of living thing that creepeth on the ground, which I have separated from you as unclean. And ye shall be holy unto me; for I the Lord am holy, and have severed you from other people, that ye should be mine " (Lev. 20: 25, 26).

The children of Israel were commanded to wash their clothes and present themselves clean unto the Lord when He descended on Mount Sinai:

" And the Lord said unto Moses: Go unto the people and sanctify them today and tomorrow, and let them wash their clothes, and be ready against the third day, for the Lord will come down in the sight of all the people upon Mount Sinai " (Ex. 19: 10, 11).

Even their clothing was to remind them of the commandments of the Lord and be an aid to holy living.

" Speak unto the children of Israel and bid them that they make them fringes in the borders of their garments throughout their generations, and that they put upon the fringe of the borders a ribband of blue, and it shall be unto you for a fringe that ye may look upon it, and remember all the commandments of the Lord and do them " (Num. 15: 38–40).

It is evident that the wilderness school conducted for forty years under the able leadership of Moses was designed of God to enable His chosen people to become an example of right and holy living—physically, mentally, and spiritually, in their new home, rich in resources and abundant in opportunities for contact with peoples of all nations passing that way by caravan in their commercial trade. Their food, their clothing, their schools, their industrial life, and their forms of worship would attract attention and create interest in those seeking to elevate their standards of living.

One of the outstanding things to be noted by the stranger would be the physical health of the children, youth, and adults, and their freedom from the diseases that were common in the surrounding nations. Israel's diet in the wilderness was the " manna " daily and miraculously provided. Some murmured and complained about the diet and longed for flesh food, which was provided for a short time on two occasions. Concerning these experiences it is recorded: "They tempted God in their hearts by asking meat for their lust" (Ps. 78: 18). "He gave them their request, but sent leanness into their soul" (Ps. 106: 15). It was God's plan to have Israel adopt the diet prescribed in Eden, so He gave them manna in the wilderness until they should enter Canaan, where they were to subsist on the herbs bearing seed and the fruits of the trees. Since they did not heartily accept God's plan of diet, He permitted them to eat animal food, restricting them to a list of clean animals, and forbidding the use of unclean animals for food.

Examples of Physical Development

We have learned that when Moses led about three million people out of Egyptian bondage, there was not a feeble person among them. What was the physical condition of Israel after forty years of wandering in the wilderness, and about to enter their promised land flowing with milk and honey? They had been provided with good food by angels. David called it "angel's food," and "the corn of heaven" (Ps. 78: 4, 5). Such good food gave promise of good health; clothing and shelter were supplied.

Just before the probably more than three million crossed the Jordan, Moses declared to his people:

"The Lord thy God led thee these forty years . . . and fed thee with manna which thou knewest not, neither did thy fathers know, that he might make thee know that man doth not live by bread only, but by every word that proceedeth out of the mouth of the Lord doth man live. Thy raiment waxed not old upon thee, neither did thy foot swell these forty years" (Deut. 8: 2–4). "I have led you forty years in the wilderness; your clothes are not waxen old upon you, and thy shoe is not waxen old upon thy foot" (Deut. 29: 5).

Nehemiah speaking of God's care for Israel in their wilderness wandering said:

"Thou gavest also thy good spirit to instruct them, and withheldest not thy manna from their mouth, and gavest them water for their thirst. Yea, forty years didst thou sustain them in the wilderness, so that they lacked nothing; their clothes waxed not old and their feet swelled not" (Neh. 9: 20, 21).

Under such constant care for their daily temporal needs, and full instruction as to their habits of daily living, Israel must have made rapid progress in physical, mental, and spiritual development, and were well prepared to enter upon God's program for them as His representatives of truth to the world enslaved by appetite, passion, and idolatry. Their children and youth must have been trained in harmony with the principles of truth they had learned in the wilderness school.

Frequent mention is made in the Scriptures of the striking physical appearance of many of the Hebrew youth.

Gideon and his Brothers. When Gideon inquired of Zalmunna and Zebah, the two Midian kings whom he had captured, "What manner of men were they whom ye slew at Tabor?" they answered, "As thou art, so were they; each one resembled the children of a king." This was a splendid testimonial from the lips of heathen rulers, and in reply to it Gideon said, "They were my brethren, even the sons of my mother" (Judges 8: 18, 19).

Joash had a wonderful family of children. Even the angel who watched Gideon for a short time while he was threshing wheat, broke forth in these words of surprising commendation: "The Lord is with thee, thou mighty man of valor" (Judges 6: 11, 12). Joash and his wife must have been exceptional parents. What a thorough, painstaking education and training must have been given to their boys, who, on reaching manhood, "resembled the children of a king"!

This resemblance noted by these Midian kings must have been physical as well as cultural, as indicated by the marginal reading: "Each one had the form of the children of a king."

In the divine plan of education, as given to ancient Israel, the physical as well as the mental and spiritual powers were to be developed. Both in the home and in the school, parents and teachers were to be faithful in giving instruction as to right habits and in requiring strict conformity to the principles of healthful living. Some of the results of this kind of education are noted in the Scriptures.

Saul. Saul's father is spoken of as a mighty man of power; while Saul is described as "a choice young man, and a goodly: . . . from his shoulders and upward he was higher than any of the people" (I Sam. 9: 1, 2). Saul was of the tribe of Benjamin, which had many who could use with equal facility the right hand or the left hand in war, and seven hundred left-handed men who "could sling stones at a hairbreadth, and not miss" (Judges 20: 16).

David. David, "when a youth," "was ruddy, and withal of a beautiful countenance, and goodly to look to." He is further described as "a mighty valiant man, . . . a comely person, and the Lord is with him" (I Sam. 16: 12, 18). David recognized God as the source of his physical skill and power; he believed that the God who enabled him to smite the lion and the bear, and thus protect his flock, would help him to smite the Philistine giant, and save his people from defeat. In the Psalms he connects God directly with his physical exertions:

"Blessed be the Lord my strength, which teacheth my hands to war, and my fingers to fight." "He maketh my feet like hinds' feet. . . . He teacheth my hands to war, so that a bow of steel is broken by mine arms." "By thee I have run through a troop; and by my God have I leaped over a wall" (Ps. 144: 1; 18: 33, 34, 29).

Esther. This queenly Jewish maid was "fair of form, and good of countenance," and she "obtained favor in the sight of all them that looked upon her" (Esther 2: 7, margin, 15).

Daniel and his Companions. When they were examined as candidates for the Babylonian university, they were found to be "children in whom was no blemish, but well favored." And when they faced the question of eating the food provided from the royal table, they purposed that they would not defile themselves with the portion of the king's meat, nor with the wine which he drank. Their condition of health, and the attitude of these youth regarding their diet, strongly suggest a thorough training during childhood in the land of their nativity. Regarding their training we have the following from a modern educator:

" Daniel and his associates had been trained by their parents to habits of strict temperance. They had been taught that God would hold them accountable for their capabilities, and that they must never dwarf or enfeeble their powers. This education was to Daniel and his companions the means of their preservation amidst the demoralizing influences of the court of Babylon. Strong were the temptations surrounding them in that corrupt and luxurious court, but they remained uncontaminated. No power, no influence, could sway them from the principles they had learned in early life by a study of the Word and works of God." [2]

The following vivid pen-picture helps us in imagination to see these noble youth in their physical fitness as they mingled with their school associates who, with unbridled appetites, feasted on the dainties provided by the king:

" In physical strength and beauty, in mental vigor and literary attainment, they stood unrivaled. The erect form, the firm, elastic step, the fair countenance, the undimmed senses, the untainted breath,—all were so many certificates of good habits, insignia of the nobility with which nature honors those who are obedient to her laws." [3]

Physical and Spiritual Development

"*Glorify God in Your Body.*" This injunction of the Apostle Paul is in keeping with the spirit of the education of Old Testament times, the outworking of which we have briefly noted in connection with the Hebrew youth mentioned above. The dignity and glory of the human body are affirmed in the words: "So God created man in his own image," and "Ye are the temple of God" (Gen. 1: 27; I Cor. 3: 16).

The awful retributions to be visited on those who refuse to acknowledge the honors conferred and the obligations imposed is expressed in the words: "If any man defile the temple of God, him shall God destroy; for the temple of God is holy, which temple ye are" (I Cor. 3: 17).

Paul recognized the futility of his efforts to win out in the conflict

---

[2] White, *Prophets and Kings,* p. 482.
[3] *Ibid.,* p. 485.

against evil unless the physical man was under control: "I keep under my body, and bring it into subjection; lest that by any means, when I have preached to others, I myself should be a castaway" (I Cor. 9: 27).

The true attitude of bodily surrender is expressed in Paul's earnest entreaty to his brethren: "I beseech you therefore, brethren, by the mercies of God, that ye present your bodies a living sacrifice, holy, acceptable unto God, which is your reasonable service" (Rom. 12: 1).

He prays that the whole man—body, soul, and spirit—may be sanctified, so that he may be preserved unto the coming of his Maker: "The very God of peace sanctify you wholly; and I pray God your whole spirit and soul and body be preserved blameless unto the coming of our Lord Jesus Christ" (I Thess. 5: 23).

The close relationship of the physical and the spiritual; and their beneficial reactions in mental diseases, were clearly stated by Doctor Hyslop, a mind disease specialist, when speaking before the British Medical Association:

" The best medicine which my practice has discovered is prayer. The exercise of prayer in those who habitually practice it must be regarded as the most adequate and normal of all the pacifiers of the mind and calmers of the nerves.

" As one whose whole life has been concerned with the sufferings of the mind, I would state that of all the hygienic measures to counteract disturbed sleep, depression of spirits, and all the miserable sequels of a distressed mind, I would undoubtedly give the first place to the simple habit of prayer.

" It is of the highest importance, merely from a physical point of view, to teach children to hold daily communion with God. Such a habit does more to quiet the spirit and strengthen the soul to overcome mere incidental emotionalism than any other therapeutic agency known to man " [4]

Teaching Health by Example

Doctor Hyslop emphasizes the great importance, "merely from a physical point of view," of teaching children to pray. Along with prayer we should teach children to watch. Jesus emphasized both: "Watch and pray, lest ye enter into temptation" (Mark 14: 38). Teach the children to be watchful lest they indulge in wrong habits of eating and drinking, loss of sleep, careless, needless exposure of the body, and in many other ways bring sickness and disease upon themselves. Then they should be warned against the use of all stimulants and narcotics. Here in the physical as well as in the intellectual and spiritual, parents and teachers must "watch for souls as they that must give an account."

There is a watchfulness on the part of children and youth that does not need stimulation, and which is continuously and keenly exercised. They watch their parents and teachers to see what and how they do, and usually are inclined to take them for an example. How unfortunate, nay, more, what a tragedy for parents and teachers to be practicing habits of intemperance in eating and drinking, the very things against which the children and youth are warned. Usually physiology textbooks warn against the use of liquor and tobacco. What must be the influence of parents and teachers who use them? In these same books, tea and coffee are considered harmful to children. But the children are wise enough to know that what is harmful for them is likewise harmful to those who are older in years. Some teachers say: " I do not indulge in tobacco and liquor in the presence of my pupils." But you advertise your use of them on your breath and in your countenance. There is only one honorable and consistent course for parent and teacher,—be what you want your children and pupils to be. In this way only can you have their full confidence and respect.

Teaching Purity of Life

While education should stress health and strength of body, it is still more important to emphasize purity of mind and heart. In this respect parents and teachers are to be inspiring examples. In this age of physical, mental and moral corruption teachers of children and youth must continually be on guard lest by word or action they suggest to the ever alert eyes and minds of those under their instruction that which may be seed that will develop into impure thoughts, words, or deeds. These find their most ready expression in sex relationship of both teacher and pupils, which becomes a topic of ridicule, or unseemly conversation. Before long the school is pervaded by an atmosphere of sexual sentimentalism which is hard to dissipate. In recent years some educators have introduced a program of sex education, beginning with the children and continuing it in modified form adapted to the youth growing into manhood and womanhood. The results of this instruction have been far from satisfactory and in some cases have aggravated the situation. A spirit of curiosity and desire for experimental knowledge has resulted in a serious protest against what is termed " sex education."

The failure of sex education results from failure to educate the whole being—a wholeness which results in holiness. As long as children and youth are drinking from the polluted streams of sensational literature and movie films whose waters are saturated with the germs of sexual aberrations, and abnormalities, how can a normal, clean, wholesome relation between the sexes be developed and maintained?

The " Education and Sex " problem is discussed by L. P. Jacks in his book *The Education of the Whole Man.* He says:

" What then can education do in this difficult matter? Of all the methods of dealing with it known to me, the least likely to effect its purpose is that of making sex knowledge a set ' subject ' of instruction to the young. . . . The most important elements in human education can never be achieved by making them into ' subjects,' but only by indirection, and no educator understands his business until he has realized that the chief ' objects ' at which he is aiming have no place in the list of ' subjects ' in his time table. Of this next to religion sex is the outstanding example.

" But in refusing to admit it as a subject, it must not be supposed that we dismiss it as an object. A wise educator has it in his mind's eye, but he says as little as possible about it. To suppose that young people will be saved from sex aberrations by ' full and frank discussion of sex ' seems to me, I must confess, a most dangerous illusion; nor would I care to be in the shoes of the teacher, man or woman, responsible for the ' full and frank discussion.' Such is the nature of the matter, that all discussion of it, especially with the young, acts by way of suggestion; the ' mystery ' of it consists partly in that. If ' discussion ' allays curiosity in one form it stimulates curiosity in another. The youth who has graduated in sex knowledge under the guidance of instructors (who themselves can hardly be exempt from danger) and has the whole ' subject ' so to speak by heart, from the fertilization of plants upwards, knows very well that his understanding of what all that means is hopelessly and painfully incomplete until he has brought it to the experimental stage. And the probability is that he will not be long in doing so. He may even be in doubt as to whether his instructors have told him the whole truth about the matter, a point on which youth is always suspicious when the moral element is strongly emphasized; in which case he will pass the more quickly to the stage of experiment, by way of finding out whether he has been humbugged or not. . . . In giving instruction in other branches of knowledge, which profess to be scientific, the need of practical experiment to complete the lesson and drive it home is acknowledged. The pupil must work the sum whose theory has been explained to him, examine the object whose nature has been described, make models and copies of it; try out in the laboratory what he has been taught in the classroom, test his knowledge by field work and so forth. But in the matter before us, this is precisely the point at which the instructor has to stop short; his object being rather to restrain experiment than to promote it. And the danger is that the blank will get itself filled up sooner than he desires, and in ways he does not desire. He is not dealing with ' cold blood ' as he is when explaining the properties of oxygen, or the processes of digestion. He is dealing with hot blood, and with blood hot for the experiment. He is playing with fire.

" The dangers to the teacher need not be elaborated. One statement must suffice. It is difficult to be sincere about sex. Yet in this matter the faintest suspicion of insincerity, which the young are quick to detect, is fatal to a good result, just as it is in the parallel case of religion.

" I think it a sound principle which regards the sex function a mystery, as nothing less august than a mystery, not in the sense of being unknowable, but as demanding high valor, and a regenerated mind in the knower, like the secret of immortality just beyond it; a thing, therefore, utterly misunderstood, and certain to be misused when reduced to its lowest elements and exhibited to the young as ' a simple natural process ' like the fertilization of plants, or the production of a hen's egg. Sound also in principle is the sharp reminder, administered by the whip, that men and women in their sex relations are not as buttercups, cooing pigeons or stock cattle, but beings whose love-making must be conducted on quite another level. Soundest of all is the care for posterity which these things betray. For it is only by preserving to sex its true character as *mysterium tremendum* (tremendous mystery) and not by diffusing a cheapened ' sex knowledge ' among the unwhipped multitudes of pleasure seekers and C3's that the high breeding of human beings has any chance of being maintained. Posterity, I imagine, has an interest in *that*. Children born as the residual products of sophisticated sex relations, when grown to adults, make indifferent ancestors.'' [5]

The above writer urges that a much neglected element in the educational process be given a larger place in the educational program. He pleads that the students be given opportunity and encouragement to do original, constructive work, which he calls creative education and which means the development of " creative skill." We give his conclusion:

'' My conclusion is, then, that the ' solution of the sex problem,' so far as it falls within the province of the educator, lies in an extension of the educational aim beyond the point represented by the acquisition of knowledge to the farther point represented by creative skill. This means, in plainer language, that Art (always understood in its catholic sense as the most excellent doing of whatever needs to be done) must find a larger and a more central place in educational practice. It means that increased weight must be thrown into the awaking and training the sense of beauty, the greatest of our lost inheritances, but the best of all prophylactics against vice, the most vitalizing and uplifting of all the positive motives that interest and actuate the *whole* man. . . .

'' If sex instruction is to be given, the parent is unquestionably the best instructor, or ought to be. All depends on the general atmosphere of the home life. If this is devitalized or poisoned, sex instruction in the home is as dangerous as it would be anywhere else.'' [6]

Creative education, the education of the whole being, and other sane human devisings are important and helpful; but they are impotent and powerless to control unbridled passion without the divine aid of Him who made men, " Every whit whole." Our children and youth with their natural and inherited tendencies to evil (see pages 72–74) must be " created in Christ Jesus unto good works," and must be guided and instructed by those who have been transformed in life by His creative power (Eph. 2: 10).

[5] L. P. Jacks, *The Education of the Whole Man,* pp. 118–122 (Harper & Brothers).
[6] *Ibid.,* pp. 125–127.

XIV

INDUSTRIAL EDUCATION

In the Home

THIS phase of education was emphasized in the Hebrew home along with physical education. As already shown, it had its place in the Garden of Eden, and outside of the garden Adam taught Cain how to till the ground and Abel how to care for the sheep. Abraham and Lot were very prosperous with their flocks and herds. Jacob for fourteen years was very successful in operating the farm of his Uncle Laban. His son Joseph received a home training that laid the foundation for fitting him to be the industrial superintendent of the greatest nation of his time during seven years of preparation for a famine that continued the same number of years. David and Solomon displayed much knowledge and skill in agriculture and architecture, the former gathering the materials and the latter superintending the construction of the grandest temple ever built by human hands. Nehemiah, cup-bearer to the king of a world empire, had knowledge and skill to serve wine, or brick and mortar as the occasion required. Daniel and Mordecai are other examples of men eminently qualified to solve the industrial and financial problems of world empires.

Not only the boys, but also the girls of Hebrew homes were trained to solve the industrial problems of life. The administration of the home life of one who had such training is recorded in the Scriptures:

" Who can find a virtuous woman? for her price is far above rubies. The heart of her husband doth safely trust in her, so that he shall have no need of spoil. She will do him good and not evil all the days of her life. She seeketh wool, and flax, and worketh willingly with her hands. She is like the merchants' ships; she bringeth her food from afar. She riseth also while it is yet night, and giveth meat to her household, and a portion to her maidens. She considereth a field, and buyeth it: with the fruit of her hands she planteth a vineyard. She girdeth her loins with strength, and strengtheneth her arms. She perceiveth that her merchandise is good: her candle goeth not out by night. She layeth her hands to the spindle, and her hands hold the distaff. She stretcheth out her hand to the poor; yea, she reacheth forth her hands to the needy. She is not afraid of the snow for her household: for all her household are clothed with scarlet. She maketh herself coverings of tapestry: her clothing is silk and purple. Her husband is known in the gates, when he sitteth among the elders of the land. She maketh fine linen, and selleth it; and delivereth girdles unto the merchant. Strength and honor are her clothing; and she shall rejoice in time to come. She openeth her mouth with wisdom; and in her tongue is the law of kindness. She looketh well to the ways of her household, and eateth not the bread of idleness. Her children arise up, and call her blessed; her husband also, and he praiseth her. Many daughters have done virtuously, but thou excellest them all. Favor is deceitful, and beauty is vain; but a woman that feareth the Lord, she shall be praised. Give her of the fruit of her hands, and let her own works praise her in the gates '' (Prov. 31: 10–31).

This is a wonderful statement of the position and honor accorded women in Israel, especially so when we consider that in the surrounding nations women were treated as slaves, and regarded on the same level as the beasts of burden. This record is worthy of careful study, especially by mothers and teachers of home-making. It will be noted that this worthy home-maker and keeper possessed knowledge, skill, and wisdom necessary to organize and maintain all the various features necessary to a prosperous, happy and influential home. This home-maker had financial ability to enable her to make wise and safe investments that would aid in providing the necessities of the family. She, as well as her husband, exerted an influence outside of the home. They co-operated fully and sympathetically in the making of the home, and the children esteemed their parents with love and respect. The mother was regarded as the queen of the home. The children rise up and call her blessed, and the father praiseth her in the gates. This woman is not named, but some belonging to her type are,—Sarah, Rebecca, Rachel, Ruth, Bathsheba, and Esther.

A modern educator gives some suggestions as to the part children may have in sharing the burdens of the home, performing such duties as their age and strength will permit:

'' The mother should be the teacher, and home the school where every child receives his first lessons; and these lessons should include habits of industry. Mothers, let the little ones play in the open air; let them listen to the songs of the birds, and learn the love of God as expressed in His beautiful works. Teach them simple lessons from the book of nature and the things about them; and as their minds expand, lessons from books may be added, and firmly fixed in their memory. But let them also learn, even in their earliest years, to be useful. Train them to think that, as members of the household, they are to act a disinterested, helpful part in sharing the domestic burdens, and to seek healthful exercise in the performance of necessary home duties.

'' It is essential for parents to find useful employment for their children which will involve the bearing of responsibilities as their age and strength will permit. The children should be given something to do that will not only keep them busy, but will interest them. The active hands and brains must be employed from the earliest years. If parents neglect to turn their children's energies into useful channels, they do them great injury; for Satan is ready to find them something to do.'' [1]

In the School

Industrial education was a feature of the training in the schools

[1] White, *Counsels to Teachers,* pp. 145, 146.

of the prophets. The students and teacher associated together in labor. We have a record of the establishment of one of these schools where the principal and his students were working together in the construction of the school building:

" And the sons of the prophets said unto Elisha, Behold now, the place where we dwell with thee is too strait for us. Let us go, we pray thee, unto Jordan, and take thence every man a beam, and let us make us a place there, where we may dwell. And he answered, Go ye. And one said, Be content, I pray thee, and go with thy servants. And he answered, I will go. So he went with them. And when they came to Jordan, they cut down wood. But as one was felling a beam, the axe head fell into the water: and he cried, and said, Alas, master! for it was borrowed. And the man of God said, Where fell it? And he shewed him the place. And he cut down a stick, and cast it in thither; and the iron did swim. Therefore said he, Take it up to thee. And he put out his hand and took it " (II Kings 6: 1–7).

This is a brief record of the establishment of this school located near the river Jordan. We learn from this brief statement the following very interesting and important points of educational value:

1. The previous location of the school (probably at Jericho) was unfavorable, and that a rural location was better adapted to the education of the youth.

2. That the students and teachers associated together in work as well as in study.

3. That the facilities for constructing the building were limited, some of the tools used being borrowed.

4. That God was interested in the establishment of this school and worked a miracle, causing the axe-head that had fallen into the water to float to the surface that the work of building should not be hindered.

Undoubtedly students were taught the dignity of labor, as illustrated in the lives of Joseph, Moses, and other patriarchs. The mingling of the teachers with the students in their daily toil served to bind them into closer sympathy than by co-operation in study alone.

The Mastery of Industries

A modern educator writes on the industrial phase of education as carried out by Hebrew parents and teachers:

" In God's plan for Israel, every family had a home on the land, with sufficient ground for tilling. Thus were provided both the means and the incentive for a useful, industrious, and self-supporting life. And no devising of men has ever improved upon that plan. To the world's departure from it is owing, to a large degree, the poverty and wretchedness that exist today. By the Israelites industrial training was regarded as a duty. Every father was required to see that his sons learned some useful trade. The greatest men of Israel were trained in industrial pursuits. A knowledge of the duties pertaining to housewifery was considered essential for every woman; and skill in these duties was regarded as an honor to women of the highest station. (Read Proverbs 31.) Various industries were taught in the schools of the prophets, and many of the students sustained themselves by manual labor.'' [2]

'' The pupils of these schools sustained themselves by their own labor in tilling the soil, or in some mechanical employment. In Israel this was not thought strange or degrading, indeed, it was regarded as a sin to allow children to grow up in ignorance of useful labor. Every youth, whether his parents were rich or poor, was taught some trade. Even though he was to be educated for holy office, a knowledge of practical life was regarded as essential to the greatest usefulness. Many also of the teachers supported themselves by manual labor.'' [3]

Christ consecrated all labor with the hands by learning and working at the carpenter's trade until He started on His ministry at about thirty years of age. Work with the hands is not confined to earth. Jesus said: "My father worketh hitherto, and I work" (John 5: 17). The prophet Isaiah was given a vision of man in his future home, and declares that he saw him engaged in labor, enjoying the work of his hands:

'' They shall build houses, and inhabit them; and they shall plant vineyards and eat the fruit of them. They shall not build and another inhabit; they shall not plant and another eat; for as the days of a tree are the days of my people, and mine elect shall long enjoy the work of their hands. They shall not labor in vain, nor bring forth for trouble; for they are the seed of the blessed of the Lord, and their offspring with them '' (Isa. 65: 21-23).

There is much uncertainty, now, about enjoying the work of our hands. Labor and capital are in controversy and the social order is much disturbed by clashes of industrial organizations. Greed, dishonesty in dealing, and the uncertainty of life make our possessions and their enjoyment uncertain.

Hebrew Industrial Life

Above it is stated that in God's plan for Israel, every family had a home on the land with sufficient ground for tilling. Every father was required to see that his sons learned some useful trade; and every daughter was to acquire the knowledge of duties pertaining to home making. From our brief study of the lives of noted Bible characters it is evident that those occupying positions of the highest honor were so trained.

In the Scriptures (Lev. 25) detailed instruction is given as to the ownership and redemption of land and houses, and also of the cultivation of the land. Treatment of the poor and the redemption of servants is given careful consideration. This chapter will bear close, careful study. In this troubled hour over agriculture and various vital industries, some of our statesmen and others vitally

[2] White, *Ibid.*, pp. 275, 276.
[3] White, *Education*, p. 47.

concerned are giving serious study to Israel's program of industrial life, and see in it a solution for our social ills. The following are a few of the factors governing the agricultural life of the Hebrews:

1. Cultivate the land six years, and let it rest every seventh year (Verses 3, 4).

2. During the seventh year nothing that grows of itself shall be gathered or gleaned (Verse 5).

3. Every sixth year under the special blessing of God the land yields enough food for three years, making ample provision for the sixth, seventh, and eighth years, or until the ninth year (Verses 20–22).

4. The land was not to be sold. "The land shall not be sold forever; for the land is mine; for ye are strangers and sojourners with me" (Verse 23).

5. Every fiftieth year the land was not to be cultivated; neither that which grew of itself was to be eaten (Verses 8–12).

6. If on account of poverty or any other reason land was sold and not redeemed, it was returned to the original owner on the fiftieth year, called the year of jubilee (Verse 10).

7. The poor and the stranger were not to be oppressed (Verses 17, 35–37, 39–43, 45, 46).

Industrial Finance

The industrial life of the Hebrews necessitated a system of exchange of commodities involving their measurement and value. Not only did this system of exchange have to do with their daily temporal affairs, but also with their spiritual life, both as to instruction and worship. The tithes and offerings in money and in materials called for exact accounting. The construction of the tabernacle and the temple required a knowledge and use of mathematics as to extension, volume, and weight. The reading of the exact and minute specifications given to Moses and recorded in the Pentateuch, indicates order and system and a knowledge of mathematical principles to successfully solve the various financial and industrial problems to be solved in building and commercial life. Treasurers were appointed as custodians of the money used in various enterprises:

" All the silver, and gold . . . are consecrated unto the Lord; they shall come into the treasury of the Lord " (Josh. 6: 19). " For these Levites . . . . were in their set office, and were over . . . the treasuries of the house of God " (I Chron. 9: 26). " And I made treasurers over the treasuries, Shelemiah the priest, and Zadok the scribe, and of the Levites, Pedaiah; and next to them was Hanan, the son of Zaccur, the son of Mattaniah; for they were counted faithful, and their office was to distribute unto their brethren " (Neh. 13: 13).

We have recorded the names of King David's treasurers, and also the superintendents of industry and the lines of work superintended by each:

" And over the king's treasures was Azmaveth the son of Adiel: and over the storehouses in the fields, in the cities, and in the villages, and in the castles, was Jehonathan the son of Uzziah: and over them that did the work of the field for tillage of the ground was Ezri, the son of Chelub. And over the vineyards was Shimei the Ramathite: over the increase of the vineyards for the wine cellars was Zabdi the Shiphmite: and over the olive trees and the sycamore trees that were in the low plains was Baal-hanan the Gederite: and over the cellars of oil was Joash: and over the herds that fed in Sharon was Shitrai the Sharonite: and over the herds that were in the valleys was Shaphat the son of Adlai: over the camels also was Obil the Ishmaelite: and over the asses was Jehdeiah the Meronothite: and over the flocks was Jaziz the Hagerite. All these were the rulers of the substance which was king David's '' (I Chron. 27: 25–31).

The names of the members of David's cabinet, consisting of six counselors and a secretary, are also given in the Biblical record:

'' Also Jonathan David's uncle was a counselor, a wise man, and a scribe: and Jehiel the son of Hachmoni was with the king's sons: and Ahithophel was the king's counselor: and Hushai the Archite was the king's companion: and after Ahithophel was Jehoiada the son of Benaiah, and Abiathar: and the general of the king's army was Joab '' (I Chron. 27: 32–34).

Those who had to do with the business affairs of the nation were pious, godly men who saw no conflict between business and religion. On the contrary they regarded religion to be the greatest essential to success. The apostle Paul makes plain the duty and privilege of serving the Lord in the transaction of business: " Not slothful in business; fervent in spirit; serving the Lord " always (Rom. 12: 11). Outstanding examples of such Christian business men were Joseph and Daniel. Daniel's administration of the business affairs of the Medo-Persian kingdom was scrutinized by two presidents and one hundred and twenty princes appointed by Darius the king; and this was their unanimous report after a most careful investigation: " The presidents and princes sought to find occasion against Daniel concerning the kingdom; but they could find none occasion nor fault; forasmuch as he was faithful, neither was there any error or fault found in him " (Dan. 6: 4). Daniel was chief of the three presidents, and the primary responsibility of the affairs of a world empire rested upon his shoulders; yet notwithstanding his busy arduous labors, he found time to pray three times a day to the God who has charge of the affairs of the universe. It was this communion with the Wonderful Counselor (Isa. 9: 6), who is " wonderful in counsel and excellent in working " (Isa. 28: 29), that made his business life faultless, and fruitful. His connection with earthly courts did not bar him from access to the heavenly courts. There to him was opened the future of world empires, with their iniquitous exploits and persecution. While beholding these he was overwhelmed temporarily with grief and fainted. Concerning this experience he leaves this record: " And I Daniel fainted and was sick certain days; afterward I rose up and did the king's business " (Dan. 8: 27). True religion, instead of unfitting, better fits a man to do business.

Hebrew Business Principles

Hebrew education provided minute, detailed instruction to guide one carrying business responsibilities; and also correct principles of dealing in the daily business transactions of life. A modern writer has truly said:

" There is no branch of legitimate business for which the Bible does not afford an essential preparation. Its principles of diligence, honesty, thrift, temperance and purity are the secret of true success. These principles, as set forth in the book of Proverbs, constitute a treasury of practical wisdom. Where can the merchant, the artisan, the director of men in any department of business find better maxims for himself or for his employees than are found in these words of the wise man? " [4]

The following are some of the instructions and a few of the principles contained in the Scriptures:

" Seest thou a man diligent in his business? He shall stand before kings; he shall not stand before obscure men " (Prov. 22: 29, margin). " The hand of the diligent shall bear rule; but the slothful shall be under tribute " (Prov. 12: 24). " Be thou diligent to know the state of thy flocks, and look well to thy herds " (Prov. 27: 23). " The Lord was with Joseph, and he was a prosperous man. . . . The Lord made all that he did to prosper in his hand " (Gen. 39: 2, 3).

In the Scriptures we have a word picture of a prosperous man— Job, one whose life was in the truest sense a success, a man whom both heaven and earth delighted to honor. He was a faithful steward of the goods entrusted to him. Speaking of his experience in the use of his goods he says:

" When the ear heard me, then it blessed me; and when the eye saw me it gave witness to me; because I delivered the poor that cried, and the fatherless, and him that had none to help him. The blessing of him that was ready to perish came upon me; and I caused the widow's heart to sing for joy. . . . I was eyes to the blind, and feet was I to the lame. I was a father to the poor, and the cause I knew not I searched out. . . . The light of my countenance they cast not down. I chose out their way and sat chief, and dwelt as a king in the army, as one that comforteth the mourners " (Job 29: 11–25).

The dishonest acquirement and the wrong use of riches are seriously condemned.

" He that getteth riches, and not by right, shall leave them in the midst of his days, and at his end shall be a fool " (Jer. 17: 11). " I will say unto my soul, Soul, thou hast much goods laid up for many years; take thine ease, eat, drink, and be merry. But God said unto him, Thou fool, this night thy soul shall be required of thee, then whose shall those things be which thou hast provided? " (Luke 12: 19, 20).

" If a man be just and do that which is lawful and right . . . and hath not oppressed any, but hath restored to the debtor his pledge, hath spoiled none by violence, hath given his bread to the hungry, and hath

4 White, *Education*, p. 135.

covered the naked with a garment; he that hath not given forth upon usury, neither hath taken any increase . . . that hath executed true judgment between man and man, hath walked in my statutes and hath kept my judgments, to deal truly; he is just, he shall surely live, saith the Lord God '' (Ezek. 18: 5–9). '' He hath showed thee, O man, what is good; and what doth the Lord require of thee, but to do justly, and to love mercy, and to walk humbly with thy God '' (Micah 6: 8). '' Ye shall do no unrighteousness in judgment, in meteyard, in weight or in measure. Just balances, just weights, a just ephah, and a just hin, shall ye have. I am the Lord your God '' (Lev. 19: 35, 36). '' A false balance is abomination to the Lord, but a just weight is his delight '' (Prov. 11: 1). '' A just weight and balance are the Lord's, all the weights of the bag are his work '' (Prov. 16: 11). '' Give and it shall be given unto you; good measure, pressed down, and shaken together, and running over shall men give into your bosom. For with the same measure that ye mete withal it shall be measured to you again '' (Luke 6: 38).

Man is not only accountable to man, but also to God for the way he transacts his business. The details of every transaction, as to motive, spirit, and ledger recordings, must pass the scrutiny of unseen auditors appointed by Him who never compromises with injustice, never overlooks evil, never condones wrong.

'' If thou seest the oppression of the poor, and violent perverting of judgment and justice in a province marvel not at the matter, for he that is higher than the highest, regardeth '' (Eccl. 5: 8). '' There is no darkness, nor shadow of death where the workers of iniquity may hide themselves '' (Job 34: 22).

The Lord gives men power to get wealth (Deut. 8: 18); and of all that they acquire He claims a specified portion—a tenth—thus acknowledging that He is the original proprietor and that we are His stewards. The Original Proprietor furnishes the capital and his stewards perform the labor required in order to make the investment profitable. He furnishes the farmer the ground to till, and the rain and sunshine to germinate and develop the seed, leaving to man the sowing, the cultivating and the gathering of the harvest. How reasonable and befitting the exhortation of the wise man: "Honor the Lord with thy substance, and with the first fruits of all thine increase;" and how gracious the promise: "So shall thy barns be filled with plenty, and thy presses shall burst out with new wine" (Prov. 3: 9, 10).

Influence of Labor on Mind and Soul

We have seen that work is essential to physical health. Useful labor promotes health more than play or recreation, because it gives the satisfaction that comes from something worth while accomplished apart from competition, which usually overexcites and often upsets the mental and, maybe, the moral balance of the participants in a game or contest. Frequently this unbalance of the mental and moral powers results in serious accident from which one may never fully recover. In athletics where competition is so keen, this is more likely to happen—resulting in some instances in the loss of life. Many educators are taking their stand against athletics—especially intercollegiate athletics, because of loss of time, money and scholarship—and, some add, loss of character. Only a handful of students benefit from the exercise (if that is profitable), and the great mass of students are idle, having no physical exercise (unless it be vocal), and the mind is under strain and tension, punctuated now and then by a thrill of joy or disappointment. When the game is over, the participants are unfitted for study and the students are so jubilant or disappointed that it is difficult to devote the mind to study and concentrated thinking.

How different the spirit and attitude on returning from the completed task of profitable work well done. The mind and spirit are ready to solve the mental and spiritual problems that are waiting for solution, and to this end physical health and exercise make a splendid contribution.

We give a few testimonials from educators as to the value of daily work in the school program, for the physical, mental, and spiritual development of the student:

" Devotion of the physical powers to amusement is not most favorable to a well balanced mind. . . . The discipline for practical life that is gained by physical labor combined with mental taxation, is sweetened by the reflection that it is qualifying mind and body better to perform the work that God designs men to do. The more perfectly the youth understand how to perform the duties of practical life, the greater will be their enjoyment day by day in being of use to others. The mind educated to enjoy useful labor becomes enlarged; through training and discipline it is fitted for usefulness; for it has acquired the knowledge essential to make its possessor a blessing to others." [5]

" No man can have either high intellectual action or definite control over his mental faculties without regular physical exercise. The want of it produces also a feebleness of will which is as fatal to moral attainment as it is to intellectual progress."—PRESIDENT WAYLAND, Brown University.

" I believe exercise to be indispensable to bodily health, and that all the operations of the mind are invigorated by health. I believe it equally promotive of moral feeling. All the benevolent impulses of the heart are quickened."—HON. JOHN QUINCY ADAMS, Mass.

Modern Manual Training Movement

The first organization to promote manual training in the United States was " The Society for Promoting Manual Labor in Literary Institutions " formed in July, 1831. Mr. Theodore D. Weld was appointed General Agent of the society and spent a year visiting "most of the large towns and leading literary institutions in the states of Ohio, Indiana, Illinois, Missouri, Kentucky, Tennessee, and Alabama,

[5] White, *Counsels to Teachers*, pp. 308, 309.

prosecuting his inquiries and calling public attention to the Manual Labor System." A report of the year's work appeared in the *American Journal of Education*, 1832.

Mr. Weld prefaces his report by saying:

" It is now a year since I accepted your appointment, and entered upon the discharge of my duties as General Agent of the Society for Promoting Manual Labor in Literary Institutions.

" In compliance with your instructions, institutions of learning have been visited; literary men in various parts of the country have been conferred with in person, and very extensively by correspondence; a great variety of details and practical results, together with a mass of testimony from the personal observation and experience of many eminent men, both literary and medical, has been collected. . . . In prosecuting the business of my agency I have traveled 4,575 miles; public conveyances, 2,630; on horseback, 1,800; on foot, 145. I have made 236 public addresses. Of these 110 were upon the subject of manual labor education, 99 upon temperance, and the remainder upon general education and other topics of public interest.''

This report includes a study of manual labor from the standpoint of the physical, mental and moral development of the student as he carries on his daily school program. The comparative values of useful labor, gymnastics, and athletics are clearly indicated.

In closing his report Mr. Weld says:

" The experience of a year has convinced me that the agency to which I was called by your appointment furnishes a field of usefulness as wide as human interests. Nothing could persuade me to leave it but the most settled conviction to duty. My heart cleaves to the manual labor system; and though I can no longer publicly advocate it as the agent of your society, I hope soon to plead its cause in the humbler sphere of personal example, while pursuing my professional studies in a rising institution at the West in which manual labor is a *daily requisition*.

" I now resign into your hands the commission under which I have acted. May He whose aid we invoked together at the commencement of our undertaking, and whose presence has sustained us in its toils and its perils, deign to bless abundantly our mutual labors.''

Luther, Zwingli, Comenius, Locke, Rousseau, Pestalozzi, Froebel, and other reformers and educators were all advocates of industrial education. Manual training as an educational feature was introduced into Finland in 1858; into Russia in 1868; into Sweden in 1870; into France in 1882; and into the schools of the United States, as a part of the common school system, in 1886. A few private technical schools were established, or departments organized in advanced institutions of learning, before this time. The first school was established in Worcester, Mass., in 1868, for students learning mechanical engineering. In 1870 the University of Illinois provided shops for teaching architecture and engineering. The Stevens Institute at Hoboken, N. J., started a similar program in 1871; and Washington University, at St. Louis, in 1872.

Principles and Practice

1. Parents should educate their children during early life to perform such duties in the home as their years and strength will allow.

2. When children are old enough to go to school, manual training should be a regular feature of their daily program. Play, work, and study should be so correlated as to insure the greatest advancement physically, mentally, and spiritually.

3. The advanced schools should provide for the youth opportunities to learn some useful trade, and this will be in part a substitute for the childhood play in the elementary schools. Physical culture exercises, preferably in the open air, will develop strength and grace of body, and the occasional recreation period will serve to break the routine of the daily program, and result in renewed vigor of body and spirit for continued effort to achieve the best and highest that the school can afford.

4. Provision should be made for instruction in agriculture, mechanical trades, manufactures, household economics, and the treatment of simple diseases.

5. The provision for capable, experienced instructors in these branches, and industrial facilities in the way of shops and tools, should be as complete as for literary and laboratory instruction.

6. Labor with the hand will be deemed as noble and honorable as that of the head and heart, for it has been dignified and glorified by the Master Mechanic of Nazareth in the learning of the carpenter's trade.

7. The one great aim of the student will be to become a " workman that needeth not to be ashamed," and one " meet for the Master's use."

Educational Literature

There is an abundance of literature on physical and industrial education, including textbooks and manuals for guidance in both shop and field work. Along with these the student should study the biographies of men and women that have been successful industrialists and household economists, who have conducted their enterprises in harmony with Biblical principles and standards.

XV

HISTORY AND PROPHECY

Man's Rule and Dominion

IN the study of the Holy Scriptures we find what God has said; in science what God has made, and in the study of physical and industrial training we learn of man's powers and ability to rule in the dominion given to him by his Creator (Gen. 1: 26–28). The psalmist David beautifully pictures man ruling in his dominion.

" What is man, that thou art mindful of him? and the son of man, that thou visitest him? For thou hast made him a little lower than the angels, and hast crowned him with glory and honor. Thou madest him to have dominion over the works of thy hands; thou hast put all things under his feet: all sheep and oxen, yea, and the beasts of the field: The fowl of the air, and the fish of the sea, and whatsoever passeth through the paths of the sea " (Ps. 8: 4–8).

Man lost his dominion and power to rule, and for nearly six thousand years has lived under the rule of the usurper—Satan. The record of man's living during these millenniums under the rule of another is history. The Creator of man has allowed Satan to carry out his plans of government which he claimed to be superior to that given to Adam. A true inspired history of this world under the rule of Satan is recorded in the Bible.

The Bible an Inspired World History

Concerning the Bible as the greatest of all books of history, a modern writer says:

" The Bible is the most ancient and the most comprehensive history that men possess. It came fresh from the fountain of eternal truth, and throughout the ages a divine hand has preserved its purity. It lights up the far-distant past, where human research in vain seeks to penetrate. In God's Word only do we behold the power that laid the foundations of the earth, and that stretched out the heavens. Here only do we find an authentic account of the origin of nations. Here only is given a history of our race unsullied by human pride or prejudice." [1]

The Bible is made up largely of biography, history, and prophecy. Biography is the record of individuals; history the record of nations; prophecy the record of individuals and nations written or spoken before the events transpire. The superior value of Bible biography, history and prophecy lies in its absolute truthfulness and reliability. The educational value of Bible biography is thus clearly set forth:

[1] White, *Education*, p. 173.

" As an educator no part of the Bible is of greater value than are its biographies. These biographies differ from all others in that they are absolutely true to life. It is impossible for any finite mind to interpret rightly, in all things, the workings of another. None but He who reads the heart, who discerns the secret springs of motive and action, can with absolute truth delineate character, or give a faithful picture of a human life. In God's Word alone is found such delineation.'' [2]

The children of the Hebrews early in life became acquainted with the fascinating stories of the lives of their illustrious and renowned ancestors, and soon learned of the deceitfulness of sin, and that " whatsoever a man soweth, that shall he also reap."

" This is why God has given so many examples showing the results of even one wrong act. From the sad story of that one sin which ' brought death into the world, and all our woe, with loss of Eden,' to the record of him who for thirty pieces of silver sold the Lord of glory, Bible biography abounds in these examples set up as beacons of warning at the byways leading from the path of life.'' [3]

Sacred History in the Schools of the Prophets

Sacred history was one of the chief subjects taught in the schools of the prophets. God by His Spirit moved some of the prophets to write the history of the reigns of several of the kings of Israel. The history of wicked kings, as well as that of good kings, was written, and the youth in studying these records learned that God is no respecter of persons; that " in every nation he that feareth him, and worketh righteousness, is accepted with him."

By reading the writings of Isaiah, Jeremiah, and other Bible prophets, we learn that they prophesied not only concerning Israel, but also of Assyria, Babylon, Egypt, and other nations. God was dealing with these nations and giving them messages of warning and reproof, pronouncing judgment upon those whose cup of iniquity was already full.

The students of the schools of the prophets must have studied these messages with intense interest, and watched eagerly the unfolding of events which fulfilled these prophecies. Not only present and future events were matters of supreme interest, but God's past dealings with kings and nations in their relation to His chosen people, formed a considerable part of the course of study in sacred history. The central thread of thought in all such study is expressed in the words: " The Most High ruleth in the kingdom of men, and giveth it to whomsoever he will " (Dan. 4: 32).

We have no secular or profane history reaching back to the times of the schools of the prophets, established by either Samuel or Elijah, and our only source of knowledge is the history in the Bible. Does the Bible give us any light on the existence of sacred historical books in the days of Samuel, David, Solomon, and Elijah? It does. Following we

[2] *Ibid.*, p. 146.
[3] *Ibid.*, p. 150.

give the information contained in the Bible regarding these sacred history books, with the names of the authors, and the subject matter dealt with in each volume:

Sacred History Books.

Volume I, " Book of the Wars of the Lord." This book contained a record of the wars fought by Israel during their sojourn in the wilderness. The first mention of this book is found in Exodus 17: 14. Moses was asked to preserve a knowledge of the victory gained by Israel over the Amalekites, by writing it " for a memorial in a book." The name of this book is given in Numbers 21: 14. Here it is declared that " the book of the wars of the Lord " contains a record of " what he (God) did in the Red Sea, and in the brooks of Arnon, and at the stream of the brooks that goeth down to the dwelling of Ar, and lieth upon the border of Moab." This sacred history volume begins with the victory of the Israelites over the Egyptians at the Red Sea, and probably contains a record of all the battles fought until Israel passed over Jordan into the Promised Land—a record of forty years of war.

Volume II, " The Book of Jasher." After Israel had entered the land of Canaan, they went to war against the Amorites. As the day was not long enough to destroy their enemies completely, Joshua, desiring more time, prayed to the Lord, and " said in the sight of Israel, Sun, stand thou still upon Gibeon; and thou, Moon, in the valley of Ajalon. And the sun stood still, and the moon stayed, until the people had avenged themselves upon their enemies. Is not this written in the book of Jasher? " (Joshua 10: 12, 13).

Just what this book contained is not fully known, but, like " the book of the wars of the Lord," it contains a record of some of the battles of Israel with surrounding nations. This " book of Jasher " is referred to as containing information concerning the use of the bow in battle; and in David's lamentations over Saul and Jonathan, mention is made of the children of Judah being taught the use of the bow according to the record contained in " the book of Jasher " (II Sam. 1: 18).

The next three books of the sacred history library treated of the life and times of David: Volume III was written by Samuel the seer. Volume IV by Nathan the prophet. Volume V by Gad the seer.

These three writers were closely associated with David from early boyhood to the end of his reign, and their counsel and advice were eagerly sought by him in administering the affairs of the kingdom. These were comprehensive volumes; for they covered David's early life, as well as the forty years of his reign and might. They treated also not only of the " times that went over . . . Israel " during the forty years of conquest and subjection of the enemies of Israel, but also of the " times that went over . . . all the kingdoms of the countries " (I Chron. 29: 26–30).

Volumes VI, VII, and VIII, " The Book of the Acts of Solomon." These volumes contain a record of " the acts of Solomon, and all that he

did, and his wisdom," covering a period of at least forty years (I Kings
11: 41–43). This history of the acts of Solomon is said to have been
written by three men, as was also the life and times of David. Each
wrote a separate book, so we have three volumes to add to the sacred
history library (II Chron. 9: 29). Volume VI was written by Nathan
the prophet. Volume VII was written by the prophet Ahijah, the
Shilonite. Volume VIII was written by Iddo the seer.

Nathan the prophet assisted in writing the history of both David
and Solomon. These prophet-historians undoubtedly wrote by inspiration. The six volumes covering the life-work of Israel's two greatest
kings, a period of eighty years, must have been filled with very interesting and important matter for the consideration of the sacred history
students in the schools of the prophets. The Scriptures do not speak of
any history written by a prophet covering the life and reign of Saul.
Undoubtedly a daily record of historical events was kept in the royal
courts, as is so often referred to by the expressions, "the book of the
chronicles of the kings of Israel," "the book of the kings of Israel and
Judah." But in addition to the records kept in the royal courts by
especially appointed secretaries, the Lord in wisdom moved upon certain
of the prophets to write the life history and reign of a few of the good
kings, and also of a few of the bad kings, that their lives might be
studied and pondered by the youth in Israel.

The life and reign of Rehoboam, son of Solomon, was written in "the
book of the chronicles of the kings of Judah" (I Kings 14: 29); but
the Lord had His life and reign also written by two of His prophets,
thus adding two more volumes to the sacred history library (II Chron.
12: 15).

Volume IX was written by Shemaiah the prophet. Volume X
was written by Iddo the seer. The latter volume contained genealogical
records which the Lord desired to have preserved for future use.

On the death of Rehoboam, Abijah his son took the throne; after his
death, another volume was added to the sacred history library. Volume
XI was written by Iddo the seer, and contained a record of "the acts of
Abijah, and his ways, and his sayings" (II Chron. 13: 22). This same
prophet wrote Volume VIII on the life of Solomon, and Volume X on
the life of Rehoboam.

Volume XII was written by Jehu, the son of Hanani, and covers the
life and reign of Jehoshaphat (II Chron. 20: 34). Jehu was a prophet
of the Lord, and reproved Jehoshaphat for joining Ahab in war against
the Syrians (II Chron. 19: 2). Several kings succeeded Jehoshaphat, of
whose reigns no special books were written. All the books written by
prophets pertained to the kings of Judah; only the records in the royal
courts were written concerning the kings of Israel.

Volume XIII covered Uzziah's reign, a period of fifty years (II
Chron. 26: 22). It was written by the prophet Isaiah, the author of the
Old Testament book bearing his name. Many important lessons were
undoubtedly drawn from the life of Uzziah, who was blessed and pros-

pered, but whose heart in his prosperity "was lifted up to his destruction."

Volume XIV was also written by the prophet Isaiah, and covered the twenty-nine years of the reign of Hezekiah. This volume contained a complete record of his kind and benevolent administration, and the prosperity that attended his reign (II Chron. 32: 32, 33). When Hezekiah died, he was greatly honored, and given the chiefest of the sepulchers as a burying place. A full and complete history of his reign was also recorded in "the book of the kings of Judah and Israel."

In addition to the sacred history library of fourteen volumes, "the book of the chronicles of the kings of Judah" and "the book of the chronicles of the kings of Israel" contained valuable material. In extent these writings really embrace many volumes, because they comprehend all the records made in the royal courts regarding the reigns of all the kings of both Judah and Israel. Undoubtedly these records were available to the prophets who taught in the schools of the prophets.

In these royal court volumes were recorded many of the religious as well as secular acts of the kings. With reference to the historical record of King Manasseh, son of Hezekiah, we read:

'' Now the rest of the acts of Manasseh, and his prayer unto his God, and the words of the seers that spake to him in the name of the Lord God of Israel, behold they are written in the book of the kings of Israel. His prayer also, and how God was intreated of him, and all his sins, and his trespass, and the places wherein he built high places, and set up groves and graven images, before he was humbled; behold, they are written among the sayings of the seers '' (II Chron. 33: 18, 19).

Surely from the Bible we glean abundant evidence of a thorough, complete course of instruction in sacred history as taught in the schools of the prophets. The fourteen volumes written by the prophets were sufficient for the pupils to gain broad, comprehensive views of "the times that went . . . over Israel, and over all the kingdoms of the countries" (I Chron. 29: 30).

The Sacred History Library

Vol. I, "Book of the Wars of the Lord," by Moses (Ex. 17: 14; Num. 21: 14).

Vol. II, "Book of Jasher," by Joshua (Josh. 10: 12, 13).

Vol. III, "Life and Reign of David," by Samuel the seer (I Chron. 29: 29).

Vol. IV, "Life and Reign of David," by Nathan the prophet.

Vol. V, "Life and Reign of David," by Gad the seer.

Vol. VI, "Life and Reign of Solomon," by Nathan the prophet (I Kings 11: 41–43; II Chron. 9: 29).

Vol. VII, "Life and Reign of Solomon," by Ahijah the prophet.

Vol. VIII, "Life and Reign of Solomon," by Iddo the seer.

Vol. IX, "Life and Reign of Rehoboam," by Shemaiah the prophet (II Chron. 12: 15).

Vol. X, "Life and Reign of Rehoboam," by Iddo the seer.

Vol. XI, "Life and Reign of Abijah," by Iddo the seer (II Chron. 13: 22).

Vol. XII, "Life and Reign of Jehoshaphat," by Jehu the prophet (II Chron. 20: 34).

Vol. XIII, "Life and Reign of Uzziah," by Isaiah the prophet (II Chron. 26: 22).

Vol. XIV, "Life and Reign of Hezekiah," by Isaiah the prophet (II Chron. 32: 32, 33).

A modern writer in speaking of the study of history in the school of the prophets says:

"There is a study of history that is not to be condemned. Sacred history was one of the studies in the schools of the prophets. In the record of His dealings with the nations were traced the footsteps of Jehovah. So today we are to consider the dealings of God with the nations of the earth. We are to see in history the fulfillment of prophecy, to study the workings of Providence in the great reformatory movements, and to understand the progress of events in the marshaling of the nations for the final conflict of the great controversy.

"Such study will give broad, comprehensive views of life. It will help us to understand something of its relations and dependencies, how wonderfully we are bound together in the great brotherhood of society and nations, and to how great an extent the oppression and degradation of one member means loss to all." [4]

The writer of the foregoing briefly contrasts the right and wrong methods of history study in the following words:

"History, as commonly studied, is concerned with man's achievements, his victories in battle, his success in attaining power and greatness. God's agency in the affairs of men is lost sight of. Few study the working out of His purpose in the rise and fall of nations."

The Bible More than a Human Book of History

Mr. Lamb, in his book, *The Making of a Man*, clearly and strikingly shows the more than human character of the Bible as a book of the world's history:

"The Bible contains the only complete compendium of this world's history. While not professedly a world's history, yet it does three things for history that would be impossible for any merely human book to do:

"1. It tells us how human history began. It gives us the origin of all things pertaining to this world—the origin of man, of nations, of sin and death, the beginnings of human history before there was any one to write history. This is the claim so ingeniously and vigorously made by Wisdom herself as personified in Proverbs 8: 22-32. . . .

"Our conclusions about 'first things' are all guesswork. We were none of us there to see the origin of this world and how human history began. God was there, and He therefore knows all about the beginnings

[4] White, *Counsels to Teachers,* pp. 379, 380.

of things, and whatever He has chosen to reveal to us in His Word is personal information, and therefore exact and reliable information,—God's wisdom about ' first things.' We may not clearly understand His statements; but we will not venture to contradict them.

" 2. The Bible in the same way is the only authority as to the end of human history. Man can only write about the past and the present. All is guesswork and uncertainty after today. But God can see into the future, the end from the beginning. Future history is as plain to Him as past history; and in the Bible we find a very complete presentation of the future of our race, an outline of the world's history until time shall be no more; and even then a wonderfully comprehensive, though brief, outline of man's eternal destiny, his relation to God's vast plans for the mighty universe; all that is necessary for us to know of the future life to furnish a basis for wise conclusions as to the true purpose of life here, as well as the highest possible inspiration and motive to attain such purpose.

" 3. And while the Bible thus reveals two things that it is impossible for human historians to know, the beginning and the end of human history, it accomplishes another purpose that is equally out of the reach of uninspired writers of history. *It traces God's hand in history.* It reveals a divine chain that links together all the important events that have transpired during the past ages, making them work out one grand eternal purpose, whose finale shall be the redemption of this ruined world from the thraldom and dominion of sin."[5]

The Bible Reveals Leading Facts of History

Quoting again from Mr. Lamb we are assured that the Bible reveals the central, crucial, pivotal facts of history:

" It (the Bible) reveals the central, crucial facts of all past history, the selection of the Jewish nation and their strange history, their relations to the surrounding nations, involving all the great nations of antiquity; the gradual preparation of the world through this chosen people for the advent of the world's Messiah and Deliverer, the record of whose life and death is not only the central fact in this world's history, but the most important event in the history of God's entire universe.

" All the great pivotal facts, in the estimation of God, so far as individuals or nations have had to do with the carrying out of His great plans for the universe, are given us in the Bible.

" For instance, the most noted men of antiquity, the men who made this world's history what it is, are largely Bible characters, and fill their conspicuous places because God raised them up and used them as a skilful player manipulates his chessmen. Not only the persons who have wrought with God, and therefore been the most successful, such as Abraham and Moses and David and Solomon and Isaiah and Daniel and Peter and Paul, but the men whom God has raised up without their knowledge and consent, and used mightily in the furtherance of His deep-laid plans, such as Pharaoh, Nebuchadnezzar, Cyrus, Alexander the Great, and the leaders of Roman history. . . .

" The Bible is God's history of this world so far as this world is related to His vast universe, so that the one who has mastered Bible

[5] F. T. Lamb, *The Making of a Man*, pp. 50–53.

history is able to view all history from God's standpoint, to get right in at headquarters, to study all important history at its base, and therefore become a wiser historian than by any other means.''[6]

The Spade Confirms Bible History

Often when Bible history has been doubted, the pick and spade have affirmed its truthfulness. Confidence in the findings of these tools of the archeologist and their witness to the veracity of Biblical history has frequently been expressed. A few of these testimonies follow:

" I believe in the spade. It has fed the tribes of mankind. It has furnished them with water, coal, iron and gold. And now it is giving them truth,—historic truth—the mines of which have never been opened till our time.''—OLIVER WENDELL HOLMES.

" Every find of the archeologist in Bible lands has gone to confirm Scripture, and confound its enemies. The stone has cried out of the wall to witness to the truth of Scripture, and to the false character of the critical attacks. Not since Christ ascended back to heaven have there been so many scientific proofs that God's Word is truth.''
—J. W. NEWTON, in *Christian Faith and Life*.

" It is a striking fact that the Bible stands in contrast to all other sacred books of the religious world in being rooted and grounded in actual history. As Dr. William T. Ellis has shown, it is pre-eminently a ' place book.' That is, its geography is definite and accurate, and as knowledge of ancient lands and ancient history increases through the discoveries of archeology, the Bible is seen to be a true record at every point.''
—ROBERT C. McQUILKIN, *The Sunday School Times*.

" Archeological research in Palestine and neighboring lands, during the past century, has completely transformed our knowledge of the historical and literary background of the Bible. . . . The excessive skepticism shown toward the Bible by important schools of the eighteenth and nineteenth centuries, certain phases of which will appear periodically, has been progressively discredited. Discovery after discovery has established the accuracy of innumerable details, and brought increased recognition of the value of the Bible as a source of history.''
—WILLIAM FOXWELL ALBRIGHT.

Hooper, in speaking of the distinct and valuable aid rendered by the archeologist, says:

" The archeologist is in a position of peculiar advantage. The spade and the pick are indiscriminate instruments of exposure; they are no respecter of persons. They bring to light of day writings and records of domestic and national life of former ages, and present them for the keenest scrutiny. In the past, men lived; kings reigned; houses were built; letters were written; records were kept; battles were fought; utensils for domestic, industrial, agricultural and military use were manufactured. They bear silent and unimpeachable witness either for or against the Bible. If these contradict the Bible record, we may be

[6] *Ibid.*, pp. 53–55.

fully assured that there will be no delay in having them brought on to the witness stand to bear testimony against the Bible. Though there has been a century of more or less active search, there has not been a single instance in which the Biblical record has not been consistently and in many instances strikingly and even dramatically sustained.''

Repeated efforts have been made and still are being made by scholars to show that Bible history is not reliable and trustworthy. As proof, the historians have denied that a nation called the '' Hittites,'' and a king named Belshazzar, both mentioned in the Old Testament Scriptures, ever existed. But the unearthing of monuments and tablet inscriptions, found in buried cities, when deciphered, plainly declare the existence of both the nation and the king. These are typical examples of the mute testimonies that are being continuallly borne that the Bible is authority in history as well as in theology.

The Philosophy of History

It is very essential that the student understand the true philosophy of history. This is well stated in the following quotation:·

'' The Bible reveals the true philosophy of history. In those words of matchless beauty and tenderness spoken by the apostle Paul to the sages of Athens, is set forth God's purpose in the creation and distribution of races and nations: He ' hath made of one blood all nations of men for to dwell on all the face of the earth, and hath determined the times before appointed, and the bounds of their habitation; that they should seek the Lord; if haply they might feel after him and find him.' ''[7]

It took Nebuchadnezzar seven years in exile to comprehend the true philosophy of history—'' that the Most High ruleth in the kingdom of men, and giveth it to whomsoever he will '' (Dan. 4: 17). He indicates his hearty acceptance of this philosophy:

'' And at the end of the days I Nebuchadnezzar lifted up mine eyes unto heaven, and mine understanding returned unto me, and I blessed the Most High, and I praised and honored him that liveth for ever, whose dominion is an everlasting dominion, and his kingdom is from generation to generation: and all the inhabitants of the earth are reputed as nothing: and he doeth according to his will in the army of heaven, and among the inhabitants of the earth; and none can stay his hand, or say unto him, What doest thou? '' (Dan. 4: 34, 35).

It is to be hoped that historians, as well as students of history, will readily and heartily accept the divine philosophy of human history as revealed in the sacred Scriptures.

The Study of Prophecy

Prophecy is history revealed in advance. To the prophets were revealed future events which had to do with individuals and with nations. With God, a thousand years are but as yesterday and as a

[7] White, *Education*, pp. 173, 174.

watch in the night (Ps. 90: 4). He knows the end from the beginning (Isa. 46: 9, 10). He mentioned by name Cyrus, a king of Persia, nearly two hundred years before his birth, and foretold the capture of Babylon, and the means employed to accomplish the seemingly impossible task. The rise of nations, their character and destiny, have been revealed through the prophets. These prophecies were studied in the Hebrew schools, and should be studied with their fulfillment in the schools of today. Fulfilled prophecy is the strongest testimony that can be produced confirming the inspiration of the Bible. The prophecies of Isaiah, Jeremiah, Ezekiel, Daniel, and of the Seer of Patmos (Book of Revelation) have been and are being fulfilled in the world events of yesterday and of today. The student of history must understand the prophecies in order to recognize their fulfillment. Human history cannot be rightly recorded nor truly understood without a knowledge of the prophetic books of the Bible. Accordingly the sacred Scriptures and secular history will be studied hand in hand. The latter is the record of human life, and the former is necessary to its right interpretation.

Methods in History

With the methods of study and teaching of history this chapter will not deal, save to hint what the Bible itself may suggest concerning method.

1. The general arrangement of Bible content is in the following order: a. Biography. b. History. c. Prophecy. d. Doctrine.

The nature and order of the material seem best suited to the growing mentality of the pupil, and would strongly suggest that the same order of arrangement be followed in developing the courses of study in history.

2. The general plan of history development should be in accordance with God's plan, unfolding through the ages, to redeem a lost world. It should not be an irregular, disconnected study of individuals, nations, and events; but beginning with man falling from his high plane of purity and innocence, trace the controversy with sin and death until man is restored, and again occupies the high and exalted position belonging to loyal subjects of the kingdom of glory. This is the plan that God followed, as recorded in Daniel 2, when He answered Nebuchadnezzar's query as to "what should come to pass hereafter." The outline of human history, as related to God's plan of unfoldment of the history of the world (Dan., chs. 2, 7, 8), was made known to Daniel through the use of beasts as symbols. These lines of prophecy close with the great controversy ended. "The kingdoms of this world are become the kingdoms of our Lord, and of his Christ" (Rev. 11: 15).

The rest of the book of Daniel is devoted to filling in the details of the great outline of human history given in Daniel, chapters 2, 7, 8.

The same general plan is followed in the book of Revelation. In

Revelation, chapters 2 and 3, the history of the true Church during the Christian dispensation is divided into seven periods of time, each reaching down to the second coming of Christ. The religious and political history of the world during the Christian dispensation is outlined under the symbols of seven seals and seven trumpets in chapters 5 to 9. The rest of the book of Revelation furnishes more detailed information of the period thrice outlined under the seven churches, seven seals, and seven trumpets.

The method God employed through the prophets to make clear to His Church the working out of His eternal purpose which He purposed in Christ Jesus, should appeal to teachers who are now called to make His eternal purpose known to their students, that they in turn may make it known to the world.

3. A history course should include a study of the dealings and providences of God with His chosen messengers and people. These were diligently studied and rehearsed, as indicated in Psalms 105 to 108.

4. Make three lists of Bible prophecies:
    (1) Fulfilled Prophecies.
    (2) Partially Fulfilled Prophecies.
    (3) Wholly Unfulfilled Prophecies.

In connection with the second list make note of events of further fulfillment; and in connection with the third list note first steps in fulfillment. In the study of history the student learns what has been and is being accomplished in the carrying out of God's plan for the redemption of the human race. In fulfilled and fulfilling prophecy the student is assured that the Most High rules in the kingdoms of men, and has full knowledge of the controversy between good and evil. This knowledge of fulfilled and fulfilling prophecy creates confidence and expectancy in the prophecies yet to be fulfilled. The student is alert and vigilant in watching the unfolding of events, and able to discern in them the signs of the times.

History Literature

History literature is abundant for textbook and reference use. Great care should be exercised in the selection of textbooks. Books that are out of harmony with Bible history ought not to be placed in the hands of immature students. The library should be provided with books written by historians who believe in the divine philosophy of history which recognizes that the Creator of the world still has His hand upon it, and will finally rescue it from the control of the usurper and the originator of all evil.

The following books are written by those who believe in the divine philosophy of history; and they are recommended as books worthy of a place in school libraries: *God's Hand in History*, 3 Vols., by C. C. J. Baron Bunsen; *The Spiritual Element in History*, by Robert Wm. McLaughlin.

XVI

THE STUDY OF LITERATURE

The Bible as Literature

AS we have seen, Hebrew education provided for a study of science and of history. While the Bible is not a treatise on science, its principles are the only safe guide in the study of science. Neither is the Bible a book on history, but it *is* history—the only authentic and absolutely reliable history that has ever been written. Equally so the Bible is not a book on literature; but it *is* literature. As literature it was one of the principal studies in the Hebrew schools. The Bible is not entirely history, but in its *entirety* it is a literary book composed of prose and poetry.

The poetical books of the Bible are five in number: Job, Psalms, Proverbs, Ecclesiastes, and the Song of Solomon. A number of poems are scattered through the remaining books of the Bible (The "Song of Moses; " the "Song of Deborah," etc.); and much of the prose is poetic in spirit, if not in form, because of the lofty and dignified themes considered, and the beautiful and striking imagery employed in giving expression to the thoughts expressed.

The first poetical expression—one of triumph—is found in Genesis 4: 23:

> " Adah and Zillah, hear my voice;
> Ye wives of Lamech, hearken unto my speech:
> For I have slain a man for wounding me,
> And a young man for bruising me.''

The Song at the Red Sea is a triumph poem, sung to celebrate the victory over Pharaoh's pursuing hosts (Ex. 15). The Song of Deborah is another triumph poem, celebrating the victory over the army of Sisera (Judges 5). Some of these poems were sung to the accompaniment of instrumental music and dancing, as when Saul and David were hailed by the women of Israel, celebrating their victories over their enemies (I Sam. 18: 5–9).

Undoubtedly " the book of the wars of the Lord " and " the book of Jasher " contained many martial poems which were sung to commemorate victories gained on the march to the Promised Land, and those also gained while subduing the inhabitants of Canaan. Other poems are mentioned; as, The Song of the Well (Num. 21: 17–20). David's Lamentation over Saul and Jonathan (II Sam. 1: 17–27). These, with many others that might be mentioned, go to show that the Hebrew literature abounded with poetry.

But in addition to the poetical fragments mentioned here, we have whole books of poetry in the Bible; one of these (Job) is believed to have been written by Moses in the land of Midian, long before the founding of the schools of the prophets. This book of poetry probably was the principal textbook of sacred poetry used in the schools of the prophets founded by Samuel and Elijah.

Other poetical books were written by two leading pupils in these schools, both of whom were kings of Israel during the period of its greatest prosperity. David wrote most of the psalms, and Solomon wrote in poetical form three thousand proverbs. A portion of these are found in the books of Proverbs and Ecclesiastes.

A Literary Master

Solomon was a man of great literary skill and ability. This literary master speaks of his painstaking efforts to produce entertaining and wholesome literature, in the following words:

" Moreover, because the preacher was wise, he still taught the people knowledge; yea, he gave good heed, and sought out, and set in order many proverbs. The preacher sought to find out acceptable words (diction): and that which was written was upright, even words of truth " (Eccl. 12: 9, 10).

Solomon then adds a few words as to the value of wise, wholesome literature: " The words of the wise are as goads, and as nails fastened by the masters of assemblies, which are given from one shepherd " (Verse 11).

The wise man offers a word of warning and caution against indiscriminate and excessive reading, of which many are guilty because of the making of " many books." He urges that all literature be measured by the unerring standard—the law of God—to determine whether it is worth our time and effort in reading; for God's law makes plain " the whole duty of man." These are his words:

" Further, by these (words of truth), my son, be admonished; of making many books there is no end; and much study (" reading," margin) is a weariness of the flesh. Let us hear the conclusion of the whole matter: Fear God, and keep his commandments, for this is the whole duty of man " (Verses 12, 13).

Another contribution from the pen of Solomon is the Song of Solomon. It is evident that the students in the schools of the prophets established by Elijah studied five poetical works: Job, Psalms, Proverbs, Ecclesiastes, and the Song of Solomon. In addition to these they studied the fragmentary poems contained in the parchment rolls of the Old Testament Scriptures, and in the historical and biographical books of the sacred history library. This abundant material provided for a thorough course in the study of sacred literature, to say nothing of the abundant material at hand for the study of the prose composition in the writings of the Hebrews.

Sacred Poetry Forms

Because the poetry of the Bible, in translation, lost largely its rhythmic and metric form, some have concluded that there were no poets among the Hebrew writers. But Hebrew poetry did not consist of a rhyming of words, but rather a rhyming of thought, which consisted of a repetition in the second line of a couplet of the thought in the first line, but expressed in different wording. This poetical form is called parallelism. It was used to give emphasis to the thought expressed.

The poems were read or sung, the readers or singers being divided into two groups. The leader of one group would recite the first line, then this would be recited by his group; the leader of the second group would recite the same thought expressed in other words in the second line, then it would be expressed by his group. The song and recitation exercise was carried on in connection with religious worship, accompanied by instrumental music. The following are a few examples of parallelism:

1. " The heavens declare the glory of God;
      And the firmament showeth his handiwork,
2. " Day unto day uttereth speech,
      And night unto night showeth knowledge " (Ps. 19).
1. " The king shall joy in thy strength, O Lord;
      And in thy salvation how greatly shall he rejoice!
2. " Thou hast given him his heart's desire,
      And hast not withholden the request of his lips.
3. " For thou preventest him with the blessings of goodness:
      Thou settest a crown of pure gold on his head " (Ps. 21).

Another poetic form found especially in the Psalms is the *strophe* and the *antistrophe,* which correspond in some degree to the stanza made up of a certain number of lines, or verses. The end of the strophe is sometimes indicated by the word " Selah." Psalm 114 will illustrate the strophe and the antistrophe.

Strophe 1:

> " When Israel went forth out of Egypt,
> The house of Jacob from a people of strange language;
> Judah became his sanctuary,
> Israel his dominion."

Strophe 2:

> " The sea saw it, and fled;
> Jordan was driven back,
> The mountains skipped like rams,
> The little hills like young sheep."

Antistrophe 2:

> " What aileth thee, O thou sea, that thou fleest?
> Thou Jordan that thou turnest back?
> Ye mountains, that ye skip like rams;
> Ye little hills, like young sheep? "

Antistrophe 1:

" Tremble, thou earth, at the presence of the Lord,
At the presence of the God of Jacob;
Which turned the rock into a pool of water,
The flint into a fountain of waters."

The strophe and the antistrophe were also recited or sung by leaders and their groups, accompanied by instrumental music, on occasions of worship, forming a very impressive religious service.

While the poetical form has largely been lost in translation, yet the spirit and power still remain. The Psalms and Proverbs seem as fresh and vigorous as if penned but yesterday. They are as applicable to life and conduct as when they were written. There are no signs of age or decay. They ring true to the experience of human life in all ages, and therefore can never grow old.

What masters of letters must those teachers in the schools of the prophets have been, who gave to the world a David and a Solomon! David was not only a ready writer, but also a ready speaker, using both the tongue and the pen with great facility. " My heart bubbleth up a good matter: . . . my tongue is the pen of a ready writer " (Ps. 45: 1, margin). A heart bubbling up with good matter was the secret of power to fulness of expression with both his pen and his tongue.

The Bible the Masterpiece of All Literature

In both prose and poetry the Bible is the masterpiece of all literature in all languages in all time. Concerning the Bible as literature the eminent Biblical scholar, Doctor Kitto, says:

" The literature of the Bible, as such, is by no means adequately appreciated in the minds of many. Owing in part to the higher claims of inspiration, its literary merits have not received generally the attention which they deserve, while the critical world, whose office it is to take cognizance of literary productions, have nearly confined their attention to works of profane authors, and left the Biblical writings to the exclusive possession of the religious public. This severance of interest is to be regretted as much for the sake of literature as of religion.

" The Bible is a book—a literary production—as well as a religious repository and charter; and ought, in consequence, to be regarded in its literary as well as its religious bearings, alike by those who cultivate literature and by those who study religion. And when men regard and contemplate it as it is, rather than as fancy or ignorance makes it, then will it be found to present the loftiest and most precious truths enshrined in the noblest language. Its poetry is one continued illustration of this fact. Indeed, but for the vicious education which the first and most influential minds in this country receive, Biblical literature would long ere now have held the rank to which it is entitled. . . .

" Nor, in our belief, can a higher service be rendered either to literature or religion than to make the literary claims of the Bible understood at the same time that its religious worth is duly and impressively set forth. The union of literature and religion is found in the Bible, and has, therefore, a divine origin and sanction. Those who love the Bible as a source of religious truth should manifest their regard both toward the book and toward Him whose name and impress it bears, by carefully preserving that union, and causing its nature, requirements, and applications to be generally understood. No better instrument can be chosen for this purpose than its rich, varied, and lofty poetry.

" In one sense the Bible is full of poetry; for very much of its contents which is merely prosaic in form rises by force of the noble sentiments which it enunciates, and the striking or splendid imagery with which these sentiments are adorned, into the sphere of real poetry." [1]

Concerning the unrivaled literary power and beauty of the Bible, a more recent writer says:

" In its wide range of style and subjects, the Bible has something to interest every mind and appeal to every heart. . . . It contains philosophy the most profound, poetry the sweetest and the most sublime, the most impassioned and the most pathetic. Immeasurably superior in value to the productions of any human author are the Bible writings, even when thus considered." [2]

" There is poetry which has called forth the wonder and admiration of the world. In glowing beauty, in sublime and solemn majesty, in touching pathos, it is unequaled by the most brilliant productions of human genius. There is sound logic and impassioned eloquence. There are portrayed the noble deeds of noble men, examples of private virtue and public honor, lessons of piety and purity." [3]

Testimonies of Scholars

The following scholars give their testimony as to the literary primacy of the Bible:

" The Scriptures contain more sublimity, more exquisite beauty, and finer strains of poetry and eloquence than could be collected from all other books that were ever composed in any age or any idiom."
—SIR WILLIAM JONES.

" The Bible, thoroughly known, is a literature of itself, the rarest and the richest in all departments of thought or imagination which exists."
—JAMES ANTHONY FROUDE.

" It is the grandest group of writings in the world, put into the grandest languages of the world, translated afterwards into every language in the Christian world, and is the guide of all the arts and acts of that world which have been noble, fortunate, and happy."—RUSKIN.

" There are no songs to be compared with the songs of Zion, no orations equal to those of the prophets, and no politics equal to that the Scripture can teach us."—JOHN MILTON.

Speaking of the Authorized Version, Huxley wrote: " It is written in the noblest and purest English, and abounds in exquisite beauties of a merely literary form."

[1] Kitto's *Cyclopedia of Biblical Literature*, art. " Poetry."
[2] White, *Education*, p. 125.
[3] White, *Counsels to Teachers*, p. 429.

Macaulay, referring to the same translation, calls it: " That stupendous work, a book, which, if everything else in our language should perish, would alone suffice to show the whole extent of its beauty and power. . . . Whoever would acquire a knowledge of pure English must study the King James Version of the Scriptures."

Green, the English historian, gave this testimony: " As a mere literary monument, the English version of the Bible remains the noblest example of the English tongue. Its perpetual use made it from the instant of its appearance the standard of our language."

The following testimonies are given with reference to the literary value of different books or chapters of the Bible:

" After perusing the book of Psalms, let a judge of the beauties of poetry read a literal translation of Homer or Pindar, and he will find in these last two such an absurdity and confusion of style, with such a comparative poverty of imagination, as will make him sensible of the vast superiority of the Scripture style."—JOHN ADDISON.

" When the philosophies of Aristotle and Plato are no longer read, the psalms of David will still be joyously sung."—RABBI LEVY.

James Anthony Froude, speaking of the book of Job, says: " An extraordinary book, a book of which it is to say little to call it unequaled of its kind, and which will one day, perhaps when it is allowed to stand on its own merits, be seen towering up alone, far away above all the poetry of the world."

Prof. Francis Bowen said of the eighteenth psalm: " Indeed I know not anything in all Greek, Latin, or English poetry, that matches in sublimity and grandeur the magnificent sweep of this description of the providence of God as manifested in the phenomena of nature."

" Follow the linked logic of St. Paul, the glowing fervor of St. John, the brilliant fancy of the Hebrew poets, the majestic eloquence of Amos, Micah, and Isaiah, especially the unapproachable simplicity, directness, and profundity of Jesus, and you will have such a mental awakening as neither Homer nor Virgil, Plato nor Seneca, Goethe nor Shakespeare, Macaulay nor Emerson, can ever give."—DR. T. HAMLIN.

Concerning the vigor of the Biblical writers, Coleridge declares: " After reading Isaiah or St. Paul's epistle to the Hebrews, Homer and Vergil are disgustingly tame to me, and Milton himself is barely tolerable."

Tennyson called the Sermon on the Mount and the parables of Jesus " perfection beyond compare."

Renan called the Gospel of Luke " the most beautiful book in existence."

Coleridge said: " I think St. Paul's epistle to the Romans is the most profound work in existence." " The most gentlemanly letter ever written by the most perfect gentleman is, in my opinion, St. Paul's epistle to Philemon."

Literary Excellence of the Bible

After noting the testimonies of these many witnesses to the superior literary excellence of the Bible, it may be of interest to note a few of the elements that contribute to its charm and power. The principal elements that characterize the literature of the Sacred Scriptures are:

1. Originality. 2. Simplicity. 3. Sincerity. 4. Purity. 5. Veracity. 6. Solemnity. 7. Dignity. 8. Authority. 9. Sublimity. 10. Majesty.

The originality and simplicity of the Scriptures are thus beautifully portrayed by Kitto:

" Its originality is also a marked characteristic of Hebrew poetry. Homer had his teachers, but who taught Moses? Yet ' the divine song of Troy ' is less divine than the ode of triumph over Pharaoh. The Hebrew poetry is original in this sense, that it is self-educed and self-developed. It is an indigenous plant in Palestine.

" Connected with its originality, as in part its cause, is the fact that the Hebrew Muse stood nearer than any other to the first days and the earliest aspects of creation, ' when the morning stars sang together, and all the sons of God shouted for joy ' (Job 38: 7). Those stars that Muse saw in the maiden purity of their earliest radiance; that song the same Muse heard when first it struck the canopy of heaven and was reverberated to earth. The rose of Sharon blushed with its first loveliness on her glad sight, and the dews of Hermon were first disturbed by her unsandaled feet. Thus there is a freshness as of morn about all her imagery. In her best days there were no stock figures of speech, no *loci communes* nor universal recipes for forming poetry. Not even at second hand did she receive her stores, but she took what she had out of the great treasure house of nature, and out of the fulness of her own heart. To be a master, therefore, to other poesies is the divine right and peculiar function of the Hebrew Muse. Other bards may borrow and imitate; the poetry of the Bible copies nature and creates.

" Hence there is a spontaneousness in its poetry. Open the psalter at any place; you find streams pouring forth like the brooks and waterfalls that trickle and gush down the hills of Palestine after the latter rain. Nature you behold at work. All therefore is ease, and, as ease, so grace. There is no constraint, no effort, no affectation. The heart itself speaks, and it speaks because it is full and overflowing.

" If we add that simplicity is another marked character of Hebrew poetry, we do little more than state that which is already implied. But such is its simplicity that it seems never to have known, in its age of purity, anything of the artificial distinctions by which critics and rhetoricians have mapped out the domain of poetry, and endeavored to supply the deficiencies of fancy by the laborious efforts of varied culture. Hebrew poetry was the voice of man communing with God. . . . It was, indeed, wholly unconscious of anything but the satisfaction of a high and urgent want, which made worship a necessity and devotion a delight.'' [4]

The Influence of Hebrew Poetry

Kitto then makes the following statement regarding the influence of Hebrew poetry on the modern world:

" It is in the main owing to the religious and devotional qualities of Hebrew poetry that the book of Psalms still, after the lapse of so many

[4] Kitto's *Cyclopedia of Biblical Literature*, art. "Poetry."

centuries, and the rise and fall of so many modes of thought and forms of social life, holds an empire over the heart of man, far wider, deeper, and more influential than what any other influence has possessed, save only that which is and will ever be exercised by ' David's Greater Son.'

" Nor is the wonder at all diminished when we learn that the Hebrew was an essentially national muse. There is no poetry which bears a deeper or broader stamp of the peculiar influences under which it was produced. It never ceases to be Hebrew. . . . The country, the clime, the institutions, the very peculiar religious institutions, rites, and observances, the very singular religious history of the Israelites, are all faithfully and vividly reflected in the Hebrew muse, so that no one song can ever be mistaken for a poem of any other people. Still it remains true that the heart of man, at least the heart of all the most civilized nations of the earth has been moved and swayed, and is still pleasingly and most beneficially moved and swayed by the strains of Biblical poesy. Others may, but we cannot account for this indubitable fact, without admitting that some especially divine influence was in operation amidst the Jews." [5]

Not only has the Bible directly influenced mankind, but many authors have consciously or unconsciously allowed it to permeate their writings, and the value of their works is accurately measured by their knowledge of the Scriptures. Dr. Eckman, in his book, *The Literary Primacy of the Bible*, after giving a long list of authors whose writings contain Scriptural quotations or allusions, says:

" A careful student of Tennyson has asserted that there are nearly three hundred direct references to the Bible in his poems. By actual count upwards of three hundred thirty references to the Bible have been found in works of Longfellow. An industrious man has reckoned that about five thousand Scripture quotations and allusions are to be found in the writings of Ruskin, who says that to the discipline of his early years in the Bible he owes ' the best part of my taste in literature, and once knowing the Bible, it was not possible for me to write superficial and formal English.' . . . Numerous writers, who seldom quote or make direct allusions to the Scriptures, obviously have been greatly affected by them. Of such is Thomas Carlyle, who, in many passages, writes like a Hebrew prophet, showing unmistakable evidences of deep study of the Bible." [6]

The Bible and the Journalist

All the scholars referred to above, and a host of others—whether writers or speakers, scientists or historians, jurists or philosophers— are unanimous in giving the Bible the highest place of honor in the field of literature. Charles A. Dana, one of America's greatest journalists, said:

" Of all books, the most indispensable and the most useful, the one whose knowledge is the most effective, is the Bible. . . . I am considering it now, not as a religious book, but as a manual of utility of professional

---

[5] *Ibid.*

[6] G. P. Eckman, *The Literary Primacy of the Bible*, pp. 38, 39. (Methodist Book Concern, New York.)

preparation and professional use for a journalist. There is perhaps no book whose style is more suggestive and more instructive, from which you learn more directly that sublime simplicity which never exaggerates, which recounts the greatest events with solemnity, of course, but without sentimentality or affectation, none which you open with such confidence and lay down with such reverence.''

It is reassuring to know that what Journalist Dana has expressed in theory has been worked out by Dr. Charles Sears Baldwin, while assistant professor of rhetoric in Yale University, in his book, *How to Write, a Handbook Based on the English Bible*. In the preface the purpose of the author is thus stated:

'' The importance of the English Bible as a model of style has been often felt, often expressed, but never, apparently, realized in systematic, practical application. Thus to apply it to the practical end of learning to write, cannot obscure or belittle its importance for other ends. Rather, the one should help the other, as in the study of the Old Testament by the writers of the New. But all that this book presumes to teach from the Bible is how to write.''

The peer of prose writers, John Ruskin, tells how, when a boy, his mother daily drilled him in reading or reciting the Scriptures, and that this program was continued until he went to Oxford. He prints the list of chapters which his mother required him to commit to memory, and " with which," he says, " thus learned, she established my soul in life." Then follows his evaluation of that early and subsequent education:

'' And truly, though I have picked up the elements of a little further knowledge—in mathematics, meteorology, and the like, in after-life—and owe not a little to the teaching of many people, this maternal installation of my mind in that property of chapters, I count very confidently the most precious, and on the whole the one essential part of all my education.''

The Bible and the Orator

Splendid examples of oratory and eloquence are found throughout the Bible. The orations of Moses contained in Deuteronomy are the first recorded orations. They are saturated with simplicity, sincerity, solemnity, dignity, authority, sublimity, and other elements contributing to the charm and power of oratory. Other examples are found in the writings of the prophets—the most notable being the orations of Isaiah, Amos, and Micah. The " Sermon on the Mount," Paul's defense before King Agrippa, and the rapturous revelations of the " Seer of Patmos" are striking examples of oratory found in the New Testament.

In modern times the orator as well as the writer acknowledges his great indebtedness to the Bible. Daniel Webster said:

'' If there is anything in my style or thoughts to be commended, the credit is due to my kind parents for instilling into my mind an early love for the Scriptures.''

It is authoritatively stated that Daniel Webster did not think himself prepared to appear before Congress to deliver his orations, "until he had taken as a tonic the eighth psalm and the fortieth chapter of Isaiah."

Edmund Burke, the greatest philosophical statesman of England, made a habit of reading a chapter in Isaiah before going to speak in the House of Commons; "for," said he, "Isaiah possesses both the blaze of eloquence and the light of truth."

The Bible the Standard in Literature

When one becomes thoroughly conversant with the literature of the Bible, he is prepared to evaluate properly all literature, outside of the Bible, for it is the standard. His powers of discrimination will be so keenly developed that he will readily discern between profitable and unprofitable literature.

We have seen that the Bible as a literary book has been the greatest factor in developing the latent powers of writers and speakers. That this fact is supported by their voluntary testimony ought to cause the educators of children and youth to see that the Bible has its rightful place in the courses of study in our elementary, secondary, and advanced schools.

Dr. William Lyon Phelps, while occupying the chair in English at Yale University, regarded the Bible as the best and only needed book for use in examining pupils as to their language qualifications for entrance into college. He said:

"If I were appointed a committee of one to regulate the much debated question of college examinations in English, I should erase every list of books that has thus far been tried or suggested, and I should confine the examination wholly to the Authorized Version of the Bible."

The Aims of Literary Study

Since the Bible is the greatest of all literary classics, and is the standard by which all other literary productions are to be measured, the aims in the study of the writings of human authors may be readily discovered in considering the aims that should motivate the student in the study of Biblical literature. We study the Bible theologically to gain a knowledge of its beautiful vivifying truths which minister to the spiritual life. We study it literarily that we may better understand and appreciate the beautiful sublime language forms in which these truths are couched. A casket is valued according to the jewels it contains. So language is magnified and glorified in proportion to the truths it reveals.

The first and primary aim of all literature study should be the discovery of truths that will develop and strengthen the spiritual in man. This being the primary aim, all literature study destitute of truth and spiritual building power is eliminated from the student's program.

Concerning the primary aim in literary study, Dr. Hiram Corson in his valuable book, *The Aims of Literary Study,* says:

" Literature is not a mere knowledge subject, as the word knowledge is usually understood, namely, that which the discursive, formulating intellect has to do. But it is a knowledge subject . . . which is quite outside of the domain of the intellect—a knowledge which is a matter of spiritual consciousness, and which the intellect cannot translate into a judgment. It is nevertheless, at the same time, the most distinct and vital kind of knowledge.''

Dr. Corson says that in educational practice the intellectual or secondary factor is made primary in the study of literature.

" But in the prevailing methods of literary study . . . the intellect or secondary factor has precedence—is, indeed, almost exclusively taken into account; and the consequence is, that students are shut off from the higher and more educating factor. And there is even a worse state of things than this, in many schools: the intellectual factor (which may be said to articulate the spiritual) is itself largely excluded by technical study, or by a study of details which rests within itself.

" When a teacher has himself assimilated the informing spiritual life of a work of genius, he is not likely to be disposed to taper his instruction into the merely technical, still less to keep the mind of his students occupied with details, and these, too, considered apart from the general vitality to which they may contribute. But very many of those who conduct literary studies in the schools have not themselves assimilated the informing spiritual life of the works studied.'' [7]

The intellectual phases of literature—its grammatical, rhetorical, and literary structures and forms—are strongly emphasized in textbooks, teachers' manuals, and students' language guide books. But that phase of literary education which is absolutely indispensable to the recognition and absorption of the spiritual life and power latent in an author's production is given but little attention, if not wholly neglected. Doctor Corson speaks of this neglect and emphasizes the importance of vocal expression, both on the part of the teacher and student, as an aid in recognizing and absorbing spiritual life and power in the study of a genuine literary production:

" How is the best response to the essential life of a poem to be secured by the teacher from the student? I answer, by the fullest interpretative vocal rendering of it. And by ' fullest ' I mean that the vocal rendering must exhibit not only the definite intellectual articulation or framework of the poem, through emphasis, grouping, etc., but must through intonation, varied quality of voice and other means, exhibit that which is indefinite to the intellect. *The latter is the main object of vocal rendering.* A product of the insulated intellect does not need a vocal rendering.

" On the part of the teacher two things are indispensable:

" 1. That he sympathetically assimilate what constitutes the real life of the poem, that is, its spiritual element as distinguished from the intellectual.

" 2. That he have the vocal cultivation demanded for a complete and effective rendering of what he has assimilated. . . .

" If the two indispensable conditions I have mentioned—a sympathetic

[7] H. Corson, *The Aims of Literary Study,* pp. 25–27 (Macmillan).

assimilation on the part of the teacher, and the vocal cultivation demanded for a full and effective rendition of what he has assimilated—if these indispensable conditions be not met, he has failed in his duty to his students. He may not know, and they may not know he has failed in his duty." [8]

Vocal Literary Interpretation

The highest and fullest literary interpretation of a masterpiece is through the human voice, whether it be in the field of letters or of music. The reading and speaking voice demands cultivation as well as the singing voice. Dr. Corson makes an appeal for voice and speech training in schools of all grades:

" There is no true estimate among the leaders in the educational world, of what vocal culture worthy of the name costs; and the kind of encouragement which it receives from them is in keeping with their estimate of it. Vocal culture should begin very early, the earlier the better. It should be one of the first things attended to in the primary schools, and should be continued through all grades of instruction up to and through the University. A system of vocal training might be instituted in the lower schools which would give pupils complete command of the muscles of articulation, extend the compass of the voice, and render it smooth, powerful, and melodious. A power of varied intonation should be especially cultivated, as it is through intonation that the reader's sympathies are conducted, and the hearer's sympathies are secured. Intonation is the choral atmosphere of reading.

" A systematic and scientific cultivation of the reading voice should be conducted with reference to the rendering of the masterpieces of poetical and dramatic literature, as that of the singing voice is conducted with reference to the rendering of the masterpieces of music. A boy's voice may be trained for the usual platform spouting; but such training would not serve for the rendering of Tennyson's ' In Memoriam ' for example, or for Milton's ' Paradise Lost.' " [9]

Dr. Corson might have added that what he terms " platform spouting " will not serve for the rendering of the originals of " Paradise Lost " and other masterpieces written by authors who caught their vision, and received their inspiration from their study of the sacred Scriptures. He finds in the Scriptures a characterization of good reading:

" Taken as it stands in the King James Version . . . a comprehensive characterization of good reading is found in the 8th chapter and the 8th verse of Nehemiah: ' So they read in the book in the law of God *distinctly* and *gave the sense*, and *caused them to understand the reading.*'

" To read distinctly, to give the sense, to cause to understand (in the Scripture sense), meet all the conditions of effective reading.

" 1. *To read distinctly.* ' Words,' says the Rev. Gilbert Austin, in his ' Chronomia,' ' are to be delivered from the lips as beautiful coins newly issued from the mint, deeply and accurately impressed, perfectly finished, neatly struck by the proper organs, distinct, in due succession and of due weight.' . . .

[8] *Ibid.,* pp. 99–101.
[9] *Ibid.,* pp. 107, 108.

"2. *To give the sense.* I have defined literature as the expression, in letters, of the spiritual, co-operating with the intellectual man, the former being the primary dominant coefficient. A production of the pure intellect does not belong to the domain of literature proper. . . .

"3. *Cause to understand.* The Scriptural use of 'understand' has reference, not to the discursive intellect, but to the understanding *heart* . . . to a sympathetic appropriation and assimilation of divine truth. So the meaning of 'cause to understand' is that the reader must by his intonation . . . by the vocal coloring, so to speak, which he gives to spiritualized thought, induce, in his hearers, a sympathetic response to the spiritual element."[10]

This Scripture quotation indicates that the Priests and Levites were skilled in the art of effective reading, for Nehemiah adds the words: "All the people wept when they heard the words of the law" (Neh. 8: 9).

As the highest example of effective reading Dr. Corson refers to Christ reading in the Synagogue from the book Isaiah:

"When it is said that 'the eyes of all of them that were in the synagogue were fastened on him,' it does not appear that He had yet spoken in His own person. And some of them did not know who He was. It was evidently the effect which His reading had upon them, which caused all eyes to be fastened on Him. I fancy that an impressive intonation came from the reader's own being—from the spiritual consciousness He had of the deep below deep in the meaning of what He read."[11]

Of the simplicity, attractive, and authoritative power of His speaking voice we read: "The common people heard him gladly" (Mark 12: 37). "All bare him witness and wondered at the gracious words that proceeded out of his mouth" (Luke 4: 22). "He taught them as one having authority and not as the Scribes" (Matt. 1: 29).

The Bible in the Study of Literature

The following are a few suggestions as to the study of the Bible as literature, and its relation to other literary writings:

1. An early acquaintance with the Bible following a program similar to that carried out by the mother of John Ruskin, previously referred to, which he briefly described as follows:

"My mother forced me by steady daily toil, to learn long chapters of the Bible by heart, as well as to read it every syllable through, aloud, hard names and all, from Genesis to the Apocalypse (Revelation), about once a year; and to that discipline—patient, accurate, and resolute—I owe not only a knowledge of the Book, . . . but much of my general power of taking pains and the best part of my taste in literature. . . .

"I have next with deeper gratitude to chronicle what I owed to my mother for the resolutely consistent lessons which so exercised me in the Scriptures as to make every word of them familiar to my ear in habitual

[10] *Ibid.*, pp. 120, 121, 126.
[11] *Ibid.*, p. 136.

music, yet, in that familiarity, reverenced, as transcending all thought and ordaining all conduct.

" This she effected, not by her own sayings or personal authority, but simply by compelling me to read the book thoroughly, for myself. As soon as I was able to read with fluency, she began a course of Bible work with me which never ceased till I went to Oxford. She read alternate verses with me, watching at first every intonation of my voice, and correcting the false ones, till she made me understand the verse, if within my reach, rightly and energetically. It might be beyond me altogether; that she did not care about, but she made sure that as soon as I got hold of it at all, I should get hold of it by the right end.

" In this way she began with the first verse of Genesis, and went straight through to the last verse of the Apocalypse, hard names, numbers, Levitical law, and all, and began again at Genesis the next day. If a name was hard, the better the exercise in pronunciation; if a chapter was tiresome, the better lesson in patience; if loathsome, the better lesson in faith that there was some use in its being so outspoken.

" After our chapters (from two to three a day, according to their length, the first thing after breakfast and no interruption from servants allowed,—none from visitors, who either joined in the reading or had to stay upstairs,—and none from any visitings or excursions except real traveling), I had to learn a few verses by heart, or repeat, to make sure I had not lost something of what was already known." [12]

The following chapters were committed by the young John Ruskin: Exodus 15 and 20; II Samuel 1: 17–27; I Kings 8; Psalms 23, 32, 90, 91, 103, 112, 119, 139; Proverbs 2, 3, 8, 12; Isaiah 58; Matthew 5, 6, 7; Acts 26; I Corinthians 13, 15; James 4; Revelation 4, 6.

2. Probably much of the work covered by the above program will be left undone in the majority of homes, and will have to be done in the Bible classes conducted in the eight grades of elementary schools. The biographical and much of the historical matter should be covered during the elementary school periods. Not only should the excellent moral lessons be impressed on the minds of the pupils, but attention should be frequently called to the simplicity, dignity, beauty, and sublimity of the language conveying these moral lessons. The students should frequently be given the opportunity to reproduce orally and in writing the story or incident, thus fixing the Bible vocabulary and style in their own minds.

3. The first history the child will learn is Bible history, and consequently the first literature the child should know is Bible literature. In the secondary school the student should become thoroughly acquainted with the Biblical authors, before becoming acquainted with English and American authors. Just as in history it is better first to learn of Adam, Noah, Abraham, and Joseph before learning of Columbus, Washington, Lincoln, and McKinley; so in literature it is better to learn of Moses, David, Solomon, and Isaiah before studying Milton, Addison, Ruskin, and Longfellow. All these writers have bor-

[12] Ruskin, *Praeterita*, Chapter I.

rowed much from the Bible, and can be better appreciated after one has gained an acquaintance with Biblical authors. All fields of literature should be entered through the gateway of the Bible. The student in this way will be prepared to decide intelligently what is worth while and what can be passed by as unworthy of his attention and study. The study of Biblical literature has provided him with a measuring rod by which he can correctly measure all literature outside of the Bible. " Man's words, if of any value, must echo the words of God."

4. In the advanced schools, the more difficult literature of the Bible, as the book of Job, the epistles of Paul, and the writings of the prophets, will be studied. After knowing what the Bible authors have written on the themes that lay on their hearts, indited by the Holy Spirit, the students can better judge of the merits of the productions of those who later have written on the same themes. " Paradise Lost," written by Moses, stimulated Milton to write on the same theme. He also wrote " Samson Agonistes " after reading of the Samson in the book of Judges. " The Burial of Moses," by Alexander; the " Ode to Absalom," by Willis; " The Destruction of Sennacherib," by Byron, were all first written in the Bible, and it was the Bible that gave to these authors their first thought and inspiration to write these beautiful poems.

5. No literature can be fully assimilated and truly appreciated until the student is capable of effectively reproducing it with the human voice in reading or recitation. Oral expression should be an integral part of literature study in all grades. The tongue is mightier than the pen.

6. The Bible should hold this place of pre-eminence, because it contains the most usable material, most aptly and most convincingly expressed. By writers and speakers it is quoted more largely than any other book, or many of them put together. This fact is strikingly expressed by the Hon. Albert J. Beveridge:

" The Bible is the most quotable book in all literature. You may take Shakespeare and Dante together, take Milton and Horace, put in the Koran and Confucius, and then boil them all down, and the quotable things in all of them put together are but a fraction of the sayings in the Bible that fasten themselves in your mind." [13]

Books on Literature

We give the titles of two books that will help teachers and students in their study of literature to discover and assimilate those elements that will contribute to their spiritual upbuilding and development: *The Aims of Literature of Study* and *The Voice and Spiritual Education*, by Hiram Corson.

[13] A. J. Beveridge, *The Bible as Good Reading*, p. 94.

XVII

THE STUDY OF MUSIC

The Highest Form of Expression

I N the previous chapter the literature of the ancient Hebrews, in both prose and poetic form, was considered, and the Bible was found to be the masterpiece, not only of the Hebrew language, but of all languages of all nations of all time. The literary beauty, both of form and of thought, as well as its power, is best exhibited and appreciated when the language is vocalized. The silent drinking from the fountain has refreshed many a soul, but the audible expression—the utterance by human lips—gives to the words of truth a re-enforcement which is lacking when no voice nor sound is heard. Reading and speaking are the more common modes of expression, but it is in the realm of music, both vocal and instrumental, that the grandest and sublimest thoughts take on their highest and most complete form of expression.

The same pen can write prose or poetry, both of which depends on the soul that moves the hand that holds the pen. So the same voice mechanism can read and speak, or it can sing, and these acts also depend on the soul that breathes upon the human cords.

Relation of Poetry to Music

Poetry and music are twin sisters. Prose is regarded as a younger brother, who rarely sings, and whose speech deals largely with the important affairs of daily life and the bare facts of useful knowledge. As already noted, several books of the Bible are poetical in form, and their subject matter readily lends itself to musical rendition and interpretation. Not only can the vocal mechanism be employed, but accompanying musical instruments re-enforce the voice, and make much more effective the rendition of the poem.

Music Among the Ancient Hebrews

That the musical arts occupied a prominent position in the life of that ancient people is evidenced by the numerous, though brief, references contained in the Bible. Music, musical instruments, and singing are spoken of again and again. It would seem that the ancient Hebrews employed music on all important occasions, in both domestic and national life.

There were the songs of labor which the people sang while about their work (Isa. 16: 9, 10). The music on funeral occasions was especially prepared, and rendered by those appointed to lament the death and eulogize the virtues of the departed (II Chron. 35: 25;

Jer. 9: 17–20; Amos 5: 16). The greatest occasion for music in the domestic life was at the wedding. Psalm 95 is thought to be a wedding song. The whole book of the "Song of Songs" is regarded as another wedding song. The bridal procession which marched through the streets to instrumental music and song is referred to in Jeremiah 7: 34.

Kings and the wealthy classes provided themselves with musical talent and instruments. In the national life, music played a very important part, and the women of Israel had the larger share in it. Victories in battle were celebrated with music. Miriam and her chorus of women, in response to the song of Moses, took up the refrain:

> " Sing ye to the Lord, for he hath triumphed gloriously;
> The horse and his rider hath he thrown into the sea."

The return of Saul and David, victorious over the Philistines, was welcomed by the women, who sang:

> " Saul hath slain his thousands,
> And David his ten thousands."

King Jehoshaphat was hailed victor over the Moabites and Ammonites, with psalteries, harps, and trumpets. The accession of a king to the throne was another occasion for song and music. So, when Solomon ascended the throne of his father, " all the people came up after him, and the people piped with pipes, and rejoiced with great joy " (I Kings 1: 40).

Music in the Schools of the Prophets

Israel's greatest achievement in music was in connection with religion. It was during the reigns of David and Solomon that the highest degree of perfection in musical organization was reached. At the dedicatory services of the temple the divine approval of the dedicatory song and instrumental accompaniment was shown by the glory of the Lord filling the temple.

The first mention of the schools of the prophets is where the recently anointed Saul, after leaving Samuel, met a company of the sons of the prophets coming down from the high place, with a psaltery, a tabret, a pipe, and a harp, playing, singing, and prophesying. When Saul met this company of students, the Spirit of God came upon him and he was turned into another man, and he prophesied among them (I Sam. 10: 5–10).

The schools of the prophets from time to time sent out students in companies, or bands, to instruct and help the people, and probably this was one of these missionary bands that Saul met as it was starting out on its mission of service. After gaining an experience and education that would qualify for efficient service, these youth were appointed as teachers and counselors, and went from city to city, instructing the people. This educational extension work was done during the reign of King Jehoshaphat, and its good results are spoken of in II Chronicles 17: 7-10. When Israel failed to provide these teachers and counselors, great loss and perplexity came to the nation (II Chron. 15: 1-6).

Sacred music was one of the four principal subjects taught in these schools; for it, along with a knowledge of the sacred Scriptures, sacred history, and sacred poetry, was considered indispensable as a means of uplifting and elevating the morals of the people:

" Music was made to serve a holy purpose, to lift the thoughts to that which is pure, noble, and elevating, and to awaken in the soul devotion and gratitude to God. What a contrast between the ancient custom and the uses to which music is now too often devoted! " [1]

A High Standard in Music

The high musical standard maintained in the schools of the prophets is thus clearly set forth:

" The art of sacred melody was diligently cultivated. No frivolous waltz was heard, nor flippant song that should extol man and divert the attention from God, but sacred, solemn psalms of praise to the Creator, exalting His name and recounting His wondrous works. Thus music was made to serve a holy purpose, to lift the thoughts to that which was pure and noble and elevating, and to awaken in the soul devotion and gratitude to God." [2]

The book of Psalms was the hymn book of ancient Israel. Only the words have been preserved, the music having been lost; but if the music was anything like the words, what soul-inspiring music it must have been! The psalmody of Israel has never been equaled, and is the basis of our best sacred music today.

The thoroughness and efficiency of the sacred music course is best attested to by considering one or two graduates from the course. David, whom we have already found to have been a great poet, evinced superior ability as an instrumentalist when only a young man. His reputation as a skilful, soulful player of the harp reached the royal courts, and he was secured to play in the presence of Saul when the evil spirit was upon him. The influence and power of the melodies, produced upon an instrument of ten strings, were so over-powering that the evil spirit could not remain in the presence of this master musician. Much of the playing on instruments today has the contrary effect, and invites the presence of the evil spirit.

Not only was the spiritual element of music emphasized, but also the technical; for David instructed the orchestra to " play skilfully with a loud noise " (Ps. 33: 3). But David's playing appealed to the heart, and through his instrument he could utter what words could not express. " I will open my dark sayings upon the harp " (Ps. 49: 4).

---

[1] White, *Patriarchs and Prophets,* p. 594.
[2] White, *Fundamentals of Christian Education,* p. 97.

Music in the Temple Service

David was not only a great instrumentalist, but a great vocalist—the "sweet psalmist of Israel" (II Sam. 23: 1). It was David who arranged the various orders of musicians and singers for the temple service:

> "David spake to the chief of the Levites to appoint their brethren to be the singers with instruments of music, psalteries and harps and cymbals, sounding by lifting up the voice with joy. . . . So the singers, Heman, Asaph, and Ethan, were appointed to sound with cymbals of brass: and Zechariah, and Aziel, and Shemiramoth, and Jehiel, and Unni, and Eliab, and Maaseiah, and Beniah, with psalteries on Alamoth; and Mattithiah, and Elipheleh, and Mikneiah, and Obed-edom, and Jeiel, and Azaziah, with harps on the Sheminth to excel. And Chenaniah, chief of the Levites, was for song; he instructed about the song, because he was skilful. . . . And David was clothed with a robe of fine linen, and all the Levites that bare the ark, and the singers, and Chenaniah the master of the song with the singers" (I Chron. 15: 16–27).

Speaking of the choir and orchestra composed of Levites, David says: "Four thousand praised the Lord with the instruments which I made . . . to praise therewith" (I Chron. 23: 5).

Of this number two hundred eighty-eight were leaders and instructors in music: "So the number of them, with their brethren that were instructed in the songs of the Lord, even all that were cunning, was two hundred fourscore and eight" (I Chron. 25: 7).

The Scriptures already cited plainly indicate that David placed a great deal of emphasis on music as a feature of religious worship. He made musical instruments, and played upon them skilfully. He composed words and sang them. The instrument and the voice were dedicated to God.

While David was a great musician, Solomon his son was, perhaps, even greater. He composed more than a thousand songs (I Kings 4: 32). The music rendered at the time of the dedication of the temple by Solomon has probably never been equaled. At least no choral assembly and orchestra has ever been accorded such divine recognition and honor:

> "It came even to pass, as the trumpeters and singers were as one, to make one sound to be heard in praising and thanking the Lord; and when they lifted up their voice with the trumpets and cymbals and instruments of music, and praised the Lord, saying, For he is good; for his mercy endureth forever; that then the house was filled with a cloud, even the house of the Lord; so that the priests could not stand to minister by reason of the cloud: for the glory of the Lord had filled the house of God" (II Chron. 5: 13, 14).

The Sacred Music Course

The course in sacred music in the schools of the prophets must have included a mastery of at least one instrument, and a thorough training of the voice. It also included a knowledge of musical composition for both the voice and the various musical instruments. We must conclude that the sacred music course was thorough, practical, and comprehensive. These schools must have led out in all lines of advancement, developing men into wise and intelligent leaders and educators in the nation.

One writer has said that it is the music of a nation that measures its standing in the grade of human civilization. What would our psalmody today be without the psalms of Israel's "sweet singer"? The psalms of David, without the music he set to them, are music still; and rendered with modern musical composition, they excel anything in modern psalmody.

The music of ancient Israel was not copied nor borrowed from the nations about them. It was an expression of the individual and national life of the chosen people of God. Their songs, both the words and the music, were composed to memorialize great events.

Examples of this kind are the song at the Red Sea, song of Deborah, etc. David felt so grateful for the successful transfer of the ark from the house of Obed-edom to Jerusalem that he wrote the words and music of a song, giving expression to his gratitude to God. He placed it in the hands of Asaph to be rendered by the choir and orchestra. "Then on that day David delivered first this psalm to thank the Lord into the hand of Asaph and his brethren" (I Chron. 16: 7). Several of the psalms David composed express his gratitude for personal deliverances from the hands of his enemies. (See Psalms 34, 52, 56, 59.)

One proof that the Hebrews produced a musical literature of their own, not copying or borrowing from the surrounding nations, was their refusal to sing their songs in the land of their captivity:

" By the rivers of Babylon, there we sat down, yea, we wept, when we remembered Zion. We hanged our harps upon the willows in the midst thereof. For there they that carried us away captive required of us a song; and they that wasted us required of us mirth, saying, Sing us one of the songs of Zion. How shall we sing the Lord's song in a strange land? " (Ps. 137: 1-4).

But the Lord, through the "weeping prophet," gave Israel another and the last song which they sang, even in a "strange land." This was a funeral song—the "Lamentations." Their former glory never returned, and their "swan song" proved to be the funeral dirge of what was once a mighty and glorious nation.

In learning and in piety, Israel reached greater heights than any other nation of her time; and this was largely due to the character of her schools.

The Bible Standard in Music

The Bible is full of instruction and suggestion to the saints, not only as to how they should pray, but also as to how they should praise God with instruments of music and with the voice. We find that the Bible raises a high standard which will entitle those reaching it to join the heavenly chorus. Below we give a few Bible principles relating to sacred music:

" Behold, I have seen a son of Jesse the Bethlehemite, that is *cunning* in playing " (I Sam. 16: 18).

" *Play skilfully* " (Ps. 33: 3).

" David and all Israel played before God with all their *might* " (I Chron. 13: 8).

" My lips shall greatly *rejoice* when I sing unto thee; and my *soul,* which thou hast redeemed " (Ps. 71: 23).

" Singing and making *melody* in your *heart* to the Lord " (Eph. 5: 19).

" Singing with *grace* in your hearts to the Lord " (Col. 3: 16).

" I will sing with *the spirit,* and I will sing with the *understanding* also " (I Cor. 14: 15).

" Is any *merry?* let him sing psalms "(Jas. 5: 13).

" Speaking (singing) to yourselves in psalms and hymns and spiritual songs " (Eph. 5: 19).

Thus we see that the Bible raises a high standard of musical attainment. It emphasizes the high and holy office of music, and indicates that the highest degree of skill is necessary to its fullest expression. But more important than skill is soul. The true artist in music is not only skilful, but soulful.

It is in the Bible that we learn that the marvelous works of creation were celebrated with music: " The morning stars sang together, and all the sons of God shouted for joy." (See Job 38: 1–8.)

It is in the Bible that we are told of the angelic chorus that broke to the world the good news of the wondrous birth of the Redeemer: " Suddenly there was with the angel a multitude of the heavenly host praising God, and saying (singing), Glory to God in the highest, and on earth peace, good will toward men." (See Luke 2: 9–14.)

It is the same Bible that tells us of " the song of Moses " and " the song of the Lamb," which will be sung by the redeemed as they go from world to world, to commemorate the completed work of creation and redemption:

" Great and marvelous are thy works, Lord God Almighty; just and true are thy ways, thou King of saints. Who shall not fear thee, O Lord, and glorify thy name? for thou only art holy: for all nations shall come and worship before thee; for thy judgments are made manifest " (Rev. 15: 3, 4).

In response will be sung the universal anthem of praise:

" Every creature which is in heaven, and on the earth, and under the earth, and such as are in the sea, and all that are in them heard I saying, Blessing, and honor, and glory, and power, be unto him that sitteth upon the throne, and unto the Lamb forever and ever " (Rev. 5: 13).

Educational Value of Music

A study of Bible songs and their history will be of great assistance in developing and establishing a high musical standard, and should be included in every course of study in music. A modern educator says:

" The history of the songs of the Bible is full of suggestion as to the uses and benefits of music and song. Music is often perverted to serve purposes of evil, and it thus becomes one of the most alluring agencies of temptation. But, rightly employed, it is a precious gift of God, designed to uplift the thoughts to high and noble themes, to inspire and elevate the soul. . . .

" The value of song as a means of education should never be lost sight of. Let there be singing in the home, of songs that are sweet and pure, and there will be fewer words of censure, and more of cheerfulness and hope and joy. Let there be singing in the school and the pupils will be drawn closer to God, to their teachers, and to one another.'' [3]

Music Principles and Practice

From the study of the Bible we may glean the following principles and practice which should be observed in pursuing a course in music:

1. Recognize your voice as a gift from God to you, and that from it He expects the largest possible returns in service.

2. Consecrate to God your voice and whatever musical talent He has given you.

3. Place yourself willingly under the discipline and training of teachers who are competent to instruct, and who are in sympathy with the high ideals which you are striving to reach.

4. Never prostitute your musical talent by using it for selfish ends, or by singing or playing music that is not pure and elevating.

5. Take the Bible principles in music as your guide.

6. Whatever other musical instrument you learn to operate, do not fail to master the instrument which God has placed in your body; for it is the most musical of instruments, and capable of the greatest possibilities.

7. Learn to operate at least one musical instrument; probably the organ or the piano is generally preferable.

8. You should be ready at a moment's notice to play the instrument or lead the singing in a religious service.

9. Many of the songs of Zion should be memorized. Time spent in this way will bring good returns, and save much embarrassment when books are lacking or scarce.

10. Let your singing and playing in religious service be always performed as an act of religious worship.

11. In singing or playing, let the message, and not the messenger, be that which shall be seen and heard.

12. Singing evangelists as well as preaching evangelists are called for in the gospel program. If God calls you, respond cheerfully and efficiently.

13. Music teachers as well as Bible, science, and history teachers are

[3] White, *Education*, pp. 167, 168.

needed in the schools. If God calls you to this sacred work, respond gladly, and remember that teaching sacred, not popular, music is your high and holy calling.

14. Those who have had a proper training will not stoop at any time to play or sing foolish or sentimental songs; and they will recognize that some music which may be properly played or sung during the week, would not be appropriate for the Sabbath.

15. More pleasure and interest will be manifested in playing and singing hymns and other sacred songs than in any other class of music.

Music in the School of the Hereafter

Music will continue to be a subject of never-ending interest in the school of the hereafter, because chiefly through its instrumentality will the never-ending gratitude to God for His abundant goodness and mercy be expressed by those who have been eternally redeemed from sin and its cruel bondage. The seer of Patmos in heavenly vision beheld the victorious redeemed saints standing " on the sea of glass, having the harps of God," and he " heard the voice of harpers harping with their harps: and they sung as it were a new song before the throne: . . . and no man could learn that song but the hundred and forty and four thousand, which were redeemed from the earth. . . . These are they which follow the Lamb whithersoever he goeth " (Rev. 14: 2–4).

XVIII

ART AND ARCHITECTURE

An Unwarranted Conclusion

MODERN scholars are well-nigh unanimous in declaring that the ancient Hebrews had but little knowledge of art, including even the mechanical arts. They cite the fact that the Israelites were bondmen in Egypt, confined to the crude art of brickmaking, and had no opportunity of acquiring a knowledge of the finer arts. Then again, it is claimed that they were prohibited by the commandment of God from making graven images, from even studying art; and that this evidence precludes all possibility of ancient Israel's having a knowledge of sculpture, architecture, weaving, embroidering, and engraving.

No one will question the truth regarding the prohibition made; but there are those who question the conclusion drawn; for the same authority that speaks of the servitude of the Israelites in Egypt and the prohibition against image worship, presents this nation released from bondage, withdrawn into the wilderness, and faced with the problem of erecting a building which required knowledge and skill in architecture, weaving, engraving, and embroidery. Furthermore, a pattern of the building to be erected, with plans and specifications, was placed in the hands of Moses on the same occasion that the two tables of stone engraved with the finger of God were committed to him.

The Building of the Tabernacle

When Moses, who " was learned in all the wisdom of the Egyptians " (Acts 7: 22), faced the problem of constructing the tabernacle with unskilled workmen, the Master Architect admonished him not to vary from the pattern. " See, saith he, that thou make all things according to the pattern showed to thee in the mount " (Heb. 8: 5). Then God revealed to Moses His plan for solving the labor problem:

" See, I have called by name Bezaleel, the son of Uri, the son of Hur, of the tribe of Judah: and I have filled him with the Spirit of God, in wisdom, and in understanding, and in knowledge, and in all manner of workmanship, to devise cunning works, to work in gold, and in silver, and in brass, and in cutting of stones, to set them, and in carving of timber, to work in all manner of workmanship. And I, behold, I have given with him Aholiab, the son of Ahisamach, of the tribe of Dan; and in the hearts of all that are wise hearted I have put wisdom, that they may make all that I have commanded thee " (Ex. 31: 2–6).

For a whole year the people were all engaged in this great enterprise of erecting the building and providing it with its wonderfully artistic furnishings and draperies, which demanded superior wisdom and skill in

187

" all manner of workmanship." Concerning the completed work Moses said:

> " According to all that the Lord commanded Moses, so the children of Israel made all the work. And Moses did look upon all the work, and, behold, they had done it as the Lord had commanded, even so had they done it: and Moses blessed them " (Ex. 39: 42, 43).

The Building of the Temple

About five hundred years later, King David conceived the idea of building a temple at Jerusalem for the worship of God. He was permitted to gather the material, but to his son Solomon was committed the work of erecting the building. The pattern of the temple, like that of the tabernacle, was not of human devising:

> " Then David gave to Solomon his son the pattern of the porch, and of the houses thereof, and of the treasuries thereof, and of the upper chambers thereof, and of the inner parlors thereof, and of the place of the mercy-seat, and the pattern of all that he had by the spirit. . . . All this, said David, the Lord made me understand in writing by his hand upon me, even all the works of this pattern " (I Chron. 28: 11, 12, 19).

Solomon, like Moses, hesitated to accept such a great responsibility, fearing that the undertaking was greater than he could successfully accomplish. But David called all the captains, officers, and responsible men of his kingdom, and asked for their co-operation in the carrying out of this great undertaking. He encouraged Solomon to accept this sacred charge from God, and assured him that he had skilful and cunning workmen to perform every feature of the work called for in the pattern:

> " Take heed now; for the Lord hath chosen thee to build a house for the sanctuary: be strong and do it." "Be strong and of good courage, and do it: fear not, nor be dismayed: for the Lord God, even my God, will be with thee; he will not fail thee, nor forsake thee, until thou hast finished all the work for the service of the house of the Lord. . . . And there shall be with thee for all manner of workmanship every willing skilful man, for any manner of service: also the princes and all the people will be wholly at thy commandment. Furthermore David the king said unto all the congregation, Solomon my son, whom alone God hath chosen, is yet young and tender, and the work is great: for the palace is not for man, but for the Lord God " (I Chron. 28: 10, 20, 21; 29: 1).

Alliance with the Nations

But in spite of all the encouragement he had received from his father, still Solomon did not believe that he had a workman with sufficient knowledge and skill to execute the more intricate and delicate features called for by the pattern. So, unlike Moses, who sought God for help in his extremity, Solomon sent a request to Hiram, king of Tyre:

> " Behold, I build a house to the name of the Lord my God. . . . And the house which I build is great: for great is our God above all gods.

But who is able to build him an house, seeing the heaven and heaven of heavens cannot contain him? who am I then, that I should build him a house, save only to burn sacrifice before him? Send me now therefore a man cunning to work in gold, and in silver, and in brass, and in iron, and in purple, and crimson, and blue, and that can skill to grave with the cunning men that are with me in Judah and in Jerusalem, whom David my father did provide '' (II Chron. 2: 4–7).

Hiram made reply to Solomon in writing as follows:

'' Because the Lord hath loved his people, he hath made thee king over them. . . . Blessed be the Lord God of Israel, that made heaven and earth, who hath given to David the king a wise son, endued with prudence and understanding, that might build a house for the Lord, and a house for his kingdom. And now I have sent a cunning man, endued with understanding, of Huram my father's, the son of a woman of the daughters of Dan, and his father was a man of Tyre, skilful to work in gold, and in silver, in brass, in iron, in stone, and in timber, in purple, in blue, and in fine linen, and in crimson; also to grave any manner of graving, and to find out every device which shall be put to him, with thy cunning men, and with the cunning men of my lord David thy father '' (Verses 11–14).

Some modern scholars claim that here is evidence that the Israelites were dependent on the Phœnicians for their knowledge of architecture, and that Solomon had to send to Hiram, the Phœnician king, for an architect to furnish the plans for the temple and superintend its construction. But it should be observed that King Hiram, in his reply, acknowledges the appointment by God to build the house of worship, and that in sending a competent, skilful workman, he is sending a man who is a son of a woman of the daughters of Dan, one of the tribes of Israel. Hiram very tactfully and indirectly reproves Solomon by telling him that he has acceded to his request, but that he is sending one of the descendants of Israel who is the leading architect in Phœnicia, thus politely indicating that it was unnecessary to send to him for an expert in architecture, for he could send him none better than a descendant of Aholiab, of the tribe of Dan, whom God endowed with special skill and wisdom for the construction of the tabernacle in the wilderness in the days of Moses.

How the Phœnicians became inheritors of the architectural knowledge and skill that God gave to Israel at the time of the building of the tabernacle, is plainly indicated by the following:

'' The descendants of these workmen (Bezaleel and Aholiab) inherited to a large degree the talents conferred on their forefathers. For a time these men of Judah and Dan remained humble and unselfish; but gradually, almost imperceptibly, they lost their hold upon God and their desire to serve Him unselfishly. They asked higher wages for their services, because of their superior skill as workmen in the finer arts. In some instances their request was granted, but more often they found employment in the surrounding nations. . . . That their selfish desires might be gratified, they used their God-given skill in the service of heathen kings, and lent their talent to the perfecting of works which were a dishonor to their Maker.

" It was among these men that Solomon looked for a master workman to superintend the construction of the temple on Mount Moriah. Minute specifications, in writing, regarding every portion of the sacred structure, had been intrusted to the king; and he could have looked to God in faith for consecrated helpers, to whom would have been granted special skill for doing with exactness the work required. But Solomon lost sight of this opportunity to exercise faith in God. He sent to the king of Tyre for a man. . . .

" The Phœnician king responded by sending Huram, ' the son of a woman of the daughters of Dan, and his father was a man of Tyre.' Huram was a descendant, on his mother's side, of Aholiab, to whom hundreds of years before God had given special wisdom for the construction of the tabernacle." [1]

" The Perfection of Beauty "

Not only Phœnicia, but undoubtedly many of the surrounding nations—Assyria, Babylonia, Medo-Persia, and Greece—became in time sharers of the knowledge and skill in architecture and the finer arts which God gave to ancient Israel. The attention of many nations was called to the building of the temple during its seven years of construction. Of the dedication of the temple and its surpassing glory and splendor, a modern writer remarks:

" Of surpassing beauty and unrivaled splendor was the palatial building which Solomon and his associates erected for God and His worship. Garnished with precious stones, surrounded by spacious courts with magnificent approaches, and lined with carved cedar and burnished gold, the temple structure, with its broidered hangings and rich furnishings, was a fit emblem of the living church of God on earth, which through the ages has been building in accordance with the divine pattern." [2]

A prophet of God, in speaking of the architectural works of Tyre, said:

" Thy builders have perfected thy beauty " (Ezek. 27: 4). The renowned city of Babylon, with its gorgeous temples, is spoken of as " the beauty of the Chaldees' excellency " (Isa. 13: 19).

But Jeremiah, when weeping over Jerusalem with its temple in ruins, declared:

" All that pass by clap their hands at thee; they hiss and wag their head at the daughter of Jerusalem, saying, Is this the city that men call The perfection of beauty, The joy of the whole earth? " (Lam. 2: 15).

The psalmist speaks of the influence of the temple at Jerusalem on the kings of surrounding nations: " Because of thy temple at Jerusalem shall kings bring presents unto thee " (Ps. 68: 29).

Copy the Temple Pattern

According to the teaching of the Scriptures, Israel exceeded the sur-

[1] Ellen G. White, *Prophets and Kings*, pp. 62, 63.
[2] *Ibid.*, p. 36.

rounding nations, not only in the knowledge of the principles of character building, but also in her knowledge and skill in temple building. Her skill in the finer arts excelled that possessed by the surrounding nations as much as the God she worshiped in her glorious temple was greater than the gods worshiped in the temples dedicated to idols of wood and stone.

That Israel gave to the world its architecture, and that the Ionic, Doric, and Corinthian columns originated in Judea in connection with the building of the tabernacle and the temple, instead of being the product of Greek architecture, a few modern architects are bold enough to declare. Nearly two centuries ago an architect of England, John Wood, a man with a national reputation for public works, wrote a book, consisting of five parts in one volume, entitled, *The Origin of Building, or the Plagiarism of the Heathen Detected*. His treatise contains an account of the rise and progress of building, from the time Cain built the first city down to modern times. He traces the progress of architecture in Egypt, Judea, Assyria, Babylon, Media, Persia, Greece, and Italy; and from the light shed upon architecture from the Bible and history he concludes that God through the building of the tabernacle and temple gave to the world the principles of architecture, including the Ionic, Doric, and Corinthian styles of columns, but that the surrounding nations appropriated this knowledge, and then took to themselves the credit of originating its principles. We give his concluding statement:

" The pagans, finding how the parts of the Jewish structures coincided with the matters contained in the history of the Israelites, soon copied those very parts, and applied them to their own idols in the temples they erected to them; which, on this account they held so sacred, that a profanation of them was punished with present death. That those pagans, not satisfied with this application, in process of time, assumed these things to their own invention, and then traduced the Jews with being blasphemers and deriders of the divinity; those people, by neglecting the real part of the law, having also forgot the symbolical, nor could they tell to what divine matters the various parts of their sacred edifices referred!

" This we have sufficiently made appear in the preceding sheets; in which we had no other hypothesis in view, nor have we any other now, but that of rendering unto Cæsar the things which are Cæsar's, and unto God the things which are God's." [3]

A little less than a century after Mr. Wood wrote his treatise, another architect, William Wilkins, A. M., R. A., D. R. S., formerly a senior fellow of Caius College in the University of Cambridge, and later Regius Professor of Architecture in the Royal Academy, wrote a work entitled, *Prolusiones Architectonicae, or Essays on Subjects Connected with Grecian and Roman Architecture*. Among the several essays written by this eminent architect, is one entitled, " The Temple at

[3] John Wood, *The Origin of Building*.

Jerusalem; the Type of Grecian Architecture." The author's purpose in writing this essay is clearly stated, as follows:

" The chief object of the present dissertation is to show the influence produced on the arts by the commencement and accomplishment of this great enterprise (the building of the Jerusalem temple), and the example it afforded to the architects of the ages immediately following, as yet unskilled in architecture, and wanting some type of great authority for their guidance. . . .

" The most brilliant era in the history of this nation is that which immediately followed the accession of Solomon, the great glory of whose reign is identified with the erection of the temple. Although this great undertaking was mainly subservient to spiritual purposes, the advantages arising from its construction were widely spread, and exercised an almost boundless influence over other important objects. It was in the reign of this prince, and a consequence arising from this act of piety, that the Hebrews first became a commercial people."

Dr. Wilkins bases his contention that the Greeks patterned their temples after the temple at Jerusalem on the close harmony existing between their measurements. The Greek temple at Pæstum varied but two inches in length and three inches in width from the Jewish temple. Other Greek temples show nearly equal harmony in their proportions.

Dr. Wilkins also furnishes drawings of ground-floor and front-elevation plans of the two halves of each temple placed in juxtaposition, for the purpose of showing with greater perspicuity the similar conformations of the essential parts of both. He then makes these significant statements:

" The great nicety of this coincidence excites our admiration, and confirms the opinion that the magnitude of both buildings was made the same by the express intention of the founder of the latter.

" A very extraordinary coincidence, both in proportion and in actual dimensions, existed between this (Jewish temple) and the temple at Pæstum, that could only have originated in the intention of the projectors of the latter to adopt the other as their model, and to adhere to it with as much precision as was consistent with the observance of different forms of worship in the two nations." [4]

Two very eminent French architects and archeologists, George Perrot and Charles Chipiez, who spent about twenty years in exploration work in Judæa and the surrounding countries, published the result of their investigations in 1890 in two volumes entitled, *The History of Art in Sardinia, Judæa, Syria, and Asia Minor*. Far the largest space is devoted to Judæan architecture, especially to the Jerusalem temple. The temple of Ezekiel's vision is fully restored by the authors and reproduced in a fine engraving. The authors apologize somewhat for devoting so much space to the Jewish temple, by saying:

" Considering the state of the area upon which once stood the temple of Jerusalem, and the scantiness of documents relating thereto, we should,

[4] W. Wilkins, *Prolusiones Architectonicae*, pp. 98, 99, 101, 105.

perhaps, have abstained from attempting its restoration, had not Ezekiel seemed to beckon to us from the holy mount, holding out to our curiosity the type, in the abstract, of the Semitic sacred building.''

'' If we have studied with a degree of care, which may have seemed too minute, the smallest relics of Jewish art and industry, it was not entirely because of the place which Israel holds in the world's annals, albeit to an inquiring mind the reason might appear sufficient; since few will be found indifferent to aught which pertains to a people ' whose religion became the stem of the general religion of the world.' ''

Then the authors speak of sculpture, "the noblest of the plastic arts," as being proscribed by the Jews, and that this "would seem to demand but a limited treatment of Jewish art; " and yet they say:

'' We could not, however, make up our minds to such a line of conduct. The Jews, though specially jealous and adverse to any innovation that interfered with their religious observances, had not the same objection to architecture; hence it came to pass that their buildings could favorably compare with those of the surrounding Asiatic nations.''

From the following statement it will be seen that these two French architects incline to the view of the two English architects noted above —that the Greeks modeled their sanctuary after the Jewish temple:

'' In our delineation of the Semitic (Jewish) temple—certainly older than the Greek sanctuary, and which may have served as its model—we showed that it was everywhere the same, though the deities that were worshipped in it might be different according to time and place.'' [5]

Much more consideration has been given to architecture than was given to the other contributions that Israel has made to the world. So generally has Israel been denied the honor due her in the field of architectural knowledge and skill, that this lengthy defense will not appear unjustifiable. Israel is entitled to the position of highest honor, not only in arkitecture (knowledge of the moral law contained in the ark), but also in architecture, or knowledge and skill in the art of building. She received directly from the divine Architect those principles that made her a master builder, whether of temples made with hands or of the greater temple of character of which the former is but a symbol.

The Spiritual in Art

The true artist will recognize that in his work he is but copying the Master Artist whose pictures are hung in the gallery of creation about him; and that these are revelations of his thoughts regarding the beautiful, the good and the true. These spiritual realities will radiate from the works of his hands, for they are experienced in his own life. He and the Master Artist are partners—the One creating, the other copying to pass it on to others less favored.

Ernest Newlandsmith, in his book *Art, Love and Life,* speaks of false and true ideals of artists and makes an appeal to all who are

[5] G. Perrot and C. Chipiez, *The History of Art in Sardinia, Judæa, Syria and Asia Minor,* Vol. I, pp. 370, 363, 368 (A. C. Armstrong & Son).

engaged in this heavenly calling to be true to their profession and to consecrate themselves anew to their sacred work.

" Here, then, is the key to the truth of the whole matter: *the supreme object of Art is to manifest God through forms.*

" Foolish men tell us that the object of Art is to portray the life and characteristics of poor fallen man and his earthbound environment. But we study humanity, as such, far too much, instead of striving to gain and express the indwelling Divine Presence. Artists talk much about expressing *themselves* in their Art. But on what grounds do they consider themselves worthy of expression? Let them rather endeavor to become self-effaced channels through which God may express Himself. Meanwhile, from the way some artists talk and act you would think that Art was a mere rubbish-heap on which to discharge their feelings, fancies and passions, good and bad and indifferent. Being attacked with various ' moods ' they strive to depict these moods on canvas, or on paper, or in sounds, quite callous as to whether the said moods are healthy or elevating. Little reck they that more often than not they are mischievously scattering mental and spiritual disease-germs throughout the world. It does not matter to them, they think it is Art, and Art is grand and noble.

" But the Art we need is the Art that makes for life and being, not the Art of morbid and neurotic temperaments. We need Art that is redolent of God, and of seas, woods, mountains, and fresh air—not the Art that savors of false civilization and London drawing-rooms. Let us insist upon Art that *says something to us,* that says that which it is good for us to hear, and which says it in as simple and direct a manner as possible."

" Let us, therefore, make a definite consecration of our whole life and being, and all our life's work to God, striving to do all to His glory. Let us endeavor to eat and drink, work and play, in the continual realization of the Divine Presence. Then our Art will become living Art; it will be impossible for it to take the downward tendency, which prevails so much in the world of today; for such Art instead of being moulded by the spirit of this or any other age, will be fashioned by the indwelling Spirit of the Blessed Trinity. It will be the voice of love—the voice of God." [6]

Let students study the lives of men and their productions in literature, music, painting, sculpture, and architecture, who received their inspiration to produce them from their study of the Bible.

The following books on Art are recommended for reading and study: Ruskin's *Modern Painters. The Divine in Art,* by Wm. Lawrence Schroeder. *Art, Love and Life,* by Ernest Newlandsmith.

[6] E. Newlandsmith, *Art, Love, and Life,* pp. 107–108, 106 (Longmans, Green & Co.).

XIX

THE STUDY OF PHILOSOPHY

Philosophy Defined

T HE word "philosophy" is formed from two Greek words which together mean a "love of wisdom"; a lover of wisdom is therefore called a "philosopher."

The Standard Dictionary gives the following definition of philosophy:

"The science of rational principles; the knowledge, in a scientific system, of the ultimate principles—elements, causes, and laws—that underlie and explain all knowledge and existence, and their application in the explanation of these."

R. W. Sellars, Professor of Philosophy in the University of Michigan, in his book, *The Essentials of Philosophy*, gives the following definition:

"Philosophy is a persistent attempt to understand the world in which we live and of which we are a part. . . . It is an effort of the intellect of man to answer fundamental problems and gain a comprehensive view of the universe." [1]

The oft-repeated and most familiar statement of the philosopher's problem is, "The solving of the riddle of the universe." Philosophy does not deal separately with the sciences, such as physics, chemistry, and biology, but as a whole. Professor Sellars quotes H. Sedgwick as to the aims of philosophy:

"It aims at putting together the parts of knowledge thus attained into a systematic whole, so that all the methods of attaining truth may be grasped as parts of one method, and all the conclusions attained may be presented, so far as possible, as harmonious and consistent."

Philosophy does not restrict itself to the natural phenomena, but enters the field of mental and moral science. History, education, and art are also within its domain. In fact, the field of its operations is the universe. Philosophy is the arbiter of all knowledge, not only as to the matter of its unification, but also of its justification to pass as knowledge. Surely, if any class of educators need not only a love for wisdom, but the gift of wisdom, it is the philosophers. This high profession demands the wisest of men.

The Ancient Hebrew Philosophers

There were three classes of teachers, or educators, in Israel: 1. The priests. 2. The prophets. 3. The sages, or wise men—philosophers.

This is attested to by both Jeremiah and Ezekiel:

[1] R. W. Sellars, *The Essentials of Philosophy* (Macmillan Co.).

'' The law shall not perish from the priest, nor counsel from the wise, nor the word from the prophet '' (Jer. 18: 18). '' Mischief shall come upon mischief, and rumor shall be upon rumor, then shall they seek a vision of the prophet; but the law shall perish from the priest, and counsel from the ancients (wise) '' (Ezek. 7: 26).

Israel had its wise men, or philosophers, who gave helpful counsel and instruction, and the names of a few of them are mentioned in the Bible. Moses and Solomon, especially Solomon, were richly endowed with the gift of wisdom. Jethro and Job, while not Israelites, gave counsel and instruction that had a far-reaching influence in developing and molding the life of the Jewish nation.

Solomon was the greatest of the Hebrew philosophers. Concerning him and other Hebrew philosophers and their philosophic viewpoint, Professor Baldwin, of the University of Illinois, in his work entitled, *Our Modern Debt to Israel,* says:

'' Of Solomon, who was regarded as the representative and embodiment of wisdom, it was said: ' He spake of trees, from the cedar that is in Lebanon, even unto the hyssop that springeth out of the wall: he spake also of beasts, and of fowl, and of creeping things, and of fishes.' All the works of the visible creation were regarded as objects of reverent study as revelations of the divine wisdom. ' O Lord, how manifold are thy works! ' cried the psalmist, ' in wisdom hast thou made them all ' (Ps. 104: 24).

'' By the observation of these ' works ' men were to understand God's ways, for God was in their thought the source of all wisdom. In the ardent panegyric upon wisdom found in Proverbs, we are told:

' The Lord by wisdom founded the earth;
By understanding he established the heavens.
By his knowledge the depths were broken up,
And the skies drop down the dew.
My son, let not them depart from thine eyes;
Keep sound wisdom and discretion;
So shall they be life unto thy soul,
And grace to thy neck.'—(Prov. 3: 19–22, R. V.)

'' By observation of even the humblest of God's creatures, men might learn wisdom:

' Go to the ant, thou sluggard;
Consider her ways, and be wise;
Which having no chief,
Overseer, or ruler,
Provideth her meat in the summer,
And gathereth her food in the harvest.'
—(Prov. 6: 6–8.)

'' Yet, while wisdom included within its range all God's creation, the department of study that offered the largest return of wisdom was human conduct. It was in the sphere of practical ethics that the sages mostly worked. Enlightened worldly wisdom, dealing with the results of an observation of human life, extended if not minute, was characteristic of Hebrew wisdom. It was never broadly speculative. The sage never, like

the modern philosopher, started with a question. It never occurred to
him to ask, Who is God? Rather, he started with an axiom: Given a God,
knowable, just, and wise, then Wisdom is to know Him so far as possible,
through observation of His works and ways, and to turn that knowledge
to practical account in our relations with Him and with our fellow men.
. . . To harmonize human life with nature by constantly connecting both
with God, was the end and aim of Hebrew wisdom.'' [2]

Bible Books of Philosophy

While philosophical principles are found here and there throughout
the Scriptures, there are three of the books of the Bible devoted entirely to philosophical thought—Job, Proverbs, and Ecclesiastes. The
book of James, in the New Testament, is by some regarded as a
fourth book on philosophy. There is no doubt that the three books of
philosophy in the Old Testament were diligently studied in the schools
of the prophets, and as a result the nation was furnished with men
qualified to act in the fear of God as leaders and counselors. Ahithophel, Hushai, and Jonathan, an uncle of David, were wise men and
counselors of the king. Concerning the wisdom and counsel of the
former we read:

" The counsel of Ahithophel, which he counseled in those days, was as
if a man had inquired at the oracle of God: so was all the counsel of
Ahithophel both with David and with Absalom " (II Sam. 16: 23).

Hebrew Philosophy

The books of Job, Proverbs, and Ecclesiastes, and such psalms as the
thirty-seventh, forty-ninth, and seventy-third, belong to the department of Hebrew literature called " The Wisdom." A study of these
books will indicate the nature and method of Hebrew philosophical
reflections. A comparison of the Hebrew and Greek methods of study
in philosophical reflection is clearly given by Prof. A. B. Davidson, as
follows:

" Hebrew wisdom differed from the philosophy of other peoples in the
point from which reflection set out. The Greek philosopher started from
the whole complex sum of things; he threw the universe into his crucible
at once. His course consisted in pursuing the currents backward, till he
reached the one source from which they all issued. His object was to
find the one thing which explained all other things, and thus his final step
was to name God. But the Hebrew thinker was at the source to begin
with. To him God was already given: his task was not to discover God
whom he did not know, but to recognize in all things God whom he knew.
He did not rise up from his thoughts of the world to thoughts of God;
his thought and knowledge of God explained to him the world and all the
events in man's history. In these he saw God everywhere fulfilling
Himself, revealing His power and wisdom, and working out His great
designs. Hence the wisdom (philosophy) became largely a doctrine of

[2] E. C. Baldwin, *Our Modern Debt to Israel*, pp. 162–164 (Sherman and
French.)

Providence; and when events in providence seemed to conflict with fundamental ideas regarding God, such as His righteousness (which was the case, for instance, when the righteous were seen in adversity, or when the wicked were prospered), the Wisdom took the shape of a theodicy—a justification of the ways of God to man. . . .

"To the wise man all things are but the reflections, infinitely various in their colors, of the mind of God. The mind and thought of God is especially reflected in the social order and moral life of man. The simple Proverbs exhibit in a great variety of ways individual illustrations of this; they are flashes of light from the infinitely numerous facets of the divine conception underlying the universe. But in chapters 1 to 9 of Proverbs, and particularly in chapter 8, this general world conception, especially on its moral side, is personified as a being called Wisdom herself.

"There is a world-plan, an articulated, moral, and intellectual framework, on which all phenomena rest. This world-plan was a conception at first in the mind of God—His thought before creation of the whole system of things, particularly of the moral human economy. The formation of this conception in the divine mind was the first of His works: 'The Lord created me as the beginning of his way, the first of his works of old. I was set up of old, from the beginning, or ever the earth was' (Prov. 8: 22, 23).

"Then the divine conception, Wisdom, is conceived as projected out of the mind of God. 'When there were no depths, I was brought forth;' 'when he established the heavens, I was there' (Prov. 8: 24, 27). And finally this Wisdom, or world-conception was God's artificer in the creation of all things. Creation was just this Wisdom realizing herself and taking form. With an intoxicating joy, Wisdom 'played' before God, and creation is the embodiment of all her movements in this play; and the sphere where her delights were highest and her realization of herself most perfect, was the habitable earth, the moral world of the sons of men.

"This chapter of Proverbs is one of the most beautiful things in Scripture. Though the wisdom here be as yet only a personification and not a person, the profound idea was taken up among the other Messianic thoughts of Israel, to which it lent depth by suggesting the relation of the Messiah to creation and the universe; and those things said here of Wisdom were afterward seen unified in the Son of God—'The Word was with God;' 'All things were made by him,' and 'He is before all things, and in him do all things subsist.'

"The conception of the Wisdom is that the world is a moral constitution, in all the phenomena of which, and of the life of men, God is present."[3]

The Hebrew philosophy acknowledged God to be the source of the wisdom and knowledge of the Hebrews, and yet it recognized the limitations of the human mind in its search and comprehension of knowledge:

"The Lord giveth wisdom: out of his mouth cometh knowledge and understanding" (Prov. 2: 6). "Great things doeth he, which we cannot comprehend" (Job 37: 5). "Lord, my heart is not haughty, nor

[3] A. B. Davidson, "Proverbs" in the *Bible Treasury*, pp. 89, 90.

mine eyes lofty: neither do I exercise myself in great matters, or in things too high for me '' (Ps. 131: 1).

Yet the Jews were diligent students in the legitimate field of thought and inquiry, for we read:

'' I gave my heart to seek and search out by wisdom concerning all things that are done under heaven '' (Eccl. 1: 13).

The proper attitude of the philosopher in his pursuit of knowledge is thus expressed by the prince of Hebrew philosophers:

'' My son, if thou wilt receive my words, and hide my commandments with thee; so that thou incline thine ear unto wisdom, and apply thine heart to understanding; yea, if thou criest after knowledge, and liftest up thy voice for understanding; if thou seekest her as silver, and searchest for her as for hid treasures; then shalt thou understand the fear of the Lord, and find the knowledge of God.'' '' The fear of the Lord is the beginning of wisdom: and the knowledge of the holy is understanding '' (Prov. 2: 1–5; 9: 10).

The comparative value of wisdom is thus described:

'' Happy is the man that findeth wisdom, and the man that getteth understanding. For the merchandise of it is better than the merchandise of silver, and the gain thereof than fine gold. She is more precious than rubies: and all the things thou canst desire are not to be compared with her '' (Prov. 3: 13–15).

Later, Solomon, the great apostle of true philosophy, became enamored of the false philosophies of the heathen nations around him, and drank from those polluted streams. He forsook the "fountain of living waters" from which he had drunk in his youth, and others were influenced by his example. He later repented of his wrong course, and the book of Ecclesiastes expresses his repentance and confession, and gives also a clear statement of the true philosophy of human life.

Severe warnings and condemnations were written by the prophets against false teachers of philosophy:

'' They have forsaken me the fountain of living waters, and hewed them out cisterns, broken cisterns, that can hold no water '' (Jer. 2: 13).

'' The wise men are ashamed, they are dismayed and taken: lo, they have rejected the word of the Lord; and what wisdom is in them? '' (Jer. 8: 9). '' Woe unto them that are wise in their own eyes, and prudent in their own sight '' (Isa. 5: 21).

'' Behold, I will proceed to do a marvelous work among this people, even a marvelous work and a wonder: for the wisdom of their wise men shall perish, and the understanding of their prudent men shall be hid '' (Isa. 29: 14).

Christ and Philosophy

The teachers in the rabbinical schools had so perverted truth, and emphasized the non-essentials of education that Christ did not attend their schools. Yet when He reached manhood and entered on His public work, they expressed great surprise at His learning and wisdom, attained without their instruction: "The Jews marveled, saying, How knoweth this man learning, having never learned (studied in our schools)?" (John 7: 15, margin).

When Jesus selected men to carry forward the work that He organized and started in behalf of mankind, He did not choose the scholars of the day. He rejoiced in the working out of His choice.

"In that hour Jesus rejoiced in spirit, and said, I thank thee, O Father, Lord of heaven and earth, that thou hast hid these things from the (worldly) wise and prudent (the philosophers and teachers of Israel), and hast revealed them unto babes; even so, Father; for so it seemed good in thy sight" (Luke 10: 21).

It was the learned "men from the East," and not the wise men in Jerusalem, who were sufficiently wise to know that the time had come for the advent of Christ to the world. "He came unto his own, and his own received him not."

Paul and Philosophy

Before "Saul of Tarsus" became "Paul, an apostle of Jesus Christ," he was one of Israel's wisest men, a member of the Jewish Sanhedrin, who had been educated at the feet of Gamaliel, a most renowned teacher. But Paul's vision of Christ on the way to Damascus (Acts 9) resulted in the scales falling from his eyes, not only physically, but intellectually and spiritually, so that the things he had reckoned as gain, he now counted as "loss for the excellency of the knowledge of Christ" (Phil. 3: 8), who became unto him "wisdom, and righteousness, and sanctification, and redemption" (I Cor. 1: 30).

Speaking of his work of building up Christ's kingdom, Paul said:

"My speech and my preaching was not with enticing words of man's wisdom, but in demonstration of the Spirit and of power; that your faith should not stand in the wisdom of men, but in the power of God" (I Cor. 2: 4, 5).

This Paul, of whom a Roman governor said, "Much learning doth make thee mad," met the learned Greek philosophers in the court of the Areopagus, where they carried on their philosophical discussions. He tactfully but fearlessly declared that their philosophical theories were unsound; for they did not recognize God as their maker, the operator of the world and the dispenser of all its blessings to mankind. As an immediate result of this lecture, we are told:

"Some mocked: and others said, We will hear thee again of this matter. . . . Howbeit certain men clave unto him, and believed: among the which was Dionysius the Areopagite, and a woman named Damaris, and others with them" (Acts 17: 32-34).

Thus it would seem that one of the chief philosophers, Dionysius the Areopagite, was won over to this larger and grander philosophy, whose fundamental principle is the recognition of God as Creator of all things and Christ as the Redeemer of lost mankind.

The apostle Paul boldly strikes the axe into the roots of the tree of worldly wisdom when he declares:

" The wisdom of this world is foolishness with God. For it is written, He taketh the wise in their own craftiness. And again, The Lord knoweth the thoughts of the wise, that they are vain " (I Cor. 3: 19, 20). "It is written, I will destroy the wisdom of the wise, and will bring to nothing the understanding of the prudent. Where is the wise? where is the scribe? where is the disputer of this world? hath not God made foolish the wisdom of this world? " (I Cor. 1: 19, 20). " Let no man deceive himself. If any man among you seemeth to be wise in this world, let him become a fool, that he may be wise " (I Cor. 3: 18).

" Not many wise men after the flesh, not many mighty, not many noble, are called; but God hath chosen the foolish things of the world to confound the wise; and God hath chosen the weak things of the world to confound the things which are mighty; and base things of the world, and things which are despised, hath God chosen, yea, and things which are not, to bring to naught things that are: that no flesh should glory in his presence: . . . that, according as it is written, He that glorieth, let him glory in the Lord " (I Cor. 1: 26–30).

The prophet Jeremiah gave this exhortation to the philosopher:

" Thus saith the Lord, Let not the wise man glory in his wisdom. . . . But let him that glorieth glory in this, that he understandeth and knoweth me, that I am the Lord which exerciseth loving kindness, judgment, and righteousness, in the earth: for in these things I delight, saith the Lord " (Jer. 9: 23, 24).

Paul lifts the danger signal against any system of philosophy that does not acknowledge Christ:

" Beware lest any man spoil you through philosophy and vain deceit, after the tradition of men, after the elements (margin) of the world, and not after Christ.'' " In whom are hid all the treasures of wisdom and knowledge.'' " And ye are complete in him, which is the head of all principality and power " (Col. 2: 8, 3, 10).

Ancient and Modern Philosophy

The ancient heathen philosophers busied themselves with the problem of world building, and did not hesitate to tell just how matter and motion were correlated in the making of the universe. They knew just what part God acted in the building process, and pointed out His limitations in relation to matter and motion. Some of these world builders did not find God so essential to the process, and gave Him a very limited part in the work of construction, while others found His services altogether unnecessary, and left Him out of their world-building schemes.

Not only did these ancient philosophers build worlds, but they built up a system of rhetoric and logic which they found absolutely necessary in order to make their theories seem plausible and thus acceptable. These ancient, self-sufficient philosophers did not profit by the interrogations addressed to an Eastern philosopher who was treading on forbidden ground:

" Who is this that darkeneth counsel by words without knowledge?
Gird up now thy loins like a man; for I will demand of thee, and answer
thou me.   Where wast thou when I laid the foundations of the earth?
declare, if thou hast understanding.   Who hath laid the measures thereof,
if thou knowest? or who hath stretched the line upon it?   Whereupon are
the foundations thereof fastened? or who laid the corner-stone thereof? ''
(Job 38: 2–6).

These interrogations of the Almighty should have borne the same
fruits of humility and repentance in the hearts and lives of philosophers
of all ages that they bore in the life of the patriarch Job:

" I uttered that I understood not; things too wonderful for me, which
I knew not. . . . Wherefore I abhor myself, and repent in dust and
ashes '' (Job 42: 3–6).

The ancient and early modern philosophers were scientists as well
as philosophers.   Francis Bacon and René Descartes believed that
philosophy was universal knowledge and included the special sciences
as its parts.   The later philosophers—Locke, Hume, Kant, Berkeley,
and others—have gradually restricted the field of philosophic inquiry,
so that today the philosopher is a specialist, dealing in the main with
the mental sciences and with the traditional metaphysical systems.

Some of the problems that the modern philosopher expects to solve
are these:

1.   To give clear and definite meanings to the concepts—space, time,
mind, matter, and causality.

2.   To make clear the working relationships that exist between the
realities indicated by the above concepts.

3.   To answer truthfully and clearly the following questions:

    a.   What is knowledge?

    b.   How is it related to consciousness?

    c.   How does it tell us about reality?

    d.   Can we have knowledge of reality outside of consciousness?

    e.   Do we really see things in the world or only in the mind?

    f.   Is mind and matter the same reality, the former being a
       more highly organized state of the latter?

    g.   What is life?

    h.   What is God?   What is right and wrong?

    i.   What are we ourselves?

    j.   Where did we come from, and whither are we bound?

Philosophers are working hard to solve these problems and to
answer these and like questions.   They are very independent in their
work, for they will not accept any outside help.   The only results acceptable to them are those that come from the reflection of their own
minds.

The Bible and Philosophy

The modern philosopher, in the main, does not believe in a revelation of God to man; consequently the Bible has no place in helping
to solve his problems.   He does not refuse to examine the pebbles of

knowledge gathered by the scientist, the historian, and other knowledge gatherers, but he scrutinizes them and casts aside those that do not fit into his reflected scheme. So the Bible and religion, if in any measure acceptable, must fit into his conception of things. The Apostle Paul describes this philosophical attitude:

" Professing themselves to be wise, they became fools. . . . And even as they did not like to retain God in their knowledge, God gave them over to a mind void of judgment " (Rom. 1: 22, 28, margin).

He tells us that there is no justifiable excuse for the philosopher's reasoning about creation independent of God:

" Because that which may be known of God is manifest in them; for God hath showed it unto them. For the invisible things of him from the creation of the world are clearly seen, being understood by the things that are made, even his eternal power and Godhead; so that they are without excuse: because that, when they know God, they glorified him not as God, neither were thankful; but became vain in their imaginations (reasonings), and their foolish heart was darkened " (Verses 19–21, margin).

The Bible, then, contains the true principles of philosophy, and is therefore the philosopher's guide as truly as it is the guide of the scientist and the historian.

The three philosophical books of the Bible will furnish food for serious, earnest thought and deep reflection. A brief statement of the philosophy of each of these books follows:

1. *Job.* God is supreme in His universe, and finite, sinful man is out of his sphere when he questions the mysterious operations of a just and all-wise Creator, in the world about him, or in His dealings with mankind. By numerous interrogations God reproves man for his unbridled curiosity and presumption that boldly demands that He let him into the secret council chamber.

2. *Proverbs.* Wisdom is exalted as the greatest gift of God, and all are exhorted to seek for this heavenly treasure. The highest wisdom is not in seeking to know the mysteries of God as revealed in creation, or in an endeavor to fathom the dealings of Providence, but rather in seeking to conform human conduct to the teachings and requirements of the Word of God.

3. *Ecclesiastes.* This book contains the confession of the prince of philosophers, who had departed from the principles of true philosophy as laid down by himself in the book of Proverbs, and a restatement of those principles, with an earnest exhortation to the young to profit by his sad and unfortunate experience. The philosophy of conduct—of morals—is far more important than the philosophy of matter and mind. This is emphatically stated in the concluding words of this book:

" Let us hear the conclusion of the whole matter: Fear God, and keep his commandments; for this is the whole duty of man. For God shall bring every work into judgment, with every secret thing, whether it be good, or whether it be evil" (Eccl. 12: 13, 14).

That the Bible contains philosophy of great value—philosophy which will require earnest thought and deep reflection to comprehend—is clearly expressed in the following words:

" It contains philosophy the most profound, poetry the sweetest, and the most sublime, the most impassioned and the most pathetic. . . . God's Word is true philosophy, true science. Human opinions . . . amount to very little. Those who are imbued with the Word of God, will teach it in the same simple way that Christ taught it. The world's greatest Teacher used the simplest language and the plainest symbols. . . . The Bible contains a simple and complete system of theology and philosophy. It is the book that makes us wise unto salvation." [4]

The blighting, soul-destroying influence of a philosophy which ignores God in His works, is thus described:

" Cold, philosophical speculations and scientific research in which God is not acknowledged, are a positive injury. And the evil is aggravated when, as is often the case, books placed in the hands of the young, accepted as authority and depended upon in their education, are from authors avowedly infidel. Through all the thoughts presented by these men their poisonous sentiments are interwoven. The study of such books is like handling black coals; a student cannot be undefiled in mind who thinks along the line of skepticism." [5]

True Philosophy to be Studied

There is a true philosophy as well as a true science, and both should be diligently studied in our schools. The philosophy contained in the Word of God is referred to principally by the term "wisdom." This wisdom is highly recommended by the greatest Bible philosopher, and the youth are strongly urged to procure this chiefest of treasures: "Wisdom is the principal thing; therefore get wisdom; and with all thy getting get understanding" (Prov. 4: 7).

Wisdom will greatly bless and reward her possessor:

" Exalt her, and she shall promote thee: she shall bring thee to honor, when thou dost embrace her. She shall give to thine head an ornament of grace: a crown of glory shall she deliver to thee " (Prov. 4: 8, 9).

" Length of days is in her right hand; and in her left hand riches and honor. Her ways are ways of pleasantness, and all her paths are peace. She is a tree of life to them that lay hold upon her; and happy is every one that retaineth her " (Prov. 3: 16–18).

Mr. Lamb, in *The Making of a Man*, gives a concrete illustration of the meaning of Bible wisdom:

" Suppose it were possible for us to be placed alongside of God, to climb up so high and get so near the throne that we could see things as God sees them, look at everything through His eyes, see this life and the

---

[4] White, *Education*, p. 125; *Counsels to Teachers*, pp. 433, 422.
[5] *Ibid.*, pp. 423, 424.

future life and their relations the one to the other, our relations to those around us now and for eternity, just as God does. Seated up there in the highest heaven and gifted with an eyesight that could sweep all worlds, and a brain that could grasp the interests of eternity, our judgment and discernment would be broad and all-comprehensive, and our conclusions therefore wise conclusions. In other words, to be able to see things from God's viewpoint would give us God's wisdom.

" This, in a measure, is to be our exalted privilege by and by. But instead of climbing up where we can see things as God sees them, let us think of God coming down to us and giving us His opinions, His conclusions, upon every important subject with which we wrestle, thus giving us the benefit of His wisdom upon each of these vast interests. This, besides being far more practical, is equivalent to lifting us up to the throne, and permitting us to look through God's all-seeing eyes and enjoy the benefit of His infinite brain and infinite heart every time we have an important question to decide, and need perfect wisdom to decide it aright.

" This is what God has done in His Word. The Bible is God's attempt to impart His wisdom to us by putting us in possession of His view of things; not of a few things, but of all matters of importance either to this life or to the life to come. It is wonderful to find how universally and how minutely the Bible enters into every possible relation in life. Scarcely a problem arises involving either our relations to each other here upon earth, or our relations to God and to the future, that is not solved in the Bible, and solved from God's viewpoint after He had considered with infinite skill all possible contingencies.

" But still more directly and personally, the Bible is the practical everyday guidebook, the one perfect rule of life. It is not simply a complete and beautiful theory, but it comes down to everyday affairs in the most practical way. It describes minutely our duties to ourselves, to our bodies, to our minds, to our spiritual natures, in childhood, youth, and hoary age; our duties to each other, husbands to wives, wives to husbands, parents to children and children to parents; it designates our neighbors, and our relations to them socially, intellectually, and religiously, our civil and our legal and all other relations. Indeed, our common laws and the common laws of every civilized country today are based almost entirely upon the Mosaic code, in many instances copied directly from the Old Testament. In fact, it would be difficult to discover any important question in life about which the Bible is silent. It is all-comprehensive, all-embracing, God's own wisdom, the conclusions He has reached upon ten thousand subjects covering every important phase of human life and human relations. And then to help us understand it all there is presented *one model life*, a perfect specimen of a man. . . .

" In brief, the word ' wisdom ' means *God's conclusions about everything becoming our conclusions.* And a careful and prayerful study of the Bible, helped by the Holy Spirit, such a careful and prayerful study as will clearly reveal God's copy, and will secure the absorption of its spirit and its life germs into our heart and life, will give us this wisdom and secure for us all the wonderful things promised." [6]

This true philosophy recognizes that man in his sinful, fallen, weakened state cannot comprehend the deep things of God, and that his

[6] Lamb, *The Making of a Man,* pp. 36–38, 55–57.

mind should be exercised principally in those fields of thought and study which will have a tendency to bring him into harmony with God and with His great plan for the salvation of mankind. It will not seek to solve the mysteries of creation and of human life in their wonderful trinity of action and reaction on body, mind, and spirit, but will be content now to " know in part," since then " we shall know even as we are known." A knowledge of the workings of conscience will be regarded as of more importance than a knowledge of the workings of consciousness. The meaning of percepts and concepts will be appreciated in proportion as they give us a clearer understanding of the precepts that should govern the life and conduct.

Abbe Pluché, in 1741, wrote a two-volume work entitled, *The History of the Heavens Considered According to the Notions of the Poets and Philosophers Compared with the Doctrines of Moses.* He considers the world-building theories of ancient and modern philosophers, and shows how they contradict Moses' account of the creation of the world. The second volume shows that the philosophy of Moses has stood the test of time and experience, and has saved its devotees from skepticism and infidelity. The author closes his discussion with the following statement regarding the field of philosophy and the guide of the philosopher:

" God gave man senses and understanding to improve everything upon the earth and to give Him praise for the same. To this point it is that experience, common sense, conscience, Moses, and all the Holy Scriptures refer us; and from this point all our great systems of physics (philosophy) seem to have labored to make us swerve, by raising us so high as to put us out of our sphere, and by busying us about what we can neither understand nor make any use of.

" Philosophy will then become amiable, accessible to every one, satisfactory, and profitable in proportion as philosophers, taking the extent (limit) of the human understanding for their rule, will renounce all learned pageantry, empty speculations, pretended profundities, and above all the illusory maxim of never admitting anything but what we evidently conceive, invariably to stick to the knowledge of facts, or the evidence of outward objects, of usages and relations. The natural consequence of the comparison which we have made of the thoughts of both the ancients and the moderns concerning the origin and design of all things, with what Moses tells us of the same, is that not only in point of religion, but also in natural philosophy, we ought to be contented with the certainty of experience and the simplicity of revelation." [7]

The true philosopher has not only an intellectual and spiritual, but also a physical reward, both in this life and in the life to come:

" A man's wisdom maketh his face to shine, and the boldness of his face shall be changed " (Eccl. 8: 1). " They that be wise shall shine as the brightness of the firmament; and they that turn many to righteousness as the stars forever and ever " (Dan. 12: 3).

[7] Abbe Pluché, *The History of the Heavens Considered*, Vol. II, p. 245.

PART FOUR

INFLUENCE OF HEBREW EDUCATION

XX

TRIUMPHS OF HEBREW EDUCATION

Educational Product

HAVING considered the educational principles and practice of the ancient Hebrews, we now come to the consideration of the products of their system and the contributions that have been made by them to the world's enlightenment and prosperity. Our first consideration will be given to the product from Hebrew homes and schools. The material is ample, for much of the Bible is devoted to the evaluation of the characters of men and women living in Bible times.

The value of the finished product of any factory does not depend on the number and size of the buildings, the amount of equipment provided, or the number of employees on the pay roll. The measure of its value is determined by its need and service. Does it meet fully the purpose for which it was produced, and supply a very urgent need? The buildings, equipment and employees are only secondary factors in determining the value of the finished product. The value primarily depends on the need it supplies, and how fully the need is met.

This is equally true of the product of any organization or institution. Accordingly we now give consideration to some of the student product of Hebrew education, as carried on in the homes and schools of that oriental people. Some of these students and their experiences have already been referred to, but we call attention to them again for a further examination of the product of the Hebrew educational system, and its influence on the leading nations of the ancient world.

Joseph

Joseph was a diligent student of a home school and lived a shepherd's life until he was seventeen years of age. Then he was sold into bondage and taken as a slave to Egypt, but soon was made overseer of his master Potiphar's household. He was cast into prison for refusing to yield to the temptation of Potiphar's wife, but was elevated to the position of assistant warden of the prison. He interpreted the dreams of two of the prisoners, which were fulfilled to the letter. Later he was called to interpret the dreams of King Pharaoh concerning the seven years' famine, and gave God the honor for interpreting the dreams. He was given a place in the kingdom next to Pharaoh, and was made food conservator and distributor for the nation. For more than sixty years Joseph was prime minister of Egypt.

This is the inspired testimony of his life-service in Egypt: " He (Pharaoh) made him lord of his house and ruler of all his substance: to bind his princes at his pleasure; and teach his senators wisdom " (Ps. 105: 21, 22). Joseph's physical education and training are attested by the organization that produced, conserved, and distributed food to nations facing starvation. His intellectual power is revealed in teaching Pharaoh's senators wisdom; his spiritual power, in resisting the sin and corruption prevailing in the royal court, and publicly acknowledging his allegiance to God.

Moses

Moses received his education at home from his mother until he was twelve years of age, and was then transferred to the royal court, after which he was educated in all the learning of the Egyptians. He refused the throne of Egypt, and became the leader and deliverer of his down-trodden people. During forty years of wilderness wandering, he faith-fully and tenderly cared for the mighty nation that God had com-missioned him to lead from Egypt into the Promised Land. In spite of abuse, insult, and murmurings, he was true to his trust, and led his people to the borders of Canaan; but because of one rash act under severe stress of conditions, he was not privileged to lead them over Jordan. However, God gave him a view of the Promised Land from Pisgah's heights, and after a brief rest and sleep in the grave, he was awakened and welcomed into the heavenly Canaan.

His early years of education according to the divine plan were nearly neutralized by the wrong education received in the schools of Egypt, so that for forty years he had to be schooled in the mountains of Midian, while caring for the sheep. There he learned how to shepherd the flock God planned for him to lead out of Egypt into the land of Canaan. Worldly education hindered for forty years the carrying out of God's plan, so that late in life—at eighty years of age—Moses began the work he might have taken up at forty. This left him but forty years of service, for he died at the age of 120. Joseph was not influenced by worldly education; he began his work as food conservator of Egypt at the age of thirty. He died at 110, and so was privileged to serve nobly for eighty years—a period double the length of Moses' service. This is a strong recommendation for the divine plan of education.

David

Like Joseph, David was early trained in the shepherd school. While learning how to contend with the enemies of his flock, he also learned lessons that were invaluable to him later in guarding the sheep of the heavenly fold. He comes from the field where he has slain the lion and the bear, and with a stone and a sling slays Goliath, the enemy of Israel, on the field of battle.

Observe the close bond of union between David's physical and spiritual powers, which is so unconsciously expressed when he affirms that the God who delivered him from his animal foes will give him victory over his human foe:

" The Lord that delivered me out of the paw of the lion, and out of the paw of the bear, he will deliver me out of the hand of this Philistine " (I Sam. 17: 37).

In God's hand he was a mighty warrior, and was used by Him to subdue all of Israel's enemies. In the time of peace, David carried forward great building enterprises, building largely the city called by his own name; he also built a large house of cedars for himself (II Sam. 5: 9–12). He desired greatly to build a house for God; but being a man of war, he was permitted only to gather the materials (II Sam. 7: 2; I Kings 8: 17; I Chron. 17: 1–12).

But David was a man of words as well as deeds. No student of the schools of the prophets ever wrote more beautiful words, more mighty, more spiritual, than David, as they appear in his psalms. Thus we see that his intellectual power was not a whit behind his physical and spiritual powers. When God found him in the sheepcote, He said, " I have found David the son of Jesse, a man after mine own heart, which shall fulfil all my will " (Acts 13: 22).

David in his home education had received such a thorough, symmetrical training that he was very highly regarded in the royal court of Saul.

" David behaved himself wisely in all his ways; and the Lord was with him." " David behaved himself more wisely than all the servants of Saul; so that his name was precious " (I Sam. 18: 14, 30, margin).

The secret of his influence and knowledge is revealed in his own words:

" I will behave myself wisely in a perfect way. . . . I will set no wicked thing before mine eyes. I hate the work of them that turn aside; it shall not cleave to me. A froward heart shall depart from me: I will not know a wicked person " (Ps. 101: 2–4).

Surely David was educated according to the divine standard, and the results of such a training are seen in his life-work.

Solomon

David's son, Solomon, was undoubtedly given every opportunity to receive an education after the divine plan. He early showed his ability to carry forward successfully great industrial enterprises requiring physical skill. This was manifest during the seven years occupied in building the temple. All nations were represented at the dedication, and saw the grandest structure that had ever been reared by human hands. The rulers of the surrounding nations returned to their kingdoms greatly impressed with its magnificence and grandeur, and endeavored in the building of their own temples to copy Solomon's work (I Kings 7: 1; II Chron. 8: 1–6). Of his industrial activities, calling into action his physical powers and those of his subjects, he says:

"I made me great works; I builded me houses; I planted me vineyards; I made me gardens and orchards, and I planted trees in them of all kind of fruit. I made me pools of water, to water therewith the wood that bringeth forth trees" (Eccl. 2: 4–6).

This industrial spirit, Solomon imbibed from the schools of the prophets, and later in life reproved the sluggard for his indolence and lack of thrift (Prov. 24: 30–34; Eccl. 10: 18; Prov. 6: 6–11; 20: 24).

His intellectual powers were equally developed with his physical powers, if not more fully. We find him a master in science, literature, and music, and his fame so spread abroad that the rulers of the surrounding nations came to inquire regarding the report they had heard, and went away convinced of its truthfulness. One of the rulers, after an interview with Solomon, said: "Behold the half was not told me: thy wisdom and prosperity exceedeth the fame which I heard" (I Kings 10: 7).

Early in life Solomon recognized his dependence upon God, and in a dream of the night acknowledged his nothingness without divine aid, and when given his choice of all gifts, chose the supreme gift—wisdom, for he said, "Wisdom is the principal thing." As long as he acknowledged God as supreme, and preserved the proper equilibrium of his physical, mental, and spiritual powers, there was none recognized greater than he. But the cup most difficult to carry is the cup that is full to the brim. Becoming proud of his physical and intellectual attainments, he neglected the culture of his spiritual powers—the balance wheel of character—and allying himself with the surrounding nations, he soon fell from the high eminence to which God had exalted him, and taking with him a whole nation of loyal and devoted subjects, they sank together into the mires of heathenism, from which Elijah, Elisha, and other prophets of God were unable wholly to extricate them.

Esther

It is interesting and encouraging to note that women as well as men, when truly educated, are fitted to occupy high and exalted positions of trust and responsibility. It was not only for Joseph and Daniel to stand "next to the king," but this was also the privilege of Queen Esther. God as well as man could trust her in that high position, for she was not only beautiful and queenly in person, but also in character. Humility and loyalty were the twin virtues that shone most brightly in her life. When being prepared for presentation to the king, she "required nothing" in apparel outside of what had been appointed her.

When her people were about to be destroyed, she, contrary to a law the penalty of which was death, obeyed the command of Mordecai, "as when she was brought up with him," and uninvited went into the presence of the king and saved her nation. Having learned loyalty and obedience at home under the training of Mordecai, she was loyal and obedient both to him and to God, "choosing," like Moses, "rather to suffer affliction with the people of God, than to enjoy the pleasures of sin for a season."

Mordecai had not neglected Esther's physical education, for the maid was fair of form and of good countenance. Her intellectual powers must have been highly developed to enable her to act as queen of a mighty empire. With great wisdom and prudence she went in and out before the people; and the divine record says: " Esther obtained favor in the sight of all them that looked upon her " (Esther 2: 15).

As already noticed, her moral and spiritual powers were strongly developed and mightily exercised in behalf of the people of God in their persecutions and sufferings. Esther was a " finished product " of God's system of education. What does her life's work say for the system?

Nehemiah

This young man occupied the honored position of cupbearer in the royal palace of King Artaxerxes. He learned through some of his own people that the work of restoring Jerusalem was at a standstill. He was much grieved by this report, and spent much time praying, fasting, and weeping. He was willing to give up his position of honor and ease to go to Jerusalem and superintend the work himself. He was filling his present position well, and the king and queen were loath to let him go. They finally consented, after he set a time for returning.

Nehemiah spent many years in earnest, vigilant toil; and the walls were finished, in spite of all that Tobiah, Sanballat, and others of his enemies could do to hinder the work. They tried several times to entice him away from the walls, but each time he sent back word: " I am doing a great work, so that I cannot come down: why should the work cease, whilst I leave it, and come down to you? " (Neh. 6: 3).

Not only did he rebuild the walls of Jerusalem, but he acted as governor of Israel for several years. To organize and establish a government with laws, and administer these with wisdom and justice, requires a high degree of mental attainment. Had he not possessed a remarkable degree of culture, he would never have been called to serve as cupbearer in the court of Persia.

As with Joseph and Moses, Nehemiah's early education resulted in the harmonious development of his threefold powers and their dedication to the service of God. His life's work, as recorded in sacred biography, vindicates the system of education that developed a man of marvelous daring and executive ability, ready for service in every good work.

Daniel and His Companions

These four young men, when hardly out of their teens, were carried captive from their Judæan homes to the land of Babylon. Of their educational attainments the divine testimony is that they were "children in whom was no blemish, but well favored, and skilful in all wisdom, and cunning in knowledge, and understanding science, and such as had ability in them to stand in the king's palace." With their physical and intellectual inheritance from the home school, is it any wonder that, after attending the Babylonian university for three years, " in all matters of wisdom and understanding, that the king inquired of them, he found them ten times better " than all the educated men in his realm? The testimony quoted says nothing of their spiritual attainments, but they must have been of a high character, for we learn that for the sake of their God and their religion they shrank not from the fiery furnace, nor from the lions' den, and were miraculously delivered. These men were exalted to high positions of trust and responsibility in governmental affairs, Daniel standing next to the king in both Babylon and Medo-Persia.

Notice how thorough was their physical education—" children in whom was no blemish, but well favored." The principles of health and physical preservation learned in childhood they would not violate, though their diet was prescribed by the king. " Daniel purposed in his heart that he would not defile himself with the portion of the king's meat, nor with the wine which he drank." Acting as mouthpiece for his companions, he made request for a more simple and healthful diet. His congenial spirit and frank, straightforward manner " brought Daniel into favor and tender love with the prince of the eunuchs," and the request was granted.

Daniel's physical and intellectual training had qualified him to solve successfully the industrial and commercial problems of great empires. He was prime minister of Babylon and was appointed head over all the wise men of Babylon. When Babylon was overthrown by Medo-Persia, Daniel's services were in great demand, and he was appointed prime minister by King Darius. Daniel was chosen to this position from three presidents, he being selected " because an excellent spirit was in him; and the king thought to set him over the whole realm."

Because of jealousy the other two presidents and one hundred twenty princes sought to find fault with Daniel's administration of the affairs of the kingdom. " But they could find none occasion nor fault; forasmuch as he was faithful, neither was there any error or fault found in him " (Dan. 6: 4).

What an illustrious example of the proper blending of the physical, intellectual, and spiritual powers in effective and efficient ministry to his fellow beings, does the life of Daniel bring to view! He who was permitted to behold visions of God until his physical being gave way, afterward " rose up, and did the king's business."

What does the life-work of these students from the schools of Israel testify with reference to the value and efficiency of the system of education given by God to the ancient Hebrew nation? Let us hear the answer of the learned Apostle Paul:

" What advantage then hath the Jew? . . . *Much every way:* chiefly because that unto them were committed the oracles of God " (Rom. 3: 1, 2). " To whom pertaineth the adoption, and the glory, and the covenants, and the giving of the law, and the service of God, and the promises " (Rom. 9: 4).

Superiority of Hebrew Education

The Hebrew system of education, which produced such splendid types as Joseph, Moses, David, Solomon, Daniel, Hananiah, Mishael, Azariah, Esther, Ezra, and Nehemiah, was on trial from the days of Abraham, down to the restoration of Israel after the seventy years of captivity. Three times it triumphed over the systems of education in the surrounding nations, and each triumph was publicly acknowledged and heralded throughout the world.

1. *The Vindication in Egypt.* It was in Egypt that the superiority of the Hebrew system of education was first vindicated. Joseph, a young Hebrew, was called from the prison house before the throne of Egypt to do what all the wise men had failed to do—interpret Pharaoh's dreams:

" Pharaoh said unto Joseph, I have dreamed a dream, and there is none that can interpret it: and I have heard say of thee, that thou canst understand a dream to interpret it. And Joseph answered Pharaoh, saying, it is not in me: God shall give Pharaoh an answer of peace " (Gen. 41: 15, 16).

Joseph not only interpreted the dreams fully, but he wisely advised Pharaoh to select a man to have charge of the production, conservation, and distribution of food throughout the whole empire:

" Pharaoh said unto Joseph, Forasmuch as God hath showed thee all this, there is none so discreet and wise as thou art: thou shalt be over my house, and according unto thy word shall all my people be ruled: only in the throne will I be greater than thou." " I am Pharaoh, and without thee shall no man lift up his hand or foot in all the land of Egypt " (Verses 39, 40, 44). " And Pharaoh took off his ring from his hand, and put it upon Joseph's hand, and arrayed him in vestures of fine linen, and put a golden chain about his neck; and he made him to ride in the second chariot which he had; and they cried before him, Bow the knee " (Verses 42, 43).

Egyptian education bowed acknowledgment to the superiority of the education given in the Hebrew patriarchal family school, of which the patriarch Jacob was the head.

2. *The Vindication in Judæa.* Solomon, a son of David, was educated in one of the prophetical schools of Israel. His education is compared with that of other men in other nations in the following words of Scripture:

" Solomon's wisdom excelled the wisdom of all the children of the east country, and all the wisdom of Egypt. For he was wiser than all men; than Ethan the Ezrahite, and Heman, and Chalcol, and Darda, the sons of Mahol: and his fame was in all nations round about " (I Kings 4: 30, 31).

His education was broad, comprehending not only morals and religion, but letters, music, and science are specifically mentioned. (See verses 32 and 33.)

His fame as a scholar spread abroad:

" There came of all people to hear the wisdom of Solomon from all kings of the earth, which had heard of his wisdom '' (Verse 34). '' All the kings of the earth sought the presence of Solomon, to hear his wisdom, that God had put into his heart '' (II Chron. 9: 23).

The queen of Sheba came from a far country and with a long train bearing gifts, yet she came with a doubting heart. But after she had communed with Solomon and had seen the royal court, with its furnishings and attendants, she said to the king:

" It was a true report which I heard in mine own land of thine acts, and of thy wisdom: howbeit I believed not their words, until I came, and mine eyes had seen it: and, behold, the one-half of the greatness of thy wisdom was not told me: for thou exceedest the fame that I heard '' (Verses 5, 6).

All the systems of education of the surrounding nations were outrivaled by the system that in Judæa produced a David and a Solomon, and its superiority was everywhere gratefully acknowledged.

3. *The Vindication in Babylon.* The early education of the four Hebrew youths carried captive to Babylon was put to a crucial test. After spending three years in mastering the Chaldean tongue and learning, they were examined by Nebuchadnezzar the king with this result: " In all matters of wisdom and understanding . . . he found them ten times better than all the magicians and astrologers that were in all his realm " (Dan. 1: 20).

Later the wisdom of Daniel, like that of Joseph, was put to the test in not only interpreting, but also in recalling to the mind of Nebuchadnezzar, the forgotten dream. All the wise men of his realm were given opportunity to solve this problem, but failed, and acknowledged their inability to meet the king's demand. The king, disappointed and enraged, was about to destroy all the wise men, when Daniel interceded, and was given opportunity to declare and interpret the dream. This he did before the king, who answered and said:

" Of a truth it is, that your God is a God of gods, and a Lord of kings, and a revealer of secrets, seeing thou couldst reveal this secret. Then the king made Daniel a great man, and gave him many great gifts, and made him ruler over the whole province of Babylon, and chief of the governors over all the wise men of Babylon '' (Dan. 2: 47, 48).

His three companions were also highly honored, being set " over the affairs of the province of Babylon: but Daniel sat in the gate of the king " (Verse 49).

Thus a third time in the history of Israel the superiority of the Hebrew system of education was fully vindicated. The learned Apostle Paul, hundreds of years later, vindicated the Jewish system of education and gave the secret of its superior strength and efficiency: " What advantage then hath the Jew? . . . Much every way: chiefly because that unto them were committed the oracles of God " (Rom. 3: 1, 2).

The psalmist attributed his superior wisdom and knowledge to the oracles of God—God's holy law:

" O how love I thy law! it is my meditation all the day. Thou through thy commandments hast made me wiser than mine enemies: for they (thy commandments) are ever with me. I have more understanding than all my teachers: for thy testimonies are my meditation. I understand more than the ancients (the sages), because I keep thy precepts " (Ps. 119: 97–100).

Did this wonderful wealth of wisdom and knowledge gathered under the Hebrew system of education pass away with the decline and fall of the nation, or was it conserved, and shared by the nations that have since come on the stage of action? Are the existing nations of earth today blessed by being partakers of this fruit borne by the tree of knowledge which flourished in Judæa in the youth-time of the world? Has the promise made to Abraham, the father of the Hebrew nation, been fulfilled: " I will make of thee a great nation, . . . and in thee shall all the families of the earth be blessed "? This important question will be considered in the following chapter.

XXI

CONTRIBUTIONS OF HEBREW EDUCATION

Service in the Nations

SOME of the illustrious Hebrew students we have found quitting themselves like men, and occupying positions of trust and honor in the nations whither they were carried captive. Prominent among these were Joseph in Egypt; Daniel in Babylon; Ezra, Nehemiah, Mordecai, and Esther in Medo-Persia. Mordecai's power and influence under Ahasuerus are graphically stated in the following words of Scripture:

" The king Ahasuerus laid a tribute upon the land, and upon the isles of the sea. And all the acts of his power and of his might, and the declaration of the greatness of Mordecai, whereunto the king advanced him, are they not written in the book of the chronicles of the kings of Media and Persia? For Mordecai the Jew was next unto King Ahasuerus, and great among the Jews, and accepted of the multitude of his brethren, seeking the wealth of his people, and speaking peace to all his seed " (Esther 10).

Our study of Bible history has clearly shown that Egypt, Babylon and Medo-Persia were greatly influenced and benefited by Hebrew education. The question may arise whether Greece and Rome were also similarly blessed. The only Scriptural reference to Greece is prophetical rather than historical:

" Turn you to the strong hold, ye prisoners of hope: even today do I declare that I will render double unto thee; when I have bent Judah for me and filled the bow with Ephraim, and raised up thy sons, O Zion, against thy sons, O Greece, and made thee as the sword of a mighty man. And the Lord shall be seen over them; . . . the Lord of hosts shall defend them . . . and the Lord their God shall save them in that day as the flock of his people; for they shall be as the stones of a crown, lifted up as an ensign upon his land. . . . Ask ye of the Lord rain in the time of the latter rain " (Zech. 9: 12–16; 10: 1).

This prophecy undoubtedly had a partial fulfillment, when, according to Josephus, Alexander the Great honored Jaddua, the high priest of the Jews, as he approached Jerusalem to plunder and destroy it because of his refusal to violate his oath of allegiance to Darius king of Persia. The following is the record of the event as given by the historian, Josephus:

" When he (Jaddua) understood that Alexander was not far from the city, he went out in procession, with the priests and the multitude of the citizens. The procession was venerable, and the manner of it different from that of other nations.
. . . " When the multitude appeared at a distance in white garments

while the priests stood clothed with fine linen, and the high priest in purple and scarlet clothing with his mitre on his head; having a golden plate whereon the name of God was engraven; Alexander approached by himself and adored that name and first saluted the high priest. The Jews also did altogether salute Alexander and encompass him about. Hereupon the Kings of Syria and the rest were surprised at what Alexander had done and supposed him disordered in his mind. However, Parmenio alone went up to him, and asked him how it came to pass, that when all others adored him, he should adore the high priest of the Jews? To whom he replied: ' I did not adore him, but that God who hath honored him with his high priesthood. For I saw this person in a dream in this very habitat, when I was at Dios in Macedonia. Who, when I was considering with myself, how I might obtain the dominion of Asia, exhorted me to make no delay, but boldly to pass over the sea thither for that he would conduct my army, and would give me the dominion over the Persians. Whence it is that having seen no other in that habit (dress) and now seeing this person in it and remembering that vision, and the exhortation which I had in my dream, I believe that I bring this army under the divine conduct, and shall therewith conquer Darius, and destroy the power of the Persians; and that all things will succeed according to what is in my own mind.'

" When he had said this to Parmenio, and had given the high priest his right hand, the priests ran along by him; and he came into the city. And when he went up into the temple, he offered sacrifice to God according to the high priest's direction; and magnificently treated both the high priest, and the priests. And when the book of Daniel was shown to him, wherein Daniel declared that one of the Greeks should destroy the empire of the Persians, he supposed that himself was the person intended. And as he was then glad, he dismissed the multitude for the present; but the next day he called them to him, and bade them ask what favors they pleased of him. Accordingly the high priest desired that they might enjoy the laws of their forefathers, and might pay no tribute the seventh year. This was readily granted. And when they entreated that he would permit the Jews in Babylon and Media to enjoy their own laws also, he willingly promised to do hereafter what they desired." [1]

Near the close of Christ's ministry Greek scholars came to His disciples saying: " Sir, we would see Jesus " (John 12: 20-22). Concerning this visit a modern educator makes the following comment:

" These men came from the West to find the Saviour at the close of His life, as the wise men had come from the East at the beginning. . . . The magi from a heathen land came to the manger with their gifts to worship the Saviour. So these Greeks representing the nations, tribes and peoples of the world, came to see Jesus. So the people of all lands and of all ages would be drawn by the Saviour's cross. So shall many ' come from the east and west, and shall sit down with Abraham and Isaac and Jacob in the kingdom of heaven ' " (Matt. 8: 11).[2]

The prophecy above quoted foretelling the controversy between Zion and Greece indicates that it will be waged during the time of the " latter rain," which ripens the harvest of the earth. During that time

---

[1] Josephus, *Antiquities of the Jews,* Book XI, pp. 417-418.
[2] White, *Desire of the Ages,* pp. 621-622.

the Elijah program of education carried out by him in the schools of the prophets will be carried forward by the sympathetic co-operation of parents and children.   This final educational movement resulting in victory and triumph to Zion is foretold by the prophet Malachi:

" Behold I will send you Elijah the prophet before the coming of the great and dreadful day of the Lord; and he shall turn the heart of the fathers to the children; and the heart of the children to their fathers; lest I come and smite the earth with a curse " (Mal. 4: 5, 6).

The triumphant influence of Christian education by Christ and His followers in the Roman Empire during the first three centuries is strongly attested by both church and secular historians.   (See pages 248–250.)

While Israel as a nation became selfish, self-centered and exclusive, and failed to be the saving light unto all nations that God had designed her to be, yet during the captivity, and subsequently, the superior wisdom, knowledge, and skill of her sons and daughters were recognized, and they became teachers and administrators in the affairs of world empires.   We find both Nebuchadnezzar and Darius acknowledging the superiority of Israel's God and of her noble captive children, and issuing world-wide decrees warning all nations and peoples not to speak anything amiss against the God of Daniel, Shadrach, Meshach, and Abed-nego, but rather that all men fear and tremble before Him.

Shall we not conclude that these nations were also greatly blessed by becoming sharers with Israel in their knowledge of the arts, sciences, and letters, and that all down through the centuries, noble Jewish men and women have been the conservators and distributors of knowledge? This is contrary to the generally accepted view.   While Israel is given credit for giving to the world a pure monotheistic religion, culminating in Christianity through the teachings of Christ, the greatest Jew, yet most scholars have constantly and persistently affirmed that we are indebted solely to Greece and Rome for most of our knowledge outside of religion and morals.   However, the learned Paul, as already noted, emphatically declared that the Jews have " much (the advantage) every way " over other nations.

Honor to Whom Honor is Due

But strange as it may seem, above the voices of the multitude of doubting scholars, other voices are sounding and being heard.   Some scholars are expressing faith in the testimony of Paul, and believe that the nations of today as well as the nations of the past are debtors to Israel in " every way " for the progress they have made.

While as a nation, Israel forsook the " fountain of living waters, and hewed them out cisterns, broken cisterns, that can hold no water " (Jer. 2: 13), yet here and there individuals drank from the unfailing fountain of wisdom and knowledge, and the nations of earth have been enlightened and uplifted by their rich and generous contributions.

The Honor Roll

It would be intensely interesting and profitable to look over the honor roll containing the names of illustrious Hebrew scholars and statesmen, noting the time when each lived, and the nations and rulers blessed by their service; and above all to learn the particular contribution each one made to the world's knowledge and advancement. This information can be gleaned from Dr. Schleiden's book previously referred to (see pp. 33–35), sometimes labeled *The Sciences Among the Jews,* and from Gustav Karpeles' work entitled *Jewish Literature and Other Essays,* in the chapter " The Jews in the History of Civilization." These writers tell us:

1.   That the greatest classic in the English or any other language— the Bible—is of Hebrew origin, and that the Jews as a nation were known as a literary people.   After the exile they were called by the Arabians, the *" Ahl ul Kitab "* (the people of the Writ).   Almost every Jew could write, and every member of the community could read the holy Scriptures.   Before the Christian era, many Jews, especially in Alexandria, spoke Hebrew and Greek.   At the time Rome ruled, they learned Latin; later Syriac; after that Arabic, and finally they added Spanish, French, and German.   During the Middle Ages there were only a few Jews, of the lower class, who did not understand at least two languages; many had complete command of five to seven languages.

Besides writing original works in science, letters, and philosophy, the Jews have been the world's most gifted translators, translating the Holy Scriptures into the Arabic and other languages, as well as works on science and philosophy.

2.   That in the field of science the Jews were the greatest physicians, being the best informed in medical knowledge.   The first works on fevers and *materia medica* were written by Jewish physicians, and translated into other languages.   Until the end of the sixteenth century the most famous physicians were largely Jews who founded and operated medical schools.   Not until the end of the seventeenth century was a line of separation drawn between medicine and natural science; therefore all medical men were students of natural science.   Mathematics and astronomy were the first to disconnect.   Many eminent astronomers and mathematicians are named among the Jewish scholars.   The astronomers developed astronomical tables; made maps showing the constellations of the stars; invented astronomical instruments; discovered the periodic revolution of Halley's comet, the parallax of the stars, the rotation of the earth on its axis, the causes of the change of the seasons, the refraction of light; wrote astronomical works, and laid the foundation for establishing in the time of Tycho Brahe and Kepler the fundamental principles of astronomy, and a correct view of the orbits of the heavenly bodies.   Jewish mathematicians originated four of the names of the ten numerals, the decimal calculation, the abacus (counting board), and assisted in the work of constructing navigation instruments to aid in traveling the trackless seas.

3. That a number of Jewish philosophers wrote on religious rather than metaphysical questions. They studied, however, the writings of the Greek philosophers, and Chasdai Crescas was the first to enter the arena against Aristotle and his authority. In his book *Or Adonai* ("The Light of God"), he combated with great acumen Aristotle's views on the universe and his "physics." This happened in 1410 A. D., considerably before any Christian scholar ventured to protest against the sway which faith in Aristotle had so long held.

4. That in statecraft the Jews have shown great skill and ability. All through the ages since the time of Daniel and Mordecai, the rulers of kingdoms and nations have chosen Jews to act as envoys, diplomats, prime ministers, and financiers in the affairs of state. Solomon's words regarding advancement and promotion have proved true with those of his brethren who have taken them to heart, and who have sought to improve upon their talents: "A man's gift maketh room for him, and bringeth him before great men" (Prov. 18: 16).

Hebrew Science

The greatest contribution made by the Hebrews to the world needs is the monothestic religion revealed in the Old Testament, and magnified in the Gospels and Epistles of the New Testament. This pure, undefiled religion embraced all knowledge; not only a knowledge of God and His word; but also of His works, the study of which is called "science." The first science in importance which was studied by the Hebrews had to do with the laws of sanitation and hygiene, or the laws of health. Today this branch of science is called the "study of medicine." It includes a study of physiology, anatomy, and hygiene, with a view to the promotion of health and health conditions and the prevention and cure of disease. David in Psalm 139 refers to this study of the masterpiece of God's workmanship:

" I will praise thee; for I am fearfully and wonderfully made: marvelous are thy works; and that my soul knoweth right well. My substance was not hid from thee, when I was made in secret, and curiously wrought in the lowest parts of the earth. Thine eyes did see my substance, yet being unperfect: and in thy book all my members were written, which in continuance were fashioned, when as yet there was none of them. How precious also are thy thoughts unto me, O God! how great is the sum of them. If I should count them, they are more in number than the sand: when I awake, I am still with thee " (Ps. 139: 14–18).

The priests and the Levites were the physicians and nurses, ministering to the physical as well as the spiritual needs of the people. Their ministry has already been considered under "Physical Education." (See pages 128–141.)

Man is not only to study God's workmanship as exhibited in his own being, but he is to carefully study all God's works over which the Creator in the beginning gave Adam and Eve dominion. David emphasizes this duty and privilege: "The works of the Lord are great, *sought out* of all them that have pleasure therein. . . . He hath made his wonderful works *to be remembered*" (Ps. 111: 2–4). This study by the Hebrews led them into all branches of science, which were not so fully classified as they are today.

Louis Gershenfield in his recent book *The Jew in Science* covers the history of science from the time of Moses to the present day. Concerning Moses as a scientist he says:

" Moses must have had a very enlarged knowledge of the sciences, to have drawn up a rational code, to consider social hygiene and the treatment of disease. . . . In the Bible we find that the priests are the sanitary police, and public health officers. Mention is made of contagious and other diseases, and the Hebrews can truly be called the founders of the prophylaxis (prevention of) of disease. Specific directions are given for the diagnosis and prevention of some of the important commonly found diseases, and isolation, disinfection, etc., were practiced. As Neuberger states, the chief glory of the Biblical science of medicine lies in the institution of social hygiene as a science.'' [3]

There is no question but what Moses gave to Israel a code of sanitary laws based on thoroughly scientific principles; however, he makes no claim of originating a code of sanitary regulations, but declares that he received them from God: " Now these are the commandments, the statutes, and the judgments which the Lord your God commanded to teach you that ye might do them in the land whither ye go to possess it " (Deut. 6: 1).

Science to the Hebrews was a sacred study, for they considered that they were studying the works of God. Even after Israel lost their national identity and were strangers in a strange land, the study of science went hand in hand with the study of the sacred Scriptures. Concerning the devotion to the study of the Scriptures and science, the author cited above says:

" The Jews did not lose interest in their religion and in investigations into the natural sciences, even when their homeland was destroyed and they lost their national independence. The fact is that they not only maintained their interest in the sciences that prevailed, but they in many instances became leaders in their promotion in those lands where they were allowed to live. Yet it is true that science throughout the early periods was inseparable from religion, which always influenced and served as a background for it.'' [4]

Some of the scientists of today have the same objectives as the Hebrews, in their study and teaching of science, but it is to be deeply regretted that many do not.

Mr. Gershenfield in his book gives the names of leading Jewish scientists down through the centuries beginning with the Christian era. Rabbi Hillel, the president of the Sanhedrin B. C. 33 to 9 A. D., was a

[3] L. Gershenfield, *The Jews in Science*, p. 32 (The Jewish Publication Society of America, Philadelphia).
[4] *Ibid.*, p. 33.

hygienist and natural scientist. Space does not permit the naming of the leading Jewish scientists that made valuable contributions to science during ancient, medieval, and modern times; but this has been ably done in the work, *The Jews in Science.*

Hebrew Literature

The Hebrew contribution in literature is far greater than in science. The Holy Scriptures is their unaided contribution—except as the writers " were moved by the Holy Ghost." Many books have been written by scholars extolling the unrivaled literary merits of the Bible. Some have discoursed on the lyric portions of the Scriptures; others on the dramatic, and still others on the prophetic. The inexhaustible depth and wealth of each is generally recognized by these literary artists, but as yet only limited opportunity has been provided in the schools for the study of these, the greatest of all literary contributions. Literature of all kinds and character, apart from Biblical literature, has a large place in school curriculums of all grades, but the *summum bonum* is given a stinted consideration, and often entirely neglected.

John Franklin Genung in his masterly work: *The Hebrew Literature of Wisdom,* emphasizes the importance and value of the study of the wisdom books of the Bible—Job, Proverbs, and Ecclesiastes in the Old Testament, and the Epistle of James in the New Testament. The purpose of this author in writing his book is thus stated in the preface:

" New light is breaking forth with almost startling rapidity, from Scripture; new windows of heaven opening for every new window of earth; this is true in our own time in a sense beyond what the world has known for centuries. If in however lowly degree the present volume may contribute some little ray to this increasing light, even though as soon as it is born it begins to die into the larger radiance that is surely dawning, the most fervent hope of the author will be realized. For he can conceive of no nobler occupation of the scholar than that which, as it inspired the ancient sages about whom he has written, has still the same power to draw men to the height of eternal truth and vision." [5]

Hebrew wisdom literature is of great value in the education of children and youth for it has to do with the conduct of daily living in the home and in the community. It makes plain and attractive right relations,—human and divine,—and gently and earnestly warns against those that are wrong.

Hebrew History

The Hebrew contribution to history is the greatest that has ever been made. Man could better dispense with all the history written aside from that contained in the Hebrew Scriptures rather than to be deprived of the history given in the Bible. With that unknown, both the past and the future are uncertain, and the destiny of the human race

[5] J. F. Genung, *The Hebrew Literature of Wisdom,* p. xviii (Houghton Mifflin Co.).

unknown. With a knowledge of Bible history and prophecy, the past is known, the present is understood, and the future is revealed. What a pity that history that makes known the past, enables one to understand the present, and reveals the future is given such meager consideration in the education of today.

Hebrew Fine Arts

In the fine arts the Hebrews made a rich contribution. As in literature, so in music the Hebrews gave to the world the best. No psalmody equals that composed and sung by " the sweet psalmist of Israel " (II Sam. 23: 1); and others associated with him in providing vocal and instrumental music for the temple service. When rendered today in the spirit of true worship, their power and influence transcends that produced by any other nation. All others, at most, are only imitations.

We have already seen that in architecture and the arts accompanying it in the building of " Solomon's Temple," the surrounding nations were greatly blest. (See p. 190.) Greece benefited most, and applied this borrowed knowledge in the building of temples to her gods. In the course of time she claimed this knowledge was the product of her own genius and refused to acknowledge her unselfish benefactor—the Hebrew nation. The fine arts were highly developed, but their use was prostituted to wicked licentious practices, in their religious and ceremonial rites, which weakened and degraded the characters of its devotees. In the course of time this nation which held the highest place of intellectual attainment among the nations, fell from her high honored position because of the prostitution of the excellent gifts that had been placed in her lap. Such will be the experience of not only nations, but individuals who prostitute to selfish ends the gifts of God.

Hebrew Polity

One of the greatest contributions made to the nations of earth by the Hebrews was that which had to do with the form and manner of government. The laws and statutes of Israel were to be an astonishment and wonder to the surrounding nations. Israel in the administration of governmental affairs was to be an example to all nations. Moses continually held this high ideal before his people:

" Behold, I have taught you statutes and judgments, even as the Lord my God commanded me, that ye should do so in the land whither ye go to possess it. Keep therefore and do them; for this is your wisdom and your understanding in the sight of the nations, which shall hear all these statutes, and say, Surely this great nation is a wise and understanding people. For what nation is there so great, who hath God so nigh unto them, as the Lord our God is in all things that we call upon him for? And what nation is there so great, that hath statutes and judgments so righteous as all this law, which I set before you this day? " (Deut. 4: 5–8).

Moses speaks of the temporal prosperity that God will give to Israel, and of the high and exalted place it will occupy among the nations:

" The Lord shall establish thee a holy people unto himself, as he hath sworn unto thee, if thou shalt keep the commandments of the Lord thy God, and walk in his ways. And all people of the earth shall see that thou art called by the name of the Lord; and they shall be afraid of thee. And the Lord shall make thee plenteous in goods, in the fruit of thy body, and in the fruit of thy cattle, and in the fruit of thy ground, in the land which the Lord sware unto thy fathers to give thee. The Lord shall open unto thee his good treasure, the heaven to give the rain unto thy land in his season, and to bless all the work of thine hand: and thou shalt lend unto many nations, and thou shalt not borrow. And the Lord shall make thee the head, and not the tail; and thou shalt be above only, and thou shalt not be beneath; if thou hearken unto the commandments of the Lord thy God, which I command thee this day, to observe and to do them '' (Deut. 28: 9–13).

The prophet Samuel wrote a book on Hebrew polity or government, and how it was to be administered:

" And Samuel said to all the people, See ye him whom the Lord hath chosen, that there is none like him among all the peoples? And all the people shouted, and said, God save the king. Then Samuel told the people the manner of the kingdom, and wrote it in a book, and laid it up before the Lord. And Samuel sent all the people away, every man to his house '' (I Sam. 10: 24, 25).

In modern times many lawyers and statesmen have written of Hebrew laws and government, extolling them in the highest terms. Concerning the Hebrew code of laws, an eminent jurist has written:

" The code bequeathed to them by their great law giver contains the only complete body of law which was ever given to a people at one time— that it is the only entire body of law which has come down to our days— that it is the only body of ancient law which still governs an existing people—that the nation which it respects, being scattered over the face of the whole earth, it is the only body of law that is equally observed in the four quarters of the globe—and, finally, that all other codes of law, of which history has preserved any recollection, were given to communities who already had written statutes, but who wished to change their form or modify their application; whereas, in this case, we behold a new society under the hands of a legislator who proceeds to lay its very foundations.''

Hebrew Philosophy

The greatest contribution of Hebrew philosophy is its insistent teaching that creation has a Creator, who upholds " all things by the word of his power " (Heb. 1: 3). Ancient and modern philosophy speak much of God's works and too little of God. The apostle Paul points out this tendency of the philosophers: "Who worshiped and served the creature (created things) more than the Creator " (Rom. 1: 25).

The French scientist Abbe Pluché in his work, *The History of the Heavens,* represents God speaking to the philosophers:

" Come, great architects, you who teach others this fabric! come, and learn of me how great is the wrong you do the disciples who listen to you. You mention my works to them, though you commonly examine only that part of them which I conceal from you. You hardly mention me to them, though you find . . . my bountiful hand and intentions everywhere. 'Tis true my name is sometimes pronounced in your conferences. You even dispute warmly when you speak of me; but you do it to bring my existence in question. You sometimes call me by the name of moving force, or of prime mover. But after having deigned to call in one first mover, to impress motion upon your dull heavy mass of an universal matter, you lose sight of me, and nature ingrosses all your attention. It is nature that makes the extract of the four elements (fire, air, water, earth); nature that unravels them; nature that constructs man, animals, plants, and fossils out of them. It is nature does all. I have as it were been a stranger in your physics. But what was the result of this? Your disciples have learned neither how to know God or His works."[6]

Abbe Pluché in the second volume of his work considers the philosophies of Aristotle, Epicurus, Gassendus, Descartes, and Newton, and tests them in the light of the "Physics of Moses." The following is his conclusion:

" It is not with the principles of Sir Isaac Newton as with the primitive matter of Aristotle, Gassendus, and Descartes. This matter, let it be presented to us under any terms whatever, as producing all things, both general and particular, by the bare impression of motion, is agreeable neither to the recital of Moses, according to which each particular being is the work of a particular will, nor to experience, according to which it is impossible for any general motion to organize a body or to produce an elementary grain; whereas Newton's physics seems perfectly agreeable to both. . . . His physics agree perfectly with the recital of Moses; since Newton, like Moses, attributed the production of the several elements, and the organization of the whole, to so many commands or intentions of the Creator."[7]

Abbe Pluché confirms his conclusion by quoting from Newton's work on *Optics:*

" In the beginning God formed matter into particles, solid, massy, hard, impenetrable, of such magnitude and figures, with such other properties, in such number and quantity and in such proportions with regard to space, as best answered the end for which He formed them."

To the above, Newton later added:

" That it seems that all material things have been composed of the above described hard and solid particles, diversely combined in the primitive formation of things by the direction of an intelligent agent, for to him who created these particles it belonged to put them in order. It would not be acting like a philosopher to pretend that the simple laws of nature may have been capable of fetching the world out of chaos, though this world, once made, may, by the help of these laws, continue to subsist for many ages."

May the contributions of Hebrew science and philosophy be more fully appreciated by educators of today, and their principles pervade all the instruction given in both of these important fields of knowledge.

<hr>

[6] Abbe Pluché, *The History of the Heavens*, Vol. II, pp. 74, 75.

[7] *Ibid.*, Vol. II, pp. 142–144.

XXII

MODERN AND HEBREW EDUCATION

Comparison and Evaluation

HAVING considered Hebrew education as to its principles, practice, product, and contributions, let us now briefly study modern education in the light of that ancient system. If those ancient educators were privileged to inspect modern systems of education, what would be their evaluation of them? It would hardly be fair to restrict the comparison of the religious system of Hebrew education to any secular system of any period of history, so the comparison will be with religious education more than with secular. The comparison is made for the purpose of seeing how fully the ancient Hebrew system is operating in modern times in Christian homes and schools.

In a previous chapter we noted that some modern educators (see page 32) are looking back and checking present-day theory and practice with that of the Hebrew system. There is a feeling that there has been a departure in some measure from ideals and methods that were steadfastly maintained by Hebrew educators, and that there should now be a return to the old paths. We give again the appeal to return made by Doctor Maynard:

" As for us, we can learn from Hebrew methods at times, from Hebrew ideals very often. In these days of machinery and complexity, of crowded tenements, highly strained modes of living, noisy, standardized pleasures, we need an education that will provide an escape for the heart and mind. The Hebrew knew where to find it, even by the waters of Babylon. Perchance if we are inspired by him, we shall know how to deal more effectively with the problem of education in theory and practice.

" The Greek with his art and his philosophy, the Roman with his law and his statesmanship, the Neo-Greek of the renaissance with his erudition and his classicism, are of less real value today than the Old Hebrew, because they did not understand as well as he, that the most important element of education is moral discipline, that the home is a place of happiness and duty, that true greatness is the righteousness which can be found only by faith in God." [1]

Lack of Morals in Education

As previously noted (see pages 22–26), the lack of morals in the education of today is generally deplored by modern educators. This was the strongest element in Hebrew education. Why this lamentable lack when the Hebrew Scriptures are accepted as the guide of Chris-

[1] Maynard, *A Survey of Hebrew Education*, pp. 57–59.

tian peoples, and the God of the Hebrews is the Christian's God? There are three serious contributing causes which, along with others not so vital, tend to neutralize and stifle efforts made in moral education and training:

1. *Doubt and Infidelity.* Much of educational effort consists in not only study and observation to discover truth; but also in testing and proving that the conclusions reached are true. This general plan of " proving all things," when applied to the study of the Scriptures, tends to infidelity and skepticism. This method had no place in Hebrew education when it came to the study of the sacred Scriptures. They were studied with reverence and humility of heart and mind, regarding them as the voice of God speaking just as truly as if it could be heard. This is an attitude of mind and spirit that must possess the parent and the teacher if it is to take possession of those under their instruction. This kind of study of the Scriptures develops in the children and youth a sense of moral responsibility to God and to those instructing them, which greatly aids in solving the problems of discipline in the home and in the school. It prepares the rising generation to carry efficiently the responsibilities of the generation they will follow.

2. *Sinful Inheritance.* An inherited sinful nature has already been shown to have a Scripture basis. (See pages 72–75.) This is denied by many educators, and their instruction of and attitude toward the children and youth has been accordingly. Holding that the child is non-moral; or, is neither good nor bad, has led parents and teachers to overlook wrong conduct, and gloss it over by saying: " The child is not responsible. It will outgrow it in time." " Let it act out its natural impulses; for if we restrict them, we hinder the natural working of the educational process." " Let the child learn from experience."

This sort of reasoning and attitude serve to strengthen wrong traits of character, and to smother any thought of responsibility to God or man. Parents and teachers are not respected or honored: and in the place of discipline and order, confusion and lawlessness reign. The children run the home, and the students run the school. If they do not like the way things are going, a strike or boycott is declared, until teacher, principal, or president is dismissed, or yields to the demands that are made.

It is true that the child is not morally responsible for wrong doing until its reasoning powers are developed sufficiently to understand matters clearly. Wrong is wrong; right is right, whether the mind of the child comprehends it or not. Evil is evil, sin is sin, whether the child has arrived at the age of responsibility or not, and the wise parent and teacher may " nip in the bud " wrong traits, and prevent their bearing a harvest of evil and woe. By divine law, bodily suffering,— corporal punishment,—was permitted if other measures failed to correct the stubborn, wilful disposition of the child.

3. *Self-Realization.* The discovery of self, the " ego," as often

spoken of in educational writings, has been emphasized by some educators during recent years. An appraisal and evaluation of one's
powers, and their fullest exercise and realization are considered necessary to progress and achievement. The potential possibilities of these
latent powers are highly extolled, so that repeated reference is made
to the "superman" that is about to appear above the educational
horizon. "Where there's a will, there's a way;" "You can if you
think so;" "I am the master of my fate;" and similar declarations
are a reflection of educational thought and conviction of some modern
educators. Scientific research and discoveries; the successful com-
pletion of great projects of construction; and the control and utiliza-
tion of great forces in nature for the benefit of man, have caused some
to feel that the lost dominion of the father of the human race is about
to be recaptured by his children after six thousand years of effort and
struggle. But now and then when the mighty forces of nature break
loose in earthquake, flood, and pestilence; and human nature rebels,
severing the ties of human brotherhood, causing revolution or ruthless
warfare; then man is again reminded of his impotency and helpless-
ness in a world where good and evil are ever in conflict.

Hebrew education recognized the limitations of man in a world of
sin. It emphasized his inability to master himself and to fully control
the forces of nature about him. It stimulated a spirit of courage,
industry and perseverance; but enjoined a spirit of humility recognizing the limitations of the human powers in study, research and
achievement.

Probably there is no greater hindrance to educational progress than
the spirit of pride and self-sufficiency. This develops a spirit of independence that causes men to lose sight of their dependence on God
for the talents and abilities He has given them. They feel that they
can acquire knowledge, and achieve success without divine aid. The
knowledge gained, the success achieved, minister to selfish ends, and
as the Apostle Paul declared: "Professing themselves to be wise, they
became fools . . . and even as they did not like to retain God in their
knowledge, Gave gave them over to a mind void of judgment to do
those things which are not convenient" (Rom. 1: 22, 28, margin).

Creative education, meaning original, constructive study and research, when carried forward in humility and integrity with a desire
to arrive at truth for the uplift and betterment of humanity and the
glory of God—is legitimate and praiseworthy. But an educational
procedure that leads men to regard themselves as creators, controllers,
and dictators of knowledge and their fellows, had no place in Hebrew
education.

The learned apostle Paul said of the true attitude and spirit of the
seeker after knowledge and wisdom:

" Knowledge puffeth up, but charity edifieth. And if any man thinketh
he knoweth (fully) anything, he knoweth nothing yet as he ought to know "
(I Cor. 8: 1, 2). " If a man think himself to be something, when

he is nothing, he deceiveth himself '' (Gal. 6: 3). '' Be not wise in your own conceits '' (Rom. 12: 16).

The Wise Man gave the same kind of counsel: "Seest thou a man wise in his own conceit? there is more hope of a fool than of him" (Prov. 26: 12).

God speaks to man and says:

'' Thus saith the Lord; Let not the wise man glory in his wisdom, . . . but let him that glorieth glory in this, that he understandeth and knoweth me, that I am the Lord which exercise lovingkindness, judgment, and righteousness, in the earth; for in these things I delight '' (Jer. 9: 23, 24).

Measuring the Human Mind

Not only have modern educators had visions of great possibilities of intellectual development; but they have devised ways and means of measuring the initial quantitative and qualitative mental endowment of the individual student. Attempts are now even being made to measure the moral powers of the student; but with less satisfactory results. Undoubtedly there is some value accruing from the wise and proper application of intelligence tests; but there is danger of placing too much dependence upon them. Because of individual differences students are divided into different groups so that each student may study to the best advantage, and not be held back by those with less mental ability. The danger point is reached in dealing with those who are short in mental endowment. The question will arise as to whether it will be worth while to provide them with educational opportunities. If so, it is suggested that the provisions be meager, and the student program such as will fit them to serve throughout life in a menial capacity. He is denied the privilege of aspiring to, and preparing for the higher callings and professions. In other words, full educational opportunities are to be provided for the few—the gifted—and the many are to be denied its full privileges and opportunities. They are compelled, as in the days of Greece, to be serfs and slaves, or as we now say, " common laborers " and " toilers."

Hebrew education gave equal privileges to all boys; and all girls were given equal educational opportunities, but not equal to that of the boys. Hebrew education, while recognizing individual differences, recognized that divine aid made up in some measure for individual differences in initial mental endowments; and also controlled personal environment. Divine power, as exercised by the ministration of the Holy Spirit and holy angels, counteracted opposing conditions and influences, provided the heart and soul was loyal to " Him in whom are hid all the treasures of wisdom and knowledge." In the youth life of Solomon we have a good example of divine aid given to increase the powers of the mind of one whose heart was right, and who was desirous of discharging his responsibilities efficiently and to the glory of his Maker.

David gave Solomon, his son, this counsel as he entrusted to him the responsibilities of the kingdom: "And thou Solomon, my son, know thou the God of thy father, and serve him with a perfect heart, and with a willing mind" (I Chron. 28: 9). As Solomon endeavored to do this, the Lord co-operated with him, increasing his mental and spiritual capacity: "God gave Solomon wisdom and understanding exceeding much, and largeness of heart, even as the sand that is on the sea shore" (I Kings 4: 29).

Nebuchadnezzar is an example of one who refused to yield mind and heart to God, and the experience following shows God's control of the physical, mental, and spiritual powers entrusted to man. (See Daniel 4.)

The healing of the body and the soul was an accepted tenet of Hebrew religion; and the healing of the mind was recognized in their educational theory and practice. The apostle Paul had much to say regarding the right and wrong exercise of the mind and heart, frequently coupling them together as though they are twin elements working together in the development of character. He exhorts: "Let this mind be in you which was also in Christ Jesus" (Phil. 2: 5); "Be renewed in the spirit of your mind" (Eph. 4: 23); "Be not conformed to this world, but be ye transformed by the renewing of your mind" (Rom. 12: 2). Not only can the mind be renewed, but divine power can restore a confused, disordered mind: "And they come to Jesus and see him that was possessed with the devil . . . sitting and clothed, and in his right mind" (Mark 5: 15). The mind as well as the soul is to be under divine control, and human teachers are privileged to co-operate with divine agencies in its training and development.

Psychology, which deals with the laws of the mind, is a very important subject, and yet unless properly studied and applied it becomes a very dangerous educational agency in dealing with children and youth. This branch of educational science has become so commercialized that its principles have been sadly misapplied to serve selfish ends. Again, as Boyd Henry Bode has shown in his book, *Conflicting Psychologies of Learning*, psychologists are far from unity in their views on this subject. The psycho-measurist and analyst have difficult problems to solve, and a recognition of the close relationship existing between the mental and moral powers of the human being will greatly aid in their correct solution.

Hebrew educators, without a technical laboratory knowledge for measuring and analyzing the human mind, seemed to be more successful than modern educators in dealing with the same problems. The proof for this is found in their educational product; and we believe that the superiority of their product was due to the recognition of the close relationship of the mental and moral powers, and the primary importance of the latter in determining educational procedure. This has already been noted (see page 215) in the experience of David who was wiser than the teachers and the philosophers because of his study of the oracles of God; and in the experiences of Daniel and his three companions (see page 211) in the university of Babylon, who were found in the final examination conducted by Nebuchadnezzar the king to be ten times wiser than all others in his realm. Their obedience and loyalty to the commandments and laws of God were demonstrated in their request for a change of the diet prescribed by the king; and their refusal to worship false gods, or to refrain from worshiping the true God. These men proved to be the most able counselors and administrators in the affairs of a world empire. Their I. Q. (intelligence quotient) was high because their M. Q. (moral quotient) was still higher. These students became extraordinary men because they were constantly in touch with extraordinary, even divine resources. One like the Son of God was in the fiery furnace; and an angel was in the lion's den. These were not the first contacts that were made with the heavenly; they were daily co-operating with the unseen.

Limitations of Mental Tests

As an indication of how impossible it is for human knowledge and foresight to measure a child or a youth's abilities and possibilities, the Scriptures speak of God looking for a man to take the throne vacated because of His rejection of Saul as king of Israel. God speaks to the prophet Samuel saying: " Fill thine horn with oil, and go, I will send thee to Jesse the Bethlehemite; for I have provided me a king among his sons " (I Sam. 16: 1). Jesse gathered together his sons and they passed before the prophet, who, when he sees Eliab the eldest, princely in his bearing, exclaims: " Surely the Lord's anointed is before Him! " The Lord rejects Eliab; and admonishes the prophet: " Look not on his countenance, or on the height of his stature; . . . for the Lord seeth not as man seeth; for man looketh on the outward appearance, but the Lord looketh on the heart " (Verses 6, 7). The remaining six sons gathered in that room were all rejected by the Lord. Then the prophet in his distress said to the father: " Are here all thy children? And he said there remaineth yet the youngest, and behold he keepeth the sheep." David is hurried into the presence of the prophet, probably in the shepherd's attire; but as soon as his feet pass over the threshold the Lord says to the prophet: " Arise, anoint him; for this is he. Then Samuel took the horn of oil and anointed him in the midst of his brethren, and the spirit of the Lord came upon David from that day forward " (Verses 12, 13).

Samuel, the seer, did not possess sufficient insight to make the right selection; and Jesse, the father, was so lacking in foresight that David was not included in the gathering of his sons, thus entirely eliminating him from a possible choice. From this incident recorded in sacred Scripture we learn:

(1) That human knowledge and wisdom is not able to discern and measure the innate mental and spiritual endowment of any human being and determine the course of training and development necessary to qualify the individual to serve his fellows in any capacity.

(2) Since this is true, that every human being should be afforded equal privileges and opportunities of education and training for service, so that human limitations shall not thwart the purpose of Him who imparts mental and spiritual endowments.

The Hebrew nation was the first nation to accord equal privileges and opportunities to all their children and youth; and their posterity (the Jews) scattered throughout the nations of earth still follow the example of their noble ancestors wherever and whenever possible.

Some modern educators, while recognizing the value of properly applied intelligence tests, are strong in their convictions that the measuring program has been carried to an unnecessary and unwise extreme, and they believe that some of the deductions made and conclusions drawn are unwarranted.

The noted educator William C. Bagley, in his illuminating work *Determinism in Education*, probably has most strongly criticized the theories put forth by the "educational determinists." In the first chapter of his book entitled, "Democracy and the I. Q.," he states the case plainly and indicates his purpose in writing his book:

" There is a prevalent conviction that the influence of education is very narrowly circumscribed by traits or capacities, which, for each individual, are both innate and in themselves practically unmodified by experience or training. This attitude is no new thing; within the past ten years, however, it has been given an emphatic sanction and a very widely extended currency, by the development of mental measurements, and particularly by the hypothesis of ' general intelligence ' which has been brought into high relief by the measurement movement.

" It is the purpose of this present paper to show that the sanction which mental measurements apparently give to this particular variety of determinism is based not upon the facts that the measurements reveal, but upon the hypotheses and assumptions that the development of the measures has involved; that these hypotheses and assumptions, while doubtless justified for certain purposes, are at basis questionable in the last degree; and that the present tendency to extend them *ad libitum* beyond a very restricted field is fraught with educational and social dangers of so serious and far reaching a character as to cause the gravest concern. The paper will also attempt to show that, even if the assumptions are granted, many of the fatalistic inferences drawn from the data in hand are not justified.''

After stating the determinist's educational propositions and assumptions, Doctor Bagley expresses his feelings and attitude toward educators who hold to the theory which he reluctantly but conscientiously opposes in his book:

" I wish to say at the outset that I have no personal animus in this discussion. For the notable achievements of those working in the field of mental measurements, I have the highest respect and warmest admiration. Many of these workers have been very cautious regarding the inferences they have drawn, whether from their assumptions, or from their facts. Many of them, indeed, are not ' determinists ' in the sense in which I use the term, and would in no case be subject to the criticisms that I shall apply to the deterministic school. Even those who are radical determinists are sincere in their beliefs; and among them are men so keen and so competent that it is with the greatest reluctance that I venture to challenge the validity of their conclusions. Were it not for my conviction that there is at stake a great ideal—an ideal that has already cost more in the terms of human striving and suffering and sacrifice than anything else in this world of ours—I would not for a moment presume to pit my judgment against the judgment of men for whom I have a respect that amounts in many cases to a veneration.

" It is sincerely with this attitude that I proceed to the tendencies of present-day determinism in our field,—tendencies which the assumption or hypothesis of a native, ' general intelligence ' is encouraging."

Before giving the conclusions reached by Doctor Bagley in his study of the significance of mental tests, we give some of the claimed discoveries of mental technicians. They tell us that twenty-five per cent. of the population is subnormal; that the average mentality of the nation is slightly over thirteen years; that only 15 per cent. are fit to go to college; and that 60 per cent. of the whole population are poorly fitted even to do high school work.

The following point of view seems to have the sanction of the educational determinists:

" Many are only fit to be hewers of wood, but they should be expert hewers. That is, those who are not fit for higher education should be thoroughly trained in the line for which they may be especially fitted. They should be told what to do, how to do it, and when to do it. They should be trained, but not educated. . . . If democracy is to come to its own by getting the best out of each, then it must do so by a scientific process of selection and elimination, thus creating an intellectual elite." [2]

Boyd H. Bode in his book *Modern Educational Theories*, makes the following comment on the above quotation:

" Without questioning the findings of the mental tests, we may be permitted to ask how he arrives at the conclusion that the less gifted part of the population ' should be told what to do, how to do it, and when to do it; ' that they ' should be trained, but not educated.' The character of the inference is not altogether clear. Is it based on an initial assumption that those who are at the top of the mental scale should rule those who are below? Or does it take for granted that only college graduates, actual or potential, are capable of self-government? Or does the writer mean to imply that education has no appreciable influence on the development of ' general intelligence,' at least when applied to those who are at the lower end of the scale?

" In the opinion of the Greeks it was eminently reasonable that the more intelligent should be the guardians of the less intelligent, and do all the thinking that was needed to be done. But it is hardly to be expected that a modern writer would care to defend this position." [3]

[2] W. D. Tait, *School and Society*, Jan. 10, 1925, p. 37.
[3] B. H. Bode, *Modern Educational Theories*, pp. 313–314 (Macmillan Co.).

Doctor Bode in his book has written an excellent chapter on the "Significance of Mental Tests." Both Doctors Bode and Bagley recognize the value of mental tests, but are opposed to some of the unrestricted applications made, and some of the interpretations of their findings. Doctor Bode closes his chapter on the "Significance of Mental Tests" with this statement:

"The mental tests are unquestionably valuable for certain kinds of classifications and predictions. Their use, however, should not blind us to the fact that life is a garment of many hues. Thinking may occupy itself with many varieties of facts and relations, and it may occupy itself with these in various ways, and with varying degrees of skill. The results of the mental tests have given new evidence for the view that education must take account of a much greater range of interest and abilities than it has done in the past. But these results have contributed nothing to shake the conviction that education in a democracy is under obligation to build on these various interests and abilities a superstructure of common attitude and common knowledge. The fulfillment of this obligation means the realization of the democratic ideal of liberal education, the ideal to which our national history has irrevocably committed us and which embodies our most cherished conception of organized social living."

Doctor Bagley in his book *Determinism in Education* shows:

1. That the I. Q. of the determinist is in direct opposition to the true principles of democracy.

2. That the Army Tests, rightly interpreted, speak with compelling force for the expansion of educational opportunity rather than for its restriction.

3. That the reaction against democracy, following the World War, has been followed by a reaction against mass education, encouraged by the determinists; and the result is rapidly developing dictatorial autocracy.

The following provisional conclusions are given in Doctor Bagley's own words:

"1. The term 'general intelligence' should be provisionally accepted as connoting the most important function of the mind—namely the ability to control behavior in the light of experience.

"2. More specifically, variations in intelligence may be taken to mean variations in the ability of individuals:

"(1) to adapt themselves through a process of judgment to new situations;

"(2) to draw or 'abstract' general inferences from specific experiences;

"(3) to apply general principles to specific situations;

"(4) to 'learn' readily. . . . .

"3. General intelligence clearly depends *in part* upon physiological functions; and inasmuch as physiological processes are functions of anatomical structures, the inference that general intelligence will be *in part* determined by original endowment or physical heredity is *a priori* incontestable. This inference is also clearly substantiated by the observed facts.

" 4. On the other hand, and just as clearly, general intelligence is determined *in part* by environmental opportunities, especially by environmental pressures, and most profoundly in all probability by those types of environmental pressure that are represented by *systematic schooling* during the period of physiological growth or maturation.

" 5. The contribution of systematic schooling to general intelligence is probably equal to the combined contributions of native endowment and the informal pressures of the average social environment.

" 6. So powerful is the influence of systematic schooling that it appears in many ways to counteract some of the differences due to original nature; to such an extent at least that one is justified in referring to general intelligence as a human trait which ' distils its own corrective ' for organic variability, and in assuming that education may be made, in a very real sense, a ' leveling up ' process.

" 7. General intelligence is not the only factor conditioning achievement, economic efficiency, leadership, and character; but it is beyond doubt one of the important factors, and it is the only factor that seems now to be under a fair degree of social control.

" 8. The importance of systematic schooling in the determination of general intelligence probably varies with the kinds of materials (experiences, disciplines, subjects of study) which the schooling represents. In general the school-pressures that stimulate the learner to *systematic and sustained mental effort toward the mastery of relatively abstract processes and toward the formation of ever-broadening concepts in ever-widening fields of knowledge* seem to yield the largest growth.

" 9. It seems that the importance of *early* training, discipline, and systematic instruction can scarcely be overemphasized. ' Educational opportunity ' means with special force care and culture during early childhood and youth. . . .

" 10. Climate apparently exerts a powerful influence upon the possibilities of developing high levels of general intelligence through universal education, and from the data now available seems to be, in general, a much more important factor than race. It is reasonable to conclude, provisionally, however, that neither climate nor race imposes an insuperable obstacle to a fairly complete integration of all peoples upon a cultural basis.

" 11. There is a close and probably a causal relationship between the level of intelligence attained through universal education by the people of a nation and the relative freedom of the nation from ' war, revolution, demagogy, despotism, degeneration.' By far the most hopeful approach to the reign of universal peace is the encouragement of universal education among all peoples.

" 12. It is probable, however, that the influence of mass-education on ' moral ' controls of conduct depends upon *quality* as well as upon the *quantity* or *extent* of the education provided. Mass-education may easily be made to intensify chauvinism (exaggerated nationalism) and thus fail to decrease the peril from war in the measure that might otherwise be possible. On the other hand, mass-education may just as easily be made to intensify individualism, and thus encourage gratification and indulgence, and discourage renunciation and sacrifice. The one extreme may be a menace to the world's peace; the other may exert an unfortunate influence upon the moral fiber of a people. While the one extreme was reflected by the spirit and ideals that governed elementary education in Germany before the War, it is also possible that the other extreme characterizes far too strongly the dominant spirit and ideals of American education today.

" 13.   The ' disciplinary ' function of systematic education is probably far more significant than is usually granted by the current interpretations of the experiments in ' transfer of training.' While it would be most unfortunate to go back to the naive conception of formal discipline that prevailed in the past, it would be the part of wisdom to go forward to a new conception which would aim to correct the unquestionable weakness, not to say flabbiness, of the position taken on this important issue by contemporary educational theory.

" 14.   The vital importance of discipline to democracy is likely to be discounted and obscured by irrelevant appeals to ' freedom,'—and its implications of ease and comfort.   Unless democracy can find a place in its theory and practice for discipline, duty, and sacrifice, it will be so seriously handicapped that its ultimate success will be a matter of the gravest question.   Whether we like it or not, we cannot deny that, in the history of the race, anything that even remotely resembles freedom (freedom not only from personal thralldom, but freedom as well from want, dread, fear, fraud, and superstition) has been a conquest, not a gift.   In a very real sense, education must reflect in each generation this element of struggle and conquest." [4]

The conclusions of Doctor Bagley, especially the danger signals raised, recall to mind similar warnings given by former President Coolidge:

" The success or failure of liberal education, the justification of its protection and encouragement by government, and of its support by society, will be measured by its ability to minister to this great cause, to perform the necessary services, to make the required redeeming sacrifices." (See pages 24, 25.)

He also questioned the reliability of mental tests in the endeavor to measure the possibilities of human development and achievement:

" Certain mental tests have been tried for the purpose of estimating the intellectual capacity of individuals, and there has been an attempt to draw the conclusion that there exists a large body of people endowed with only a moderate mentality.   But the capabilities of these people to respond to educational training is still unknown, and no one has yet put a measuring-stick on the possibilities of the human soul."

We quote again from Lucia Barton Morse that part of her statement (see pages 37, 38) which bears upon intelligence tests:

" Out of the chaos of opinion as to what constitutes the whole child, what may be the real meaning of intelligence, . . . may we not look over the ages to that one child whose influence has been indelibly stamped upon our time, because in some way he increased toward perfection in mind and body, and in his spiritual and social relationships. . . .

" It is this contact with the spiritual which in the modern world of

---

[4] W. C. Bagley, *Determinism in Education,* pp. 157–160.   (Warwick and York, Baltimore.)

materialism we fail to make vital. Busying ourselves with providing the means for measuring a child's intelligence, we lose our vision of wisdom.

" Our children of today are free and fine and beautiful, but they lack that poise that comes with the deliberate choice of principle to direct their lives. They think and act independently, and creatively, but too often they are afforded no background for judgment beyond that intelligence that can be measured. . . .

" It may be a solution to our problem if among other educational activities we faithfully water and nourish this seed which is the soul of every child, that he may naturally grow and wax strong in spirit. For whatever form the idea of God may take in our minds, we can but know there are no figures which may determine how much of the kingdom of heaven a child can manifest.''

" The child (Jesus) grew, and waxed strong in spirit, filled with wisdom " (Luke 2: 40), and became the Teacher and Saviour of the world. Did the Master Teacher leave to under-teachers any instruction that will help to solve the problems of the educational determinist regarding mental abilities,—acquired and inherited; those deserving of educational opportunities, and others who are entitled only to training? He " needed not that any should testify of man, for he knew what was in man " (John 2: 25).

Christ gave two parables which educators can very profitably study. The " Parable of the Talents " and the " Parable of the Pounds." In the first parable the servants of the king were made stewards of his goods. Unto one he gave five talents, to another two, and to another one, to every man according to his several ability (Matt. 25: 15). In the second parable a nobleman " called his ten servants and delivered unto them ten pounds (a pound each) and said unto them, Occupy until I come " (Luke 19: 13). These parables represent the principles of the kingdom of heaven, as expressed and interpreted by the Master Teacher. Let us consider their application in the field of education and training for service:

1. While the " talents " and " pounds " of the parables had reference to money, yet they are equally applicable to all acquired or inherited capabilities, gifts, or endowments—physical, mental, or spiritual. It is in that broad, all-inclusive sense that the word talent is used today.

2. These abilities, gifts, and endowments are inherited or acquired, and all of them must be put to use if they are retained, enlarged and strengthened.

3. These abilities and gifts are bestowed by the ministration of the Holy Spirit: " Now there are diversities of gifts, but the same Spirit. . . . For to one is given by the Spirit the word of wisdom; to another the word of knowledge by the same Spirit, to another faith by the same Spirit; to another gifts of healing by the same Spirit; to another the working of miracles; to another prophecy; to another discerning of spirits; to another divers kind of tongues; to another the interpreta-

tion of tongues " (I Cor. 12: 4, 8–10; see also I Cor. 12: 28–30; Rom. 12: 6–8; Eph. 4: 11–13).

4. Christ speaks of this work of the Holy Spirit: " Howbeit when he, the Spirit of truth, is come, he will guide you into all truth " (John 16: 13). " He shall teach you all things, and bring to your remembrance all things whatsoever I have said unto you " (John 14: 26).

5. The Holy Spirit not only determines the number and size of the gifts individually bestowed, but also aids in their cultivation and operation: " But all these worketh that one and the selfsame Spirit, dividing to every man severally as he will " (I Cor. 12: 11). " To every man according to his several ability " (Matt. 25: 15). " And there are diversities of operations, but it is the same God which worketh all in all. But the manifestation of the Spirit is given to every man to profit withal " (I Cor. 12: 6, 7).

6. Parents and teachers have nothing to do in the bestowal of gifts, but only with their cultivation and operation. Even in these respects they are but co-partners with the Holy Spirit in the providing of equal opportunities for the education and training of all.

7. The " Parable of the Talents " represents the placing of responsibilities in accordance with varying inherited and acquired abilities. The results in individual effort show the same percentage of efficiency —100%. The greater the abilities, the larger the responsibilities carried; but the degree of efficiency is constant, each meriting the " well done " of their employer.

8. In the " Parable of the Pounds " are represented those with equal inherited and acquired abilities (one pound), but varying in environmental conditions or educational opportunities, or both, which seems to be the probable explanation for the varying success of each of the custodians.

9. These two parables present both phases of the educational problem:

(1) The parable of the talents, spoken to the twelve disciples, who had unequal inherited abilities, but all had the three and one-half years of educational opportunity under the Master Teacher.

(2) The parable of the pounds was spoken to the multitude— the common people,—with meager but equal inherited abilities (one pound each), and who had varied educational opportunities and environments.

10. The twelve disciples, who were to carry forward the work Christ had begun, were encouraged to faithfulness in bearing their individual responsibilities, being assured that approval did not depend upon the number of talents possessed, but on their faithful use.

11. Those of the multitude that thronged Christ, though possessing but the " one pound," must have been encouraged when they learned that by diligent improvement of their opportunities they could multiply

it and would receive the approval, "Well done, good and faithful servant."

The Three Dimensions Test

The principles and methods of pedagogy and psychology, as revealed in the teachings and ministry of Christ and the learned apostle Paul, indicate the impossibilities as well as the possibilities of human achievement. Christ declared to His disciples: "Without me ye can do nothing" (John 15: 5). Paul, on the other hand, triumphantly affirms: "I can do all things through Christ which strengtheneth me" (Phil. 4: 13). Both of these statements plainly reveal the futility of human effort apart from divine aid. The degree of divine aid given depends upon the attitude of the learner. Christ said: "If any man will to do his will he shall know" (John 7: 17). Paul echoes this thought: "If there be first a willing mind it is accepted according to that a man hath" (II Cor. 8: 12). There is human and divine co-operation: "It is God which worketh in you both to will and to do" (Phil. 2: 13). From the above Scriptures it is plainly evident that the attitude of the learner is a large determining factor governing progress and achievement in learning. There are three leading factors, which must be taken into account in measuring learning power and ability:

1. General intelligence—the native or inherited mental endowment.
2. Environment, including all educational opportunities.
3. Attitude of mind and spirit of the learner.

A large mental endowment, with abundant educational opportunities, avails little or nothing without strong persevering attitudes, stimulating study, and research. (See page 234.) But on the other hand, even with limited mental endowment and educational opportunities; a strong persevering attitude of study and research will result in greater progress and advancement in learning and achievement.

No accurate measurement of human abilities and capacities is possible, without consideration of the divine contributions of moral and spiritual power. These are difficult to measure and efforts to do so have not been successful. Two dimensions (length and breadth) give area, or surface measurement, but another dimension (height or depth) is necessary to reveal volume or content. So in measuring the human mind, and its possibilities, three factors must be considered: (1) mental endowment (length); (2) educational opportunity (breadth); (3) mental and moral attitudes (height or depth). With these three factors understood and applied, mere surface measurement will be avoided, and content, forshadowing achievement, will be revealed. These are the terms of measurement employed by the Apostle Paul in evaluating the personality of Christ: "That . . . ye may be able to comprehend . . . what is the breadth and length, and depth, and height; and to know the love of Christ which passeth knowledge" (Eph. 3: 17–19).

Christ was the truest interpreter of Hebrew ideals and methods of

Hebrew education. A number of modern educators have given study to the pedagogy and psychology of the Master Teacher as revealed in the Four Gospels containing His teachings, and several excellent books have appeared, deserving of careful study.

Methods of Hebrew Education

We have given considerable space to the consideration of Hebrew educational ideals and methods. As already quoted (see pages 37, 38), Doctor Maynard tells us: "As for us, we can learn from Hebrew methods at times, from Hebrew ideals very often." Methods may properly change with changing times, but ideals that are true and ennobling do not change and should constantly beckon us on to higher and nobler living.

While methods may properly change with the changing times, yet the changes made should never becloud or obscure the ideals. The principles and methods of teaching and discipline of the Hebrews, as already noted (see pages 64–83), not only contributed to wisdom receiving and knowledge gathering, but also to character building. They were also careful to select good material for study and observation. Good material and good methods result in the development of good character. Today much of the crime and lawlessness is laid at the door of bad material used in study and observation in the schools. The character of much of the educational literature studied; of some of the plays enacted; and of many of the films projected are seriously questioned; while the methods employed are generally recognized to be good.

Hebrew education centered largely in the family and therefore was not formal nor routine in character. It was a natural accompaniment in the program of daily living. It made living more vital and progressive. To the Hebrews education was not so much a preparation for a better life as it was living a better life day by day in the home, in the community, and in the nation. In modern education a continuous effort is being made to fit the student to act his part in the social order, and methods and material are being devised and arranged to that end. The "socialized recitation," the "project method" of study, the "extra-curricular" activities are examples of efforts in that direction. These methods and activities are applauded by some and criticized by others. Some think these methods and activities are too strongly emphasized and overworked,—the result being an unbalanced education.

Doctor Bode in his valuable book, *Modern Educational Theories*, gives a critical analysis of various methods of instruction and investigation. In the chapter "Scientific Method and Higher Education" he says:

" It would be stupid as well as perverse, not to acknowledge unreservedly the tremendous debt which modern education owes to science. Nevertheless a survey of the situation leaves one with the uncomfortable sense that all is not well in Zion. Our educational system has been reorganized in the direction of accommodation to every variety of human capacity and interest. We might expect, therefore, that our courses of study would prove a great adventure for every normal individual; that at some point or other he was bound to strike fire; that sooner or later he would thrill to a glimpse of human achievement and of human destiny. An unsophisticated bystander might imagine a college as a place where brainstorms and concentrated rushes on the library were among the normal incidents of the day.

" It is not necessary to explain at length that this is hardly a true picture of higher education. In fact the discrepancy is great enough to suggest that our enthusiasm for science and scientific method must have left something important out of the reckoning. The organization may be a triumph of scientific achievement but it is lacking in soul. The machine has not been sufficiently humanized. How else can we account for the fact that just at the time when our colleges and universities are showing such startling enrollments, when higher education is in demand as never before, the charge of a prevailing lack of intellectual seriousness should be most emphasized? Our students don't read, says one critic. They don't think, says another. They have no industry or ambition, says a third. They come to college at great expense of time and money, and then make it necessary to apply methods of forcible feeding if they are to get what they came for. By some strange irony ' student activities ' is a phrase used to denote almost everything except study. Jazz, movies, fraternities, football—these be thy gods, O Israel! It is distressing to find that our educational progress seems to have created an alarming indifference to, if not a positive dislike for, what we have been accustomed to call a liberal education." [5]

Another modern educator speaking of the dangers that threaten the peace and safety of liberal education, says:

" The number and the proportion of the careless and the idle and the stupid and the unfit of those who are passively floating in the educational current and come to college because just now there is nothing else to do; of those whose fathers send them because of a faith in education, but who themselves do not set particular value upon it or upon anything else whose acquisition involves labor or character; of those who are attracted by the promise of good times in fraternity or sorority; of those who want the imagined social prestige conferred by the diploma; of those who are not entirely sure that a Saturday-Evening-Post-Short-Story husband or wife may not be the outcome—the number and proportion of these have increased until they threaten the peace and safety of liberal education and are disturbing the technical school as well. . . . The slovenly spelling, the slovenly handwriting, . . . the slovenly expression, the slovenly thinking, the slovenly besmudged page, the evidences of no capacity, no interest, and no industry, that a large minority (I am not saying majority) of the students will unblushingly hand him (the instructor) would be a disgrace to the meanest institution. This is the sort of rottenness that exists beneath the goodly outside of ' the most perfect educational system the

5 B. H. Bode, *Modern Educational Theories*, pp. 272, 273.

world has ever seen.' The toleration of it is an offense that is rank and smells to heaven.'' [6]

This is a discouraging picture of modern higher institutions of learning, and unfavorable criticisms have been made of secondary and elementary schools by those connected with them. There should be an earnest, careful reconsideration of the ideals, study materials, student activities, subject matter, and methods that obtain in modern education from the kindergarten up to and including the university, to discover and to replace the weak links of the educational chain, that it may hold and bind together the human family in purity, integrity, unity, happiness and prosperity.

The Hebrew system of education points the way, and its weaknesses and failures were not the fault of the system, but resulted from the failure of its custodians to fully carry it out. Christ in His life and ministry fully demonstrated the superiority of the system of education which He gave to the Hebrew nation; and in the closing chapter of this book we consider Christ in Hebrew and Modern Education, believing that He is "the way and the truth and the life" for all Christian peoples in all their endeavors to educate their children and youth.

[6] Grant Showerman, '' Intellect and Undergraduate,'' *School and Society*, Feb. 26, 1921, p. 5.

XXIII

CHRIST AND EDUCATION

The Prince of Educators

THE almost universal testimony regarding Christ's life on earth is, that He was the " Prince of teachers," the " Master of Educators." This has been attested to frequently throughout the pages of this book. The period of child and youth training under Mary and Joseph has been referred to again and again. The plans, methods, and spirit of the training and development of Jesus have been approved and extolled by educators down through the centuries, since the closing of the home school in Nazareth. As we have seen, (see pages 30, 31, 36, 38, 54–58), modern and present-day educators are pointing back to Nazareth for an illustration of the methods of instructing and training the child. The superiority of the psychological and pedagogical principles and methods employed by Christ in teaching His disciples and the people (see pages 30, 54) have been and are being affirmed, and emphasized by prominent educators.

In the sacred Scriptures we have briefly but clearly and vividly revealed the child and youth life of Jesus and the education and training He received that prepared Him for His three and one-half years of ministry as the Teacher and Saviour of the world. He freely and willingly came into this world, a babe born in Bethlehem. He grew from infancy to manhood in Nazareth under the care and training of earthly parents. He was one of several brothers and sisters in this large family. His heavenly Father loaned Him to the world for a time to be an example of true human growth and development, and He closed His human life on the cross to atone for the sins of the world. After His resurrection He returned to heaven, and His Father sent the Holy Spirit to continue the work that He and His disciples had carried on for a little more than three years. Christ for nearly two thousand years has been directing His work on earth from heaven, using the Holy Spirit and ministering angels as His agencies to carry it forward. All this is clearly revealed in the Scriptures.

The question naturally arises as to Christ's relation to the human family before He was born in Bethlehem. He has had close contact with the human family during the nearly two thousand years since His resurrection and ascension, but how about His relation to the world during the four thousand years that preceded His coming to this world in human form? Christ said to the Jews who were boasting that Abraham was their father: " If ye were Abraham's children, ye would do the works of Abraham. . . . Abraham rejoiced to see my day; and he saw it, and was glad. . . . Before Abraham was, I am " (John 8: 39, 56, 58). On another occasion speaking of Moses, Christ said: " Had ye believed Moses, ye would have believed me; for he wrote of me. But if ye believe not his writings, how shall ye believe my words" (John 5: 46, 47). So Christ was known and recognized in the time of Abraham and Moses as the Son of God and the Saviour of the world.

The Apostle Paul speaking of Christ and His relation to the children of Israel and Moses their leader, said:

" This is he, that was in the church in the wilderness . . . which spake to him (Moses) in the Mount Sinai, and with our fathers; who (Moses) received the lively oracles to give unto us " (Acts 7: 38). " I would not that ye should be ignorant, how that all our fathers were under the cloud, and all passed through the sea, . . . and did all drink the same spiritual drink; for they drank of that spiritual Rock that followed them, and that Rock was Christ " (I Cor. 10: 1–4).

Christ and Hebrew Education

From the above Scriptures, it is evident that the Christ of Bethlehem, before taking human form, communicated with patriarchs and prophets; and enshrouded in glory and majesty from Mount Sinai proclaimed with audible voice His holy law, committing it to Moses engraved on two tables of stone. For forty days Moses was in the mount, receiving from Christ the statutes, laws, and judgments that were to direct and govern His chosen people in their physical, mental, and spiritual growth and development. These Moses wrote in a book which was placed " in the side " of the ark which contained the two tables of stone written by Christ, the great Lawgiver, who, nearly two thousand years later on the Mount of Olives, declared: " Think not that I am come to destroy the law or the prophets; I am not come to destroy, but to fulfil " (Matt. 5: 17).

These laws and statutes which Christ gave at Sinai, He obeyed as a child and youth in Nazareth, and taught them to the people during His three and one-half years' ministry. Israel, as we have noted, (see pages 319–355) prospered, and not only became a mighty nation, but her teachers were the teachers of the world as long as they were obedient to these laws. But the chosen nation proved untrue to the sacred trust committed to her and desired to be like the surrounding nations. Her kings formed alliances with some of these nations, which proved in the end to be the undoing of a nation so highly honored of God. Ten of the twelve tribes of Israel were carried into captivity by the Assyrians, and never returned. Later the two remaining tribes (Judah and Benjamin) were carried captives to Babylon by King Nebuchadnezzar; but were privileged to return to build anew their temple and city after seventy years of captivity and bondage. For a time under the leadership of Ezra and Nehemiah there was peace and prosperity; but later, entangling alliances resulted in weakness and confusion.

Christ was the author of the Hebrew educational system, and wherever or whenever it was faithfully and fully adhered to, peace, prosperity, enlightenment and continual advancement were not only experienced by the chosen nation; but also were reflected in the life and experience of the neighboring tribes and nations, who marveled at the display of such wisdom, knowledge, and power.

Christ and Jewish Education

On the return of the Israelites, after the seventy years' captivity, they were called " Jews" by the surrounding nations. The Jews continued the educational activities so successfully carried out by Ezra the priest and scribes (see pages 106–108); and synagogue schools in large numbers sprang up throughout Palestine, where the children were gathered for instruction. Not only were synagogue schools provided for the education of the children, but more advanced schools were provided for the instruction of the youth. Concerning the higher schools conducted by sages and scribes (Soferim), Rabbi Meyer J. Rosenberg says:

" The scribes, who had been coming more into prominence even before the Exile, had before 300 B. C. E., become an important order. As the name and function of the scribe was open to all, it is to be regarded as a lay order like the schools of the prophets. A priest or Levite might be a scribe, but the profession was not confined to any order. Men of various occupations were also scribes. Ezra, fifth century B. C. E., was both priest and scribe. After return from the captivity, the scribe class gradually increased in number. They became in fact the learned and legal class, and as such the more eminent of them were teachers and expounders of the Law. They also extended the Law by their interpretations. The prophets were thus practically superseded by a written Law, and an authoritative oral interpretation, out of which came the Talmud." [1]

Jewish and Greek Education

The Jews, like their forefathers, the Hebrews, were tested as to their loyalty to the divine plan of education given at Sinai. Dr. Swift says: "The faithful Jews not only remained indifferent to the physical, esthetic, and intellectual interest of their pagan conquerors, but studiously excluded them from their schools and from their ambitions." (See page 34.) Rabbi Rosenberg, speaking of the conflict between Hellenic culture, ideals and institutions, and those of Judaism, says:

" The two types of life were bound to clash. Hellenism was a social movement, kindling patriotism, inspiring decadent people to a higher and broader type of life, preaching the brilliant, joyous, virile, artistic use of power. Judaism was a religious faith, sturdy, serious, believing in moral ideals and issues, and cultivating holiness. To a Jew a Greek seemed lightminded, unmoral, often godless; to a Greek a Jew seemed intolerant, narrow, and stupid, concerned with trifles. The greatest difference was that the Greek ideal was at heart a selfish one; the Hebrew ideal was at heart sacrificial." [2]

Speaking of the struggles of Judaism during the four hundred years previous to the Christian era, Rabbi Rosenberg says:

[1] M. J. Rosenberg, *Historical Development of Hebrew Education*, pp. 97, 98 (the Author).
[2] *Ibid.*, p. 78.

" Within three centuries Judaism received a testing which was indeed a baptism of fire. The Persian empire gave way before the swift resistless attack of the Grecian conqueror, Alexander the Great. The Jewish people became subjects of various Grecian powers. This brought Judaism as the characteristic expression of the Jewish mind and heart into contrast, and at last into conflict with Hellenism as the embodied idealism and ambition of the aggressive Greeks. Out of this struggle emerged a stronger Judaism, improved in some respects, but stimulated in several unhealthy tendencies, which developed disadvantageously." [3]

Some of the "unhealthy tendencies which developed disadvantageously" were the selfish exclusive attitude and spirit which resulted in a superiority complex toward peoples of other nations. The Jews regarded themselves as the chosen nation with a royal priesthood (as indeed their fathers were); but they looked upon all others as barbarians unworthy of their notice and respect. They were very diligent in establishing schools to educate their children and youth in their laws and traditions; but they ceased to be a light to the world, and to put forth efforts to enlighten and uplift others whom they considered less favored by their God.

The Schools of Hillel, Shammai and Gamaliel

Many schools for the training of scribes were established, called "Schools of the Soferim," probably suggested by "the schools of the prophets," in the days of Samuel, Elijah and Elisha. The purpose of the schools of the Soferim is set forth by Doctor Swift:

" From earliest times it was necessary for prospective Soferim (scribes) to receive special professional training. The increase after the Exile, in the functions of the Soferim, in their numbers, importance, and in the body of literature to be mastered by them, made necessary prolonged and careful training. Those who were called upon daily to declare and administer the Law must possess not merely a superior knowledge of the Law itself. They must know all possible interpretations, methods of interpretation, and the precedents created by former decisions and applications. In temple court or in synagogue noted scribes gathered about themselves groups of youth and men. In time each famous scribe appears to have had his own group or school. In some cases the distinctive character of the master's teaching resulted in the development of rival schools, such as those of Shammai and Hillel. The latter's grandson, Gamaliel, it will be recalled, was the teacher of Saul of Tarsus." [4]

The school of Hillel was the greatest of the Schools of Judiasm when Christ was born in Bethlehem, and its master was still living, having died A. D. 10. For nearly five centuries these schools were perpetuated by the descendants of its founder. His grandson, Gamaliel, " a doctor of the law," having " reputation among all the people," on one occasion stood up in the council and saved the apostles from death (Acts 5: 33–42). The apostle Paul tells us that he was brought up " at the feet of

[3] *Ibid.*, p. 77.
[4] F. H. Swift, *Education in Ancient Israel to 70 A. D.*, p. 100.

Gamaliel and taught according to the perfect manner of the law of the fathers, and was zealous toward God " (Acts 22: 3).

Concerning Hillel's work and influence, we quote the following from *The Encyclopedia Britannica* under "Hillel":

" Hillel is especially noted for the fact that he gave a definite form to the Jewish traditional learning, as it had been developed and made into the ruling and conserving factor of Judaism in the latter days of the second Temple, and particularly in the centuries following the destruction of the Temple. He laid down seven rules for the interpretation of the Scriptures, and these became the foundation of rabbinical hermeneuties (Scripture interpretation). . . . The tendency of his theory and practice in matters pertaining to the Law is evidenced by the fact that in general he advanced milder or more lenient views in opposition to his colleague Shammai, a contrast which after the death of the two masters, but not until after the destruction of the Temple, was maintained in the strife kept up between the two schools named the House of Hillel and the House of Shammai."

Christ and the Rabbinical Schools

When Christ was born, Hillel and Shammai were living and were the teachers in Jewish education. Rabbi Akiba was a prominent educator who perished when the Temple was destroyed A. D. 70. He prepared a Hebrew primer (see pages 31, 32), used in teaching the children. Philo, who, in A. D. 40, was advanced in years, " went from Alexandria to Rome at the head of a Jewish embassy to persuade the Emperor Gaius to abstain from claiming divine honor of the Jews." He was the leading Jewish philosopher of his day, and while firmly contending that the writings of the Pentateuch were a divine revelation from God to Israel, yet he endeavored to so interpret the law and the prophets that the Greeks would be won to Judaism. On the other hand he endeavored to so explain the philosophy of Plato, the Stoics and the Pythagoreans, that the Jews would readily accept the Greek philosophies. His writings were voluminous, and his influence was strongly felt among both the Jews and the Greeks.

Christ was reared in the atmosphere of educational and ecclesiastical thought sponsored largely by these three leading Jewish teachers— Hillel, Shammai, and Philo. His parents, brothers, and sisters were influenced by it. We have already briefly considered Christ's reaction to the rabbis and their teaching. (See pages 100, 102.)

He who gave to the Ancient Hebrews their system of religion and education was now a child born in Jewry, subjected to the influences of Judaism. The Jews were the inheritors of the " oracles of God " delivered to their fathers, and the rabbis endeavored to direct and mould the education of the Christ child who before His incarnation had given them the true principles of religion and education. He refused to have any part in their educational program. His education was imparted by His earthly parents, and the co-operation of divine agencies. While performing His mission, He was opposed by Scribes,

Pharisees, Sadducees, and Herodians,—the educational elite of His time. The most talented, the shrewdest and the bitterest of His enemies endeavored to entangle Him in words; but failed in their efforts. Finally they subjected Him to mockery, physical suffering, and ignominious death. "He came to his own, but his own received him not."

Christ and Christian Education

Early Christian Education.

While Christ was rejected by His own people as a nation, yet there were those who were loyal and true. The twelve apostles, later joined by the apostle Paul and others, went everywhere preaching Christ, and "the multitude of them that believed were of one heart and of one soul" (Acts 4: 32). "And believers were the more added to the Lord, multitudes both of men and women" (Acts 5: 14). "And the disciples were called Christians first in Antioch" (Acts 11: 26).

In a comparatively short time the gospel of Christ was carried to the then civilized countries and a large body of Christians accepted the teachings of Christ. The apostle Paul, speaking of the wide spread of the gospel in his day, said that it "was preached to every creature which is under heaven" (Col. 1: 23); and speaking of the gospel heralds, said "their sound went into all the earth, and their words to the end of the world" (Rom. 10: 18).

Did the early Christian Church prove true to the Founder of Christianity? The apostle Paul before his death expressed fears of disloyalty on the part of some of the shepherds of the Christian fold:

"Take heed, therefore, unto yourselves, and to all the flock. . . . For I know this, that after my departing shall grievous wolves enter in among you, not sparing the flock. Also of your own selves shall men arise speaking perverse things to draw away disciples after them" (Acts 20: 28–30).

The following warning seems to apply particularly to erroneous teaching in the field of education:

"Beware lest any man spoil you through philosophy and vain deceit, after the tradition of men, after the rudiments of the world, and not after Christ" (Col. 3: 8).

The apostle Paul, after his acceptance of Christ, thus evaluates his learning from Jewish teachers:

"What things were gain to me, those I counted loss for Christ, yea, doubtless, and I count all things but loss for the excellency of the knowledge of Christ Jesus my Lord" (Phil. 3: 7, 8). "O the depths of the riches, both of the wisdom and the knowledge of God!" (Rom. 11: 33).

Some of the Christian teachers proved untrue to the principles of Christian education, but Paul with prophetic insight foretold its victorious conquest over Judaism, and over every opposing power:

"For ye see your calling, brethren, how that not many wise men after the flesh, not many mighty, not many noble are called, but God hath chosen . . . the weak things of the world to confound the things which are mighty; and base things of the world, and things which are despised, hath God chosen, yea things which are not, to bring to naught things that are; that no flesh should glory in his presence '' (I Cor. 1: 26–29).

A modern educator briefly reviews the conflict and the victory of Christian education during the first three centuries:

"A son was born into a peasant carpenter family, belonging to a race whose glory and power had departed. The family lived in honest poverty and obscurity among the wood workers and shepherds of a mean Syrian village. This son was disowned by His people, rejected by His synagogue, and finally crucified between thieves on a hill outside of the Jerusalem wall. Yet within scarcely more than three hundred years after His birth this unknown, despised carpenter became the major intellectual and spiritual influence in the mightiest empire the world had ever known. . . .

"Neither the pride of power nor the cruelty of imperial Rome could halt the march of Christ's cross. Its victory was symbolized in the death of Julian the Apostate, a nephew of Constantine, who having returned to heathenism, sought in vain to stay the rising tide of Christianity. He died on a battlefield in 363 A. D. with a Persian arrow in his bosom. He is said to have cried out in his suffering and rage while casting dust into the air: ' Oh Nazarene, thou hast conquered.'

"It was in these suffering centuries that millions of humble Christians testified to their supreme devotion in martyrdom. The annals of history have no parallel to this period of sorrow and moral heroism through which the early Christian church triumphantly passed."[5]

After such a splendid victory, how sad that the conqueror compromised with the conquered, which resulted in the union of the false and the true in religion and in education. Christianity and Paganism plunged the world into the long gruesome period known as the "Dark Ages." The lamp of truth burned low, flickered, but its flame was not entirely extinguished. A few great Christian personalities emerge in the outline of this dark picture.

Charlemagne, the Frankish king, caught a vision of the possibility of the return of culture, and revived in his counselors and subjects the hopes of a higher and more unified order of society. He learned late in life to read, yet this noble man of God towers in the landscape as the most significant figure in education, religion, and government during a period of five hundred years. He urged a diligent study of the Bible. He gathered about him what few poets and scholars he could find and established schools in every surviving cathedral. When his life-work closed in 814 a new day had dawned.

Another great towering personality of this dark period was Alfred the Great, who reigned from 871 to 901. Concerning his personal equipment and great undertaking, Doctor Covert says:

"He was devout, learned, and imperially minded. His name is ever to be associated with the leadership of a great intellectual and spiritual experience of the period. He set out to educate the people in religion and

[5] W. C. Covert, *Christ and Culture*, pp. 28, 29 (Harper & Brothers).

in the arts, and devoted one-eighth of his income to this work. He gave them portions of the Scripture in their rude Anglo-Saxon tongue. He found Alcuin, the greatest school master of the period. The school he organized at York was a beacon whose shining touched the whole of Western Europe! Here gathered men of learning, teachers, poets, singers, copyists, and missionaries!

"In 1901, on the 1000th anniversary of Alfred's death, a bronze statue was erected at Rochester cathedral; its inscription gives a clue to the scope and character of his work. It reads:

> ' Alfred found learning dead,
>   and he restored it:
> Education neglected,
>   and he revived it:
> The laws powerless,
>   and he gave them force:
> The church debased,
>   and he raised it;
> The land ravaged by a fearful enemy,
>   from which he delivered it.'

"Down through the devastated centuries till the dawn broke with Dante, Petrarch and Savonarola, and till liberty and learning found new meaning in the reformation of Martin Luther and John Calvin, names of scholars and devout defenders of the truth shine out of the darkness." [6]

Since the emergence from the darkest period of the ages, surrounded by the ever increasing radiance and power of Him " in whom are hid all the treasures of wisdom and knowledge," how have the under teachers acquitted themselves in carrying on the work the Master Teacher left them to do? What answer can they give today to His searching question: "Where is thy flock that was given thee, thy beautiful flock?" (Jer. 13: 20). He expects, and will be satisfied with but one answer: "Behold I and the children whom the Lord hath given me are for signs and wonders in Israel from the Lord of hosts, which dwelleth in Mount Zion" (Isa. 8: 18). He who gave to the Hebrews, the Jews, and to the Christians His divine plan for the education of the children and youth throughout the ages will have an accounting with His educational stewards,—parents, teachers, preachers, and those who enact laws providing educational opportunities.

Modern Christian Education.

The educators of the past century have had exceptional opportunities for the education of the children and youth. This has been especially true for those who have had unobstructed opportunities to give a Christian education. The Hebrews and Jews had such an opportunity more than any other nation in history. They were signally called of God to carry out His divine plan of education. We have noted their successes and failures. The Christians under the leadership of Christ and the apostles had greater difficulties and obstacles to en-

6 *Ibid.*, pp. 50, 51.

counter. These Christian followers after nearly three centuries of struggle finally won; but elated with their victory, and compromising with their conquered enemies, they formed alliances which robbed them of their physical, mental, and spiritual strength. The long dark night of oppression, tyranny and degeneration followed, with only flickering lights of truth shining here and there. The Reformation pierced the darkness, and the clear blaze and light of truth has been shining for more than a century. The few years that have passed of this twentieth century have been fruitful and especially marked with progress and advancement along all educational lines of endeavor. Improved methods of instruction, better facilities in buildings, libraries and laboratories, higher standards of teaching are strongly emphasized and realized everywhere.

But in spite of all this onward progress, for a few years past, there has developed a feeling of unrest and uncertainty regarding our educational program. This has been especially true since the World War. The startling events, developments, and outbursts in the social, political, financial, and religious world since that world catastrophe occurred, are causing thoughtful, serious men and women in private and public life to question the validity and security of our educational program. This has been quite fully considered in some of the early chapters of this book. The general consensus of opinion of educators, both secular and religious, is that our educational program lacks in character building power, and that that is the main cause for the direful situation in the social, political, financial, and religious world.

In the early history of America, colleges and universities were established by various religious denominations; and the Bible was given a large place in the curriculum. Daily in these institutions, students and teachers assembled for the reading of the Scripture and prayer. Some of the schools made very prominent the training of young men and women for the ministry and other phases of gospel service. The members of the faculties of these institutions of learning were earnest, praying, God-fearing men and women who carried a burden of soul for their students and for the heathen world lying in darkness and superstition. Many of these schools now disclaim any denominational affiliation, and claim an undenominational or non-sectarian status. This was a necessary step, it is said, in order to secure contributions from some who refused to contribute to, or to endow a school connected with a religious organization. Again it has been found necessary in some instances to eliminate in large degree Bible instruction if their work was to be recognized by state universities and colleges, and accrediting organizations. Whether consciously or unconsciously, these two concessions made by these institutions have changed in great measure the spirit and character of their work. The Faculty has been shorn of spiritual power, the chapel hours of worship have been cut down or entirely eliminated, and the spiritual atmosphere of the school has largely, if not altogether, dissipated. Teachers are now on the Faculties who make no profession of religion, and some of these are bold to make light of religion, both in private and public.

It is no wonder that the spirit and objectives of such an institution have changed. This condition of things would not be so surprising in state supported schools where religious instruction is not properly allowed because of parents and students who have no desire for such instruction. But it seems almost unbelievable that such a condition could prevail in a Christian institution.

Andrew D. Harmon, former president of Transylvania College, in *Current History* for December, 1930, speaks of these untoward influences which have worked in the experiences of church colleges. He says that in their effort to keep pace with the standards and ideals of secular education they have exalted intellectualism above spirituality, and thus lost their distinctive character:

" The hitherto undisputed claim that the church college carried a more wholesome moral and spiritual atmosphere has been a compelling argument in its favor. But this claim is seriously questioned today. The requirements of standardizing agencies have compelled church colleges to shift their emphasis from morality to scholarship. This has changed the whole mental pattern and modified the spirit of church colleges. They have not developed in recent years along lines that express the urge and soul of vital Christianity. They have given up their natural element of greatest strength, religion, and taken up the tax-supported institution's element of greatest weakness, standardization."

This change in the church colleges of various denominations did not come in a day. It took years to bring about the transformation. Regarding this, Professor Harmon declares:

" Today there are definite trends indicating the removal of the historic church college from the field of education. The forces that terminate institutions have a long drift, but they move inexorably. Usually the change is at hand before society is aware. The passing of the church college is now taking place, and most of its devotees are looking upon the transition; some even players in the drama, and do not recognize it."

If Christ were to visit the Christian education temples of today, how would He be received and what would be His attitude toward these institutions founded in His name? Would He approve or cleanse them? A modern educator gives the following answer:

" Should Christ enter our institutions for the education of the youth, He would cleanse them as He cleansed the Temple, banishing many things that have a defiling influence. Many of the books which the youth study would be expelled, and their places filled with others that would inculcate substantial knowledge and abound in sentiments which might be treasured in the heart, in precepts that might govern the conduct."[7]

Would Christian educators resent His cleansing work and crucify Him as did His own people? A recent publication, *Christ Crucified in Our Colleges*, indicates that some educators feel that the crucifixion

[7] White, *Christian Education*, p. 174.

is now going on even in some of the temples and schools dedicated to His Name. What a tragedy for this to occur in any age, but especially so in this unequaled period of progress and enlightenment.

Education and Character

The world today, perhaps, more than ever stands in need of men and women of noble, upright character. The need and kind are well stated in the following appeal:

" The greatest want of the world is the want of men,—men who will not be bought or sold; men who in their inmost souls are true and honest; men who do not fear to call sin by its right name; men whose conscience is as true to duty as the needle to the pole; men who will stand for the right though heavens fall." [8]

Such men and women were Joseph, Moses, Daniel, Ruth and Esther, educated and trained under the Hebrew system of education. Such were the disciples trained by Christ, Timothy and Titus under the instruction of the Apostle Paul. Such men and women are needed as leaders in solving the weighty, serious problems of today.

The above writer clearly indicates the relative value of knowledge and character in developing wise, capable leadership:

" True education does not ignore the value of scientific knowledge or literary acquirements; but above information it values power; above power goodness; above intellectual acquirements, character. The world does not so much need men of great intellect as of noble character. It needs men in whom ability is controlled by steadfast principle. . . . Character building is the most important work ever entrusted to human beings; and never before was its diligent study so important as now. Never was any previous generation called to meet issues so momentous; never before were young men and women confronted with so great perils as confront them today." [9]

The Charge of the Master Teacher

Just before Christ's ascension to heaven He gave this twofold charge for the carrying forward of His work on earth: " Feed my lambs " and " Feed my sheep." He said that in doing this they would show their love to Him (John 21: 15–18). The work of the true teacher is a service of love. The lambs and the sheep will be provided with good food, properly prepared and served, and well adapted to the varying stages of their physical, mental and spiritual development. To give parents and teachers a clearer vision of this high and sacred service has been the one object of the author in the writing of this book.

The divine plan of education as revealed in and through Jesus Christ to ancient and modern Israel regards:

(1) The Bible as the voice of God speaking to His earthly family.

(2) Science as a revelation of God, working visibly in the created world in behalf of man and the creatures that inhabit it, and man's

[8] White, *Education*, p. 57.
[9] *Ibid.*, p. 225.

efforts to understand the laws of creation and co-operate with them for his personal benefit and to the honor of his Maker.

(3) Physical and industrial education as man's fitness and ability to co-operate with God in providing the temporal blessing of life.

(4) History as a record of God's dealing with individuals and nations, and their response to His kind providences.

(5) Literature as the study of language forms that reveal the character of God; and man's written and vocal expressions as a revelation of his attitude toward his Creator and his fellow-beings.

(6) Music as a higher and more exalted form of expression than literature, revealing the attitude of the soul toward God and man.

(7) The fine arts as an expression of God's love of the beautiful and the true in nature and human life, and the efforts of man to reproduce it in painting, sculpture and architecture.

(8) Philosophy as a revelation of the Creator's wisdom, power, and love in creating the world and the universe, and His purpose in so doing as related to His intelligent creatures.

Many parents and teachers are earnestly desiring and longing for an educational program which will be conducted on a broader and higher plane both as to its aims and its efficiency. The following is a typical expression of this desire and purpose:

" Our ideas of education take too narrow and too low a range. There is need of a broader scope, a higher aim. True education means more than the perusal of a certain course of study. It means more than a preparation for the life that now is. It has to do with the whole being, and with the whole period of existence possible to man. It is the harmonious development of the physical, the mental, and the spiritual powers. It prepares the student for the joy of service in this world, and for the higher joy of wider service in the world to come."—White, *Education*, p. 13.

The source of such an education is brought to view in these words of Holy Writ: " In him (Christ) are hid all the treasures of wisdom and knowledge . . . and ye are complete in him " (Col. 2: 3, 9).

Such a program of study and teaching would soon remove the charge of a " Christless," " Godless " education being given in the schools, and as one writer has truly said: " Christ will be the center of all teaching and study." Such a plan of education will be abundantly justified by its product; for true " wisdom is justified of her children."

The plan of education set forth in this book cannot be fully applied, except in Christian homes and schools; but it can be fully lived in the lives of all who are privileged to teach, whatever their environment. If the reading of this book inspires parents and teachers to a greater appreciation of their high calling; a stronger resolution to impart only the education that truly educates; and to a fuller consecration of their powers and abilities to inspire and uplift the children and youth of the rising generation, the author will feel abundantly justified in this effort.

BIBLIOGRAPHY

Education of Ancient Israel, F. H. Swift, Open Court Pub. Co., Chicago.

Survey of Hebrew Education, J. A. Maynard, Morehouse Pub. Co., Milwaukee, Wis.

Historical Development of Hebrew Education, Rabbi Meyer Rosenberg, author and publisher.

Pedagogics of the Talmud, Sir Hermann Gollancz, Oxford University Press, London.

The Jews in Science, Louis Gershenfield, Jewish Pub. Society of America, Philadelphia.

Hebrew Literature of Wisdom, J. Franklin Genung, Houghton, Mifflin Co., N. Y.

Our Modern Debt to Israel, E. C. Baldwin, Sherman French & Co., Boston.

Pedagogy of Jesus, in the Twilight of Today, A. W. Squires, Harper & Bros., N. Y.

The Education of the Whole Man, L. P. Jacks, Harper & Bros., N. Y.

Modern Educational Theories, B. H. Bode, Macmillan Co., N. Y.

Determinism in Education, William C. Bagley, Warwick & York, Inc., Baltimore.

The Essentials of Philosophy, R. W. Sellars, Macmillan Co., N. Y.

Art, Love and Life, Ernest Newlandsmith, Longmans, Green & Co., N. Y.

Aims of Literary Study, Hiram Corson, Macmillan Co., N. Y.

Christ and Culture, W. C. Covert, Harper & Bros., N. Y.

The Revolt Against Mechanism, L. P. Jacks, Macmillan Co., N. Y.

The Way Out of Confusion in Education, John Dewey, Harvard University Press, Cambridge, Mass.

How to Write, C. S. Baldwin, Macmillan Co., N. Y.

Visualized History of Education, Louise Tucker, Hinds, Hayden & Eldridge, N. Y.

America's Great Need of Education, Calvin Coolidge, Houghton, Mifflin Co., Boston.

History of Art in Sardinia, Judea, Syria and Asia Minor, Perrott & Chipiez, A. C. Armstrong and Son, N. Y.

Literary Primacy of the Bible, G. P. Eckman, Methodist Book Concern, Chicago.

The Making of a Man, M. T. Lamb, Hazlett, Harrison & Co., Trenton, N. J.

The Freedom of Man, Arthur Compton, Yale University Press, New Haven, Conn.

The Bible as Good Reading, Hon. Albert Beveridge, Houghton, Mifflin & Co., Boston.

Higher Learning in America, Robert Maynard Hutchins, Yale University Press, New Haven, Conn.

Judaism, Geo. Foot Moore, Harvard University Press.

Counsels to Teachers, Ellen G. White, Pacific Press Pub. Ass., Mountain View, Calif.

What Do We Mean by Education? James Welton, Macmillan Co., Ltd., London.

Christ and Science, Francis H. Smith, Fleming H. Revell Co., N. Y.

Education, Ellen G. White, Pacific Press, Mountain View, Calif.

The Philosophy of Christian Education, H. H. Horne, Fleming H. Revell Co., N. Y.

Fundamentals of Christian Eduation, Ellen G. White, Pacific Press, Mountain View, Calif.

The Legacy of Israel, Bevins & Singer, Clarendon Press.

Christ's Object Lesson, Ellen G. White, Pacific Press, Mountain View, Calif.

AUTHORS QUOTED

INDEX

A

Abraham, the school of, 82, 83
Adam and Eve, the school of, 53, 61
Agencies of moral education, 26
American education, 16
Angels, as teachers, 64
Architecture, Hebrew, 187–8; of Tyre and Babylon, 188–90
Art, Hebrew, 187; the spiritual in, 193

B

Bible, guide in Education, 29; and men of learning, 34; authority in education, 40, 46; educational principles in, 41, 59; quickens the intellect, 57; inspired world history, 153, 158; masterpiece of all literature, 167; literary excellence of, 169; and the journalist, 171; and the orator, 172; in the study of literature, 176
Bible history, leading facts revealed in, 159; spade confirms, 160
Biblical literature, testimonies of scholars, 168
Body, influence of labor on, 149
Books, sacred history, 155
Business principles, Hebrew, 148–9

C

Character and education, 253
Christ and modern education, 105; and science, 113; and education, 243; the Prince of Educators, 243; and Rabbinical Schools, 247; and Christian education, 248; The Master Teacher, 253
Christian education, Christ and early, 248; Christ and modern, 250
Conduct and education, 79
Confusion in education, 27–8
Conservation of the soil, 145, 146
Contributions of Hebrew education, 32, 216
Creation, and revelation, 110; vital questions concerning, 111; and the Creator, 121–4
Creative education, 37, 72, 227–8

D

Daniel, education and training of, 211
David, education and training of, 208
Development, educational, 53; physical, mental, spiritual and social, 55, 137
Discipline, principles of, 72; methods of, 74
Disease, and health, 131
Dominion of man, 153

E

Eden, the school in, 53, 61
Education, a vital question, 13; Greek, 14; in England, 14; in America, 16; European, 16; quality and quantity, 18; confusion in, 21, 27; moral, neglected, 22; creative, 37, 227; danger signals, 24; guide-book in, 29, 40; Hebrew system of, 32, 36; comparison of Hebrew and Greek, 35–41; Bible, authority in, 40, 60; relation of Bible to, 40; origin of Hebrew, 45; wisdom, primary element in, 47; and redemption, 54; and the social life, 55; and the Talmud, 58; methods in Hebrew, 68, 240; and conduct, 79; antediluvian, 80; patriarchal, 82; Christ and modern, 105; physical, 128, 136–7; industrial, 91, 142; influence of Hebrew, 207; comparison of Hebrew and modern, 226; Christ and, 243; Christ and Christian, 248; character and, 253
Educational, verdict, 20; unity lacking, 21; systems compared, 35–6, 40; theory of the Hebrews, 35, 40, 49; principles in the Bible, 41; value of music, 183–4; development and processes, 53; determinism, 229–39
Educator, Ezra as an, 62, 108
Educators, criticise education, 17; recognize the problem, 25
Elijah and Elisha established schools of the prophets, 93

257